LIFE-ON-THE-HYPHEN

LIFE
ON THE
HYPHEN

The Cuban-American Way

GUSTAVO PÉREZ FIRMAT

UNIVERSITY OF TEXAS PRESS
AUSTIN

Requests for permission to reproduce material from this
work should be sent to Permissions, University of Texas
Press, Box 7819, Austin, TX 78713-7819.

∞ The paper used in this publication meets the
minimum requirements of American National Standard
for Information Sciences—Permanence of Paper for
Printed Library Materials, ANSI Z39.48-1984.

LIBRARY OF CONGRESS
CATALOGING-IN-PUBLICATION DATA

Pérez Firmat, Gustavo, date.
    Life on the hyphen : the Cuban-American way / Gustavo
Pérez Firmat.—1st ed.
        p.   cm.
    Includes bibliographical references and index.
    ISBN 0-292-71153-0 (cloth).—ISBN 0-292-76551-7 (paper)
    1. Cuban Americans.   2. Popular culture—United
States.   3. Cuban Americans—Florida—Miami.   I. Title.
E184.C97P47   1994
973'.04687291—dc20   93-33590

Owing to limitations of space all acknowledgments for
permission to reprint previously published material may be
found on page 217.

FOR MARY ANNE,   *who loves
Ricky too*

Contents

Illustrations

Acknowledgments

Many friends (and some enemies)
offered much valuable information and advice during the time that this
book was in the thinking and making. Among the friends I should
mention Nivia Montenegro, Enrico Mario Santí, Mark Couture,
Ricardo Castells, Lesbia Varona, Ana Rosa Núñez, Antonio Prieto,
José Muñoz, Jorge Febles, Jorge Duany, and Cathy Cheron. Jorge
Olivares, Roberto González Echevarría, and Antonio Benítez Rojo—
also friends—read the entire manuscript and made many insightful
suggestions (some of which I actually followed). Theresa May, of the
University of Texas Press, was supportive of the project from the
beginning. Kathy Lewis provided wise and expert copyediting.

I owe a special debt to Willie Chirino, Jorge Oliva, and Gloria and
Emilio Estefan for allowing me to reproduce cover art and song lyrics.
Lucie Arnaz graciously gave me permission to quote from her father's
unpublished materials. José Kozer does not usually agree with my inter-
pretation of his poems, but he lets me cite them anyway. René Touzet,
Rolando Laserie, Rosendo Rosell, and Israel "Cachao" López spent sev-
eral hours sharing with me their vast knowledge of Cuban music. Dan
Ishkowitz lent me his father's cha-cha records.

I would also like to thank my colleagues in the Department of
Romance Studies at Duke University for creating a work environment
that made it much easier for me to stay home and write. The Interli-
brary Loan staff at Perkins Library was invariably helpful and efficient.
Jane Snyder, of the Film and Video Department, located some hard-to-
find films. Lynn Olssen, of the San Diego State University Library,
made valuable manuscript and film material available to me.

Finally, my children, David and Miriam, endured my moods and my mambos with a patience that belies their age. And Mary Anne Pérez, whose book this is, not only spent countless hours in the library but helped me to understand that life on the hyphen is everything I say it is, and more.

LIFE-ON-THE-HYPHEN

RICKY TO LUCY: *"Lucy, honey, if I wanted things Cuban I'd stayed in Havana. That's the reason I married you, 'cause you're so different from everyone I'd known before."*

Introduction # THE-DESI-CHAIN

A couple of years ago the cover story of an issue of *People* magazine was devoted to Gloria Estefan, who is well known as the most important moving part in the Miami Sound Machine. At the time, Estefan was staging what the magazine termed an "amazing recovery" from a serious traffic accident that had left her partially paralyzed. Gloria herself was upbeat about her prospects, and the point of the story was to reassure all of the rhythm nation that little Gloria would conga again.[1]

I begin with this anecdote for two reasons: the first is that Estefan's celebrity gives a fair indication of the prominent role that Cuban Americans are playing in the increasing—and inexorable—latinization of the United States; by now, few Americans will deny that, sooner or later, for better or for worse, the rhythm is going to get them. My other reason for bringing up the *People* story has to do with the photograph on the cover, which shows Gloria holding two dalmatians whose names happen to be Lucy and Ricky (Fig. 1). Like one of the Miami Sound Machine's recent albums, the photograph cuts both ways: it suggests not only the prominence but also the pedigree of Cuban-American pop culture. After all, if Gloria Estefan is the most prominent Cuban-American performer in this country today—a "one woman Latin boom," as the *New York Times* put it[2]—Ricky Ricardo is certainly her strong precursor. Surprising as it may seem, Desi Arnaz's TV character has been the single most visible Hispanic presence in the United States over the last forty years. Indeed, several generations of Americans have acquired many of their notions of how Cubans behave, talk, lose their temper, and treat or mistreat their wives by watching Ricky love Lucy.

FIGURE 1   *Gloria Estefan with "Lucy" and "Ricky." Photograph from* People Weekly, *© 1993 Acey Harper; used by permission.*

Just last semester, I had a Cuban–American student who claimed he had learned to be a Cuban male by watching *I Love Lucy* reruns from his home in Hialeah.

But the connection between Estefan and Ricky goes further than this. The Miami Sound Machine's first cross-over hit was "Conga"— the 1986 song that contained the memorable refrain:

> *Come on shake your body, baby, do the conga,*
> *I know you can't control yourself any longer.*

Well, the person who led the first conga ever danced on American soil was none other than Desi Arnaz, who performed this singular feat in a Miami Beach nightclub in 1937.[3] Alluding to this historic (and quite possibly hysteric) event, Walter Winchell later said, in a wonderful phrase, that a conga line should be called instead a Desi Chain. It is well to remember, then, that a few years ago when Gloria Estefan entered the *Guinness Book of World Records* for having led the longest conga line ever, she was only following in Desi's footsteps, only adding another kinky link to the Desi Chain.

I can summarize the significance of this photograph by saying that it illustrates in a particularly clear manner the two forces that shape Cuban-American culture, which I will call *traditional* and *translational*. As a work of tradition, the photograph points to the genealogy of Cuban-American culture; it reminds us that Gloria Estefan is only the latest in a long line of Cuban-American artists who have come, seen, and conga'd in the United States. As a work of translation, it reminds us of the sorts of adjustments that have to occur for us to be able to rhyme "conga" and "longer." In this the photograph is typical, for ethnic cultures are constantly trying to negotiate between the contradictory imperatives of tradition and translation.

"Tradition," a term that derives from the same root as the Spanish *traer*, to bring, designates convergence and continuity, a gathering together of elements according to underlying affinities or shared concerns. By contrast, "translation" is not a homing device but a distancing mechanism. In its topographical meaning, translation is displacement, in Spanish, *traslación*. This notion has been codified in the truism that to translate is to traduce (*traduttore, traditore*); implicit in the concept is the suggestion that to move is to transmute, that any linguistic or cultural displacement necessarily entails some mutilation of the original. In fact, in classical rhetoric *traductio*—which is of course Spanish for translation—was the term used to refer to the repetition of a word with a changed meaning. Translation/*traslación*, traduction/*traducción*—the misleading translation of these cognates is a powerful reminder of the intricacies of the concept.

The subject of this book is how tradition and translation have shaped Cuban-American culture, which is built on the tradition of translation, in both the topographical and linguistic senses of the word. My name for this tradition will be the Desi Chain, since Desi Arnaz is its initial link. To be sure, the Cuban presence on the North American continent is at least as old as the Florida city of St. Augustine, which was founded in 1565.[4] But it is one thing to be Cuban in America, and quite another to be Cuban American. My subject is the latter, a contemporary development. The scope of this book is limited, therefore, to the last half-century, for it is during this period that Cuban-American culture has evolved into a recognizable and coherent cluster of attitudes and achievements.

Another thing that Desi Arnaz and Gloria Estefan have in common is that both left Cuba before they reached adulthood. Born in Cuba but made in the U.S.A., they belong to an intermediate immigrant generation whose members spent their childhood or adolescence abroad but grew into adults in America. Because this group falls somewhere between the first and second immigrant generations, the Cuban sociologist Rubén Rumbaut has labeled it the "1.5" or "one-and-a-half" generation.

> *Children who were born abroad but are being educated and come of age in the United States form what may be called the "1.5" generation. These refugee youth must cope with two crisis-producing and identity-defining transitions: (1) adolescence and the task of managing the transition from childhood to adulthood, and (2) acculturation and the task of managing the transition from one sociocultural environment to another. The "first" generation of their parents, who are fully part of the "old" world, face only the latter; the "second" generation of children now being born and reared in the United States, who as such become fully part of the "new" world, will need to confront only the former. But members of the "1.5" generation form a distinctive cohort in that in many ways they are marginal to both the old and the new worlds, and are fully part of neither of them.*[5]

One of the theses of this book is that Cuban-American culture has been to a considerable extent an achievement of the 1.5 generation. Many of the links in the Desi Chain are made up of one-and-a-halfers, for their intercultural placement makes them more likely to undertake the negotiations and compromises that produce ethnic culture. Life on the hyphen can be anyone's prerogative, but it is the one-and-a-halfer's destiny. I diverge from Rumbaut, though, in stressing the beneficial consequences of this intermediate location. Although it is true enough that the 1.5 generation is "marginal" to both its native and its adopted cultures, the inverse may be equally accurate: only the 1.5 generation is marginal to *neither* culture. The 1.5 individual is unique in that, unlike younger and older compatriots, he or she may actually find it possible to circulate within and through both the old and the new cultures.

While one-and-a-halfers may never feel entirely at ease in either one, they are capable of availing themselves of the resources—linguistic, artistic, commercial—that both cultures have to offer. In some ways they are *both* first and second generation. Unlike their older and younger cohorts, they may actually be able to choose cultural habitats. The one-and-a-halfer's incompleteness—more than one, less than two—is something that I will have occasion to discuss later on; but for now I want to highlight the opportunities for distinctive achievement created by this fractional existence.

One-and-a-halfers are translation artists. Tradition bound but translation bent, they are sufficiently immersed in each culture to give both ends of the hyphen their due. As a one-and-a-halfer myself, I realize that this view is self-serving; but it does not seem unusual that hyphenated cultures should emerge from a sensibility that is not universally shared within an immigrant group. Only those immigrants who arrived here between infancy and adulthood share both the atavism of their parents and the Americanness of their children. I see it in my own family. My parents, who are now in their early seventies, have no choice but to be Cuban. No matter how many years they have resided away from the island—and if they live long enough soon there will come a time when they will have lived longer in Miami than they did in Havana—they are as Cuban today as they were when they got off the ferry in October 1960. My children, who were born in this country of Cuban parents and in whom I have tried to inculcate some sort of *cubanía*, are American through and through. They can be "saved" from their Americanness no more than my parents can be "saved" from their Cubanness. Although technically they belong to the so-called ABC generation (American-Born Cubans), they are Cubans in name only, in last name. A better acronym would be the reverse: CBA (Cuban-Bred Americans). Like other second-generation immigrants, they maintain a connection to their parents' homeland, but it is a bond forged by my experiences rather than their own. For my children Cuba is an enduring, perhaps an endearing, fiction. Cuba is for them as ethereal as the smoke and as persistent as the smell of their grandfather's cigars (which are not even Cuban but Dominican).

In order to describe the blending of cultures that has taken place in many parts of the world, and particularly in the Americas, anthropologists have employed the terms "acculturation" and "transculturation." Acculturation stresses the acquisition of culture; transculturation calls attention to the passage from one culture to another.[6] Drawing on these two notions, I will use the term "biculturation" to designate the type of blending that is specific, or at least characteristic, of the one-and-a-half generation. In my usage, biculturation designates not only contact of cultures; in addition, it describes a situation where the two cultures achieve a balance that makes it difficult to determine which is the dominant and which is the subordinate culture. Unlike acculturation or transculturation, biculturation implies an equilibrium, however tense or precarious, between the two contributing cultures. Cuban-American culture is a balancing act. One-and-a-halfers are no more American than they are Cuban—and vice versa. Their hyphen is a seesaw: it tilts first one way, then the other. The game ends at some point (the one-and-a-half generation passeth away), and the board then comes to rest on one side. But in the meantime it stays in the air, uneasily balancing one weight against the other.

I realize that mine is not a fashionable view of relations between "majority" and "minority" cultures. Contemporary models of culture contact tend to be oppositional: one culture, say white American, vanquishes another, say Native American. But the oppositional model, accurate as it may be in other situations, does not do justice to the balance of power in Cuban America. I like to think of Cuban-American culture as "appositional" rather than "oppositional," for the relation between the two terms is defined more by contiguity than by conflict. I am not referring here to the political relations between Cuba and the United States, to which this statement, obviously and sadly, does not apply. And neither do I want to discount the persistent anti-Americanism that has loomed so large in the island's history. My context of reference is the experience of Cubans in this country, lives lived in collusion rather than collision. Over the last several decades, in the United States, Cuba and America have been on a collusion course. The best products of this collaboration display an intricate equilibrium between the claims of each culture. Equilibrium does not necessarily mean stasis, however, and I am not talking about dull, motionless coexistence. Fractions are fractious, and one-and-a-halfers are notorious for being restless and uppity.

I am also not talking about anything that a given individual or community actually elects. Before becoming a prerogative, biculturation is a fate—the fate typical of individuals who reach this country too young to be Cuban and too old to be American. But this fate, once it is accepted and assumed, becomes a prerogative. It's an election after the fact. You choose what you cannot avoid. You elect what you cannot elude. You rearrange fate into feat. A Cuban proverb says: "Si del cielo te caen limones, aprende a hacer limonada." If God gives you lemons, learn to make lemonade. In many ways the interstitial placement of the one-and-a-half generation is a lemon, since you do not feel entirely at home in either setting. Spiritually and psychologically you are neither *aquí* nor *allá*, you are neither Cuban nor Anglo. You're "cubanglo," a word that has the advantage of imprecision, since one can't tell where the "Cuban" ends and the "Anglo" begins. Having two cultures, you belong wholly to neither one. You are both, you are neither: *cuba-no/ america-no*. What is more, you can actually *choose* the language you want to work, live, love, and pun in. For myself, there have been many times I wish I didn't have this option, for choosing can be painful and complicated—those lemons were really limes, weren't they? Nonetheless, the equipment that comes with the option creates the conditions for distinctive cultural achievement. One-and-a-halfers gain in translation. One-and-a-halfers feed on what they lack. Their position as equilibrists gives them the freedom to mix and match pieces from each culture: they are "equi-libre."

An immigrant group, especially if the expatriation has been involuntary, passes through three stages in its adaptation to a new homeland. Initially the immigrant tries to deny the fact of displacement. I will call this first stage "substitutive," for it consists of an effort to create substitutes or copies of the home culture. This is translation in the topographical sense only, an undertaking that engenders all of those faint doubles of foreign places that speckle the American urban landscape—the little Italies and little Haitis and little Havanas with which we are all familiar. But the adjective "little" here is equivocal, for it says not only that these enclaves are smaller than their models but that they are diminished in ways more important than square miles or population. What's "little" about little Havana is not only its size (Miami is actually the second most populous Cuban city), but its diminished status as a deficient or incomplete copy of the original. No matter how great the effort, substitution is always partial. In Miami one can find stores and restaurants that claim lifespans much in excess of the duration of the Castro regime. These claims rest on a particular kind of historical elision that overlooks personal, historical, and geographical discontinuities. The Miami version of a restaurant called El Carmelo does not have a whole lot in common with its Havana homonym; it's not the same *place*, and it's not even the same *food*, for the Miami menu by now includes such offerings as the Nicaraguan dessert *tres leches*.

Yet the substitutive impulse of newly arrived exiles makes them ignore the evidence of the senses, including their taste buds. Because the reality of exile may be too costly to accept, the exile aspires to reproduce, rather than recast, native traditions. No immigrant ever arrives with only the clothes on his or her back. Even those Cubans who arrived penniless brought with them all kinds of baggage. Willie Chirino, a popular Cuban-American singer and composer, says in a song that he left Cuba with the following: Beny Moré, the Trío Matamoros, Miguelito Cuní, a *colibrí*, a palm tree, a *bohío*, and a book by José Martí. He even "relocalized" in Miami his native province of Pinar del Río. Chirino did not bring much luggage, but he certainly arrived with a lot of baggage, for his list is a gallery of Cuban icons. Most revealing about the list is that several of the people it mentions, like Beny Moré and the surviving members of the Matamoros Trio, never did leave Cuba. Typically his bill of cultural goods denies political and geographical ruptures. The speaker of Chirino's song inhabits, or would like to inhabit, a Cuba of the mind, a fantasy island untouched by time or history.

The compensatory theme of the substitutive stage is "we are (still) there." This is why, even after more than thirty years of exile, it sometimes seems that Little Havana exists in a time warp. This phenomenon is related to what Lisandro Pérez has termed "institutional completeness."[7] An "ethnic enclave" like Miami provides for all of its members' needs. As Pérez points out, your life begins in the hands of a Cuban obstetrician and it ends in the hands of a Cuban undertaker. In between, you have little need of contact with the outside, non-Cuban world. The completeness of the enclave has enabled the reproduction in Miami of what many still call, whimsically, *la Cuba de ayer* (yesterday's Cuba). I find this effort to recreate yesterday's Cuba in today's America both heroic and pathetic. Heroic because it tries to rise above history and geography. Pathetic because it is doomed to fail. No matter how intense and persistent, substitution cannot go on forever. At some point—after months or years or maybe decades—the immigrant begins to find it impossible to sustain, even precariously, the fiction of rootedness. Unsettling events reimpose a sense of reality. Someone dies and has to be buried outside the Cuban family plot; your children bring home friends (or worse: spouses!) who cannot trill their *r*s; the old radio sta-

tions switch to music that follows a different beat. The enclave is no longer *en clave*.

When events like these become habitual, the substitutive fantasy collapses. No amount of duplicate landmarks can cover up the fact that you are no longer there, and what's more, that you may never return. This is the clever point of Arturo Cuenca's *This Isn't Havana* (Fig. 2), where the colloquial English-language phrase is placed over a photograph of the Little Havana restaurant La Esquina de Tejas, which was modeled after the one in Cuba. Barely visible, the overlaid text is a ghostly presence, a geographical reality-principle that says, "You're not there." The name of the restaurant, "The Corner of Tiles," refers to a street corner in Havana, not Miami; and the fact that "Tejas" is also Spanish for Texas adds to the equivocal geography of this uncommon place. Tile Corner or Texas Corner—either way, it isn't Havana. If René Magritte's *Ceci n'est pas une pipe* underscores that the copy is not the thing, Cuenca's *This Isn't Havana*—whose title perhaps alludes to

Magritte's painting—makes the related point that the exile needs to live and reside in the same place. You can't have your *coquito* in Cuba and eat in Miami too.

The Cuban-American poet Ricardo Pau-Llosa once wrote, "The exile knows his place, and that place is the imagination."[8] I would add that the exile is someone who thinks imagination is a place. The problem is, imagination is *not* a place. You can't live there, you can't buy a house there, you can't raise your children there. Grounded in compensatory substitutions, the recreation of Havana in Miami is an act of imagination. But imaginings cannot sustain one indefinitely. Sooner or later reality crashes though, and the exile loses the place that never was. His or her reaction to the collapse of substitution is vertigo, disorientation. If La Esquina de Tejas is not Havana, what is it? If you aren't there, where are you? I do not mean that exiled individuals literally do not know where they are, but that emotionally they have gotten used to believing otherwise. The painful knowledge that they live in exile has been attenuated by the comforting feeling that they never left. You walk into a restaurant on Eighth Street and not only does it have the same name as one in Cuba, but it probably has a map of Havana on the wall and a Cuban flag over the counter. You *know* you're in Miami, but still you *feel* at home.

But as exile lengthens, these feelings begin to fray. Gradually the awareness of displacement crushes the fantasy of rootedness. This ushers in the second stage, for which I will use the term "destitution." In its common usage a destitute person is someone bereft of wealth or possessions; but since destitution derives from *stare*, to stand, it literally means not having a place to stand on. This is what second-stage exiles feel: that the ground has been taken out from under them, that they no longer know their place, that they have in fact lost their place. Rather than nostalgic, they now feel estranged and disconnected. The provisional comforts of substitution have vanished. Now every time you drive by La Esquina de Tejas, in your mind's eye you see a sign that says instead, "This Isn't Havana." If the theme of the first moment was "we are there," the theme of the second moment is "we are nowhere." (Later in this book we will come across several examples of destitution, expressed in the images of displacement and itinerancy that haunt Cuban-American music to this day.)

Mercifully, time passes and "nowhere" begins to feel like home. While the ground under your feet may be unfamiliar, it's still ground, a place to stand on. As the years go by the foreign country loses its foreignness and "nowhere" breaks down into a "now" and a "here," into a concrete time and place. If this isn't Havana, it must be someplace else. Destitution gives way to institution, to the establishment of a new relation between person and place. To institute is to stand one's ground, to dig in and endure. Thus, the theme of the third stage is not "we are there" or "we are nowhere," but rather, "here we are." I take this phrase from Emerson, for this is an Emersonian moment, a moment to lay foundations. For many years there has been a popular Cuban-American band in Miami called Clouds; in 1984 the band changed its name to Clouds of Miami. The addition of the locative phrase signals the transition from destitution to institution. Whereas the band's original name signified uprootedness, the feeling of being up in the air, the revised name brings Clouds down to earth by anchoring them in a specific locale. The cover of Clouds' first album after the name change showed cumuli drifting against the Miami skyline. Although the sensation of rootlessness does not dissipate altogether, it acquires a name and an address.

Since these three moments or stages chart an individual's or a community's slow acceptance of life in a new country, they tend to succeed each other. In Miami the three moments have roughly corresponded to the three decades since the Cuban Revolution. The sixties was a time of nostalgia and substitution; by the seventies, when it had become evident that Castro was there to stay, the prevailing attitude was destitution; and in the eighties, with the maturation of a younger generation of Cuban Americans, destitution gave way to institution. But this chronological progression belies the crucial fact that these attitudes commingle and alternate. For one thing, not everybody reaches exile at the same time or at the same age; for another, individuals as well as communities swing back and forth from one moment to another. It may be, in fact, that all three attitudes are already present from the moment one steps on foreign soil. Even then, feelings of nostalgia and disorientation are probably tempered by a sense of emplacement. Nonetheless, there has been a discernible evolution in the attitudes of Cubans in the United States. Once an exile, always an exile; but it doesn't follow that once an exile, always *only* an exile. What changes is the relative prominence of these attitudes. To this day Cuban Miami is by turns nostalgic, estranged, and foundational; but it used to be far more nostalgic than it is now.

Although I will be discussing all three stages, I will pay most attention to the institutional moment. I am especially interested in locative gestures, in Cuban America's creation of a sense of place inside (but not entirely inside) and outside (but not entirely outside) U.S. culture. What I'm after is a cultural map of Cuban America, that hybrid "nowhere" whose spiritual center is materialistic Miami. At the same time, I want to show that Cuban America is larger and older than Little Havana, and so I have striven to locate and study cultural expressions that antedate the massive exodus that began in 1959.

The first three chapters of the book, thus, are devoted to pre-Castro figures. The subject of Chapter 1 is Ricky Ricardo, the television character from the *I Love Lucy* show. As I hope to show through a discussion of one of the most popular programs in the history of American television, Ricky Ricardo is the tutelary spirit, the *orisha* of Cuban-American culture. He embodies an openness to otherness, a liking for unlikeness that defines Cuban America as a whole. By loving Lucy, Desi renounces regression, using the word in both the sense of *regreso* and *regresión*. As Ricky himself stated, to love Lucy is to embrace the unfamiliar in the form of an *americana* who stands, more generally, for Americana. I draw similar lessons from Desi Arnaz's career in the years before and after he loved Lucy, which forms the subject of Chapter 2. Arnaz was not only a successful actor and a shrewd businessman; he is also the author of *A Book* (1976), which I regard as a significant work of Cuban-American literature. Desi Arnaz may not be Oscar Hijuelos, but it is enough to read *A Book* and to go through the notes and papers that Arnaz left behind after his death to realize that the stereotype of him as a mindless conga-playing lothario who made a living by sponging off his wife is far from the truth. Chapter 3 reconstructs the biography of the mambo in order to show its receptivity to heterogeneous musical traditions. Born in Cuba but made in the U.S.A., the mambo is itself a one-and-a-halfer. I do not mean that the mambo was invented by a one-and-a-halfer—no one individual "invented" the mambo—but that its hybrid, hyphenated musical form allies it with other 1.5 creations. Like Cuban-American culture, the mambo is a music of acceptance, not resistance.

Beginning with Chapter 4, my argument moves from Hollywood to Little Havana and from the 1950s to the 1960s and beyond. The last episode of *I Love Lucy* (which by then was called *The Lucille Ball–Desi Arnaz Show*) was first broadcast in April of 1960, the same month of the failed Bay of Pigs invasion. This coincidence may serve to separate the contemporary history of Cuban America into two periods. Even though reruns of *I Love Lucy* continue to be popular to this day, it is difficult to imagine a character as innocent as Ricky Ricardo in the

Castro era. The Cuba occasionally evoked in *I Love Lucy* is a place without history; watching the episodes, one has no idea of the turbulence of Cuban political life during the 1950s. In *I Love Lucy* Cuba remained that paradise next door depicted in the so-called maraca musicals. But after the much-publicized Revolution, the image of Cubans surely changed: the stereotype of the Latin lover was supplemented by that of the guerrilla fighter and, somewhat later, by that of the drug dealer.

The subject of Chapter 4 is the "sound of Miami," Cuban America's most recent answer to the musical question of biculturation. In this chapter I have tried to tell the story of Cuban Miami through an examination of its song lines. I will look especially closely at Gloria Estefan and Willie Chirino, two performers whose careers are to me exemplary, in order to draw attention to the way in which Cuban American one-and-a-halfers negotiate the contradictory imperatives of tradition and translation. Chapters 5 and 6 offer contrasting case studies of two writers, novelist Oscar Hijuelos and poet José Kozer, who fall just outside the one-and-a-half generation. Arguably the two most important Cuban-American writers, Kozer and Hijuelos will take us to the outer limits of the generational spectrum. Oscar Hijuelos, who is contemporary with the one-and-a-halfers, is much closer in outlook to the second generation. Born in 1950 in New York of Cuban parents, Hijuelos was never an exile, and he writes from the point of view of a hyphenated but anglophone American. His work is a complex and moving valedictory to Cuban culture. By contrast, for José Kozer (born in Havana in 1940), Cuban-Jewish essence precedes American residence. Although he was a young man when he arrived in the United States in 1960, his poetry remains decidedly exilic. Yet Kozer's prolonged residence in New York has inflected his poems in striking ways, with the result that he is a Cuban-American writer in spite of himself.[9]

These six chapters are supplemented by six short interchapters that I have called "mambos." In a salsa arrangement, a mambo has two functions: first, it serves as a bridge between sections; second, it provides brief and brassy variations on the themes of the song. The verbal mambos also have these two aims. On the one hand, they facilitate transitions; on the other, they expand or qualify some of the arguments in the book.

In both chapters and interchapters my argument draws heavily on forms of popular culture. Cuban-American culture is shamelessly materialistic and resolutely middle-brow. As a fascinating mixture of class and crass, of *kitsch* and *caché*, it honors consumers over creators; or rather, it treats consumption like a creative act. You will find Cuban America not only in museums, concerts, and bookfairs, but also, and perhaps primarily, in shopping malls, restaurants, and discotheques. Cuban America defines itself by a way of dressing and dancing and driving; it expresses itself not only in novels and plays, but in fashion and food, in jewelry and jacuzzis, in advertising slogans and in popular music. For this reason, I have not hesitated to take my texts and topics from wherever I could find them: malls as well as museums, boutiques as well as bookstores.

                      I hope it is clear from the foregoing that I write neither from nostalgia nor from estrangement, though these attitudes are certainly not foreign to me. The institutional moment carries within it the memory of the first two stages, and I do not want to overplay generational differences among Cubans in this country. The founding of Cuban America is by no means an adamic undertaking; the kind of cultural landscape that I am talking about is fought for, agonized over, and achieved in response to nostalgia and disorientation. Whatever the "American Adam" may think, the Cuban-American Adam knows that history is his (or hers) to assume, not shed. To say "here we are" is in some sense to begin anew; but this beginning is driven and riven by a past that does not go away. This book is written from the perspective of someone who is neither old enough to be Cuban nor young enough to be American, but who is exactly old and young enough to be Cuban American. In this sense the pages that follow are themselves part of the landscape that they describe. Early on I realized that I could not keep myself out of this book no matter how hard I tried, so I didn't try. The book's map of Cuban America certainly reflects what one calls a personal agenda. At least it is not a hidden agenda. I have tried to fashion a narrative that allows me to make sense of the general circumstances of my own life. But since I share these circumstances with other Cuban-American baby boomers, the story I tell may be personal, but it is not idiosyncratic.

In order to explain Cuban America to myself, I have endeavored to explain it to others who are not like me. Whatever the book's real audience, I have for the most part assumed that its fictive audience is not Cuban or Cuban American. The advantage of proceeding this way is that fewer things go without saying. Addressing an audience of strangers, one takes fewer shortcuts, for the fund of shared values and information is smaller. While working on this book, I often found that you cannot explain the obvious without first exploring the subtle. Translation also attempts to explain the obvious, and it also is full of subtleties and ambiguities.

But I also write with another audience in mind. Fundamentally this book is a community-building enterprise, and in this respect my primary audience is made up of Cuban Americans like myself. Like myself? I'm not really sure; but I hope my discussion does strike a generational chord. I do not claim for Cuban America a fixed habitation or a permanent address, for I am fully and painfully aware that, in this era of mobile homes and shifting borders, one's sense of place is provisional at best. Like other borders, those of Cuban America are makeshift and movable. It cannot be otherwise for a domain built upon acts of translation. But it *is* a domain, a cultural abode, and by now it has its own history and customs.

When pondering the shakiness of my foundations, the mobility of my cultural home, I take consolation and courage from the knowledge that insular Cuban culture also rests on shifting grounds. La Esquina de Tejas certainly isn't Miami, but it isn't quite Havana either. This is the other point of Cuenca's photograph: given that "Tejas" is also a toponym, the Cuban corner itself has an uncertain geography. How did "Texas" end up deep in the heart of Havana? The mixing and matching that creates equivocal names and incongruous displacements has been a part of Cuban history almost from its inception. The reasons for this are complex, but the principal ones have to do, on the one hand, with the extinction of Cuba's aboriginal population, and, on the other, with the island's strategic location at the entrance to the Americas. This has meant that Cuban culture has always lacked a stable core or essence, a situation that Jorge Mañach summarized with the aphorism that Cuba is a "patria sin nación," a homeland without nationhood.[10] Like the United States, Cuba is a country of immigrants; unlike the United States, it is a country of immigrants many of whom reached the island on the way to other places (including the United States). As the great Cuban ethnologist Fernando Ortiz pointed out many years ago, Cuba is a land of migratory birds, *aves de paso*. Ortiz's famous metaphor for Cuba was that of the *ajiaco*—an indefinitely renewable stew that accepts the most diverse ingredients.[11] This is why atavistic calls for cultural and linguistic purity on the part of some Cuban exiles have always struck me as singularly inappropriate. There are no pure people in Cuba; in

Cuba even the purée is impure. Cubans have always been hyphenated Americans. Stretched across the Caribbean, Cuba itself looks like a hyphen on the way to becoming a question mark. *Life on the Hyphen* could also have been the title of a book about the Cuban condition.

For this reason, I do not find only discontinuity between "Cuban" and "Cuban American." The Cuban American, and in particular the one-and-a-halfer, is one of the possible forms that the Cuban talent for hyphenation can assume. Cuban America is also an *ajiaco*, except that in some Miami restaurants the name is now "tropical soup." The evolution from Cuban to Cuban American, from *ajiaco* to tropical soup, and from Cuban Spanish to Cuban English, does not involve the denaturing of a putative "essence." For Cubans residence precedes essence, and essence is aroma. In our case, the hyphen is not a minus sign but a plus; perhaps we should call ourselves "Cuban + Americans."

I realize that my views will probably strike some as unpatriotic and even assimilationist, but it is not assimilation that I am talking about. Cuban-American culture heightens and draws out certain tendencies inherent in mainland island culture—most prominently, the tendency toward hyphenation. We Cubans have a peculiar relation to our roots: we eat them. What is the *ajiaco* if not a root roast, a kind of funeral pyrex? You take your favorite aboriginal roots—*malanga, ñame, yuca, boniato*—and you cook them until they are soft and savory. In keeping with your roots' roots, you might even cook them in a hole in the ground. But then you consume them. You don't freeze them. You don't preserve them. You don't put them in a root museum. You don't float them down a root canal. You eat them in the knowledge that such conspicuous consumption will let you remain faithful to—what else?—your roots.

This is why the acronym YUCA (for Young Urban Cuban American) is both ironic and apt. A YUCA is a self-consuming vegetable. An English-speaking YUCA who parks his beamer, hooks a beeper into his belt (or slings a cellular phone into her purse), and goes into a pricey Coral Gables restaurant also called Yuca to eat *nouvelle cuisine ajiaco* is not less Cuban but more American. Again, it is a question of addition not subtraction: Cuban + American. The *agria cultura*, the acrid culture of the YUCA, consists of uprootings and reroutings. I don't believe in assimilation, but I live by translation. Life on the hyphen: the one-and-a-half generation is also the one-and-a-hyphen generation. Paraphrasing José Ortega y Gasset: you are you plus your *rayita*, your hyphen.

A few years ago I met a Spanish-American man who wanted to know where I was from. I replied that I was *cubano* (when I'm asked the same question by Americans I always reply that I am American). "Pero ¿cubano de dónde?" he said, "Cuban from where?"—as if being Cuban did not mean hailing from a certain island in the Caribbean. I said that I was "cubano de North Carolina," Carolina Cuban, and he was satisfied with that rather bizarre answer. For this man—who was himself a Nicaraguan from Coral Gables—Cuba is less a place on a map than the label for a certain ethnic or cultural group. Just as there are Cubans from Havana, there are Cubans from Miami or New Jersey or North Carolina. I have mentioned Ortiz's view of Cubans as *aves de paso*, birds of passage, which is also the title of Michael Piore's well-known book on American immigrants. It may be that the criteria that define Cubanness are those of ethnicity rather than of nationhood.

The occasional urgency of my tone in the following chapters stems from my conviction that, precisely because of its link to a specific generation, the varieties of Cuban-American culture that I will discuss here have a limited life expectancy, what Lisandro Pérez calls an "expiration date." As the name already indicates, the one-and-a-half generation is something of a novelty; and its culture is a novelty culture. Like other sorts of novelties—"novelty songs" and "novelty acts" come to mind—it is clever, entertaining, original, but in the end ephemeral. At the level of community, the three-stage evolution I outlined previously contains a fourth stage, embodied in the second immigrant generation and its sequels. Considerable evidence suggests that second-generation Cuban Americans have been fairly resilient in retaining their parents' and grandparents' culture. Nonetheless, with the graying of the one-and-a-halfers, Cuban America will undoubtedly change complexion and lose some of its Cuban color. What has happened to other ethnic groups will happen to us: we will have a sentimental, rather than a vital, link to our culture of origin. Cubanness will be something we acquire, not something we absorb. It is at this point that one starts inventing holidays, digging for roots, and signing up for mambo classes. For better *and* for worse, one-and-a-halfers do not need to look far in search of their origins. They carry their roots wherever they go. They were to the mambo born.

But mambos are not forever, and even in Miami things are already changing. These are the last days of Little Havana. Signs of the transformation are visible all over town. The phenomenon is complex and owes not only to the natural evolution of the Cuban exile community, but also to the arrival in the city of significant numbers of other Hispanics. As I write this in 1993, Miami is more Hispanic than ever but less Cuban than ten or fifteen years ago. When I wax nostalgic, it is for the "old" Miami that I mostly long, not for Cuba. Walking around the Kendall suburb of Miami, one gets the distinct feeling that José Vasconcelos's prediction of a *raza cósmica*, a cosmic race, is going to be realized not in South America but in Southwest Dade. The spawning ground for the cosmic race may well be the Town and Country Mall in Kendall, a dazzling diorama of designer clothes, aerobicized bodies, and tanned tan skin. I do not view this as a bad thing. Whatever is lost in translation will be gained in translation.

The other determinant of the future of Cuban America is, of course, the political situation in the island. Once the current regime disappears, the landscape of Cuban America will be different from what it has been for the last three decades. Those Cubans who decide to stay, probably the large majority, will no longer be able to view the world through the lens of exile. Once the "real" Cubans go back to the island, those of us who remain here will have no choice but to realize that we are Americans, with or without the hyphen. Perhaps then most of the anguish and disorientation of exile will recede definitively into the past.

Or perhaps it will be more acute than ever. Exile is distressing, but actually having the possibility of return may be more distressing still, for it will call into question the comforting fictions that one has lived by for many years. Exiles who can return and do not lose their identity. So what do they become then, Cuban ex-exiles? And what will happen to Cuban-American culture in Miami once there is unrestricted travel to and from Cuba? After Castro Miami may well be more "Cuban" and less "American" than it was during the lifetime of the Revolution. With more communication and traffic with the island, Little Havana may well deepen its Cuban roots. Perhaps Kendall will end up as a suburb of Santos Suárez after all. What *is* certain is that, for all of these reasons, the present borders of Cuban America will not remain fixed for long.

I thus write with the sense that I am describing ways of speaking, writing, acting, and living that will soon undergo a profound transformation. Although I believe that there is a peculiarly Cuban-American way of assuming United States culture, and that this way preceded my generation and will continue beyond it, the phenomena that I will describe in the mambos and in the Miami chapters of this book may well have reached their definitive form during the last several years. I chronicle the present with the disquieting awareness that it may quickly become a thing of the past. Hence, I sketch the contours of Cuban America in the hope of keeping my "country" on the map a little longer.

But the primary purpose of these pages is not to defer or deny the transformation but to try to cope with it. After the welcome demise of the Cuban Revolution, the question of what it means to be Cuban in America will become more rather than less urgent. Many years ago Miami Cubans used to group their fellow exiles into two camps, those who would be allowed to return to a free Cuba and those who would not. Of someone in the latter camp, it was said, "ése no tiene regreso," literally, "he has no return." The not-so-wholesome idea behind the labeling (which varied according to your own political persuasion) was to weed out from a future Cuban polity either sympathizers of the Batista regime or former collaborators of the Revolution. For myself, I know that I belong in the category of those for whom there is no going back—*no tengo regreso*—but for personal rather than political reasons. Paradoxically, for someone like myself, returning to Cuba would be tantamount to going into exile a second time. By recovering a long-standing tradition of Cuban-American cultural achievement, I am looking for a way to make sense of my life as a Cuban-American man in the post-Castro era, a time when I will no longer be able to rely on the structures of thought and feeling that I have used for three decades.

I should say something here of earlier studies about Cuban Americans. For the most part, books in this area have tended to be scholarly monographs analyzing the economic, demographic, and class profile of the Cuban-American community in the United States.[12] Although these books have been indispensable to my own work, I am less interested in data than in details. One learns a great deal from graphs and statistics, but sometimes stories and impressions can be equally instructive. Closer to what I have in mind are the books about Miami by Joan Didion and David Rieff.[13] I like Rieff's better than Didion's, though it is revealing that both use the protocol of the travel journal, as if visits to Miami were expeditions into a foreign country. Already in the title, Rieff's *Going to Miami* evokes a formula common in travel writing; but it is Didion's book in particular that resembles nothing so much as a nineteenth-century ethnographer's report on an exotic Amazonian tribe. For Didion, Cuban Americans are picturesque but fundamentally unintelligible. Cuban-American women, especially, mystify her. She goes to a party and remarks that the women looked like "well-groomed mangoes." Upon reading this, one gets the distinct impression that Didion is no fan of tropical fruits.

This book is not a travel journal but a user's guide. My discussion is shaped by somewhat different tastes, for I write from the perspective of someone who not only grew up among well-groomed mangoes, but who would be pleased to be considered a well-groomed mango himself. (Alternate title: My Life as a Mango.) One of the points I want to get across is that, contrary to most reports from the field, there is nothing particularly zany or exotic about Cuban Americans. Multicultural pieties aside, the Cuban-American way is not inconsistent with the American way. A well-groomed mango (like a well-crooned mambo) can be just as American as apple pie. The Desi Chain may move to the beat of the conga, but with each step it advances deeper into the American heartland.

Lost in Translation

MAMBO NO. 1   *Take the phrase literally. Turn the commonplace
into a place. Try to imagine where one ends up if
one gets lost in translation. When I try to visualize
such a place, I see myself, on a given Saturday
afternoon, in the summer, somewhere in Miami.
Since I'm thirsty, I go into a store called Love
Juices, which specializes in nothing more salacious
or salubrious than milk shakes made from papayas
and other tropical fruits. Having quenched my thirst,
I head for a boutique called Mr. Trapus, whose
name—trapo—is actually the Spanish word for
an old rag. Undaunted by the consumerist frenzy
that has possessed me, I enter another store called
Cachi Bachi—a name that, in spite of its chichi
sound, is a slang word for a piece of junk, cachi-
vache. And then for dinner I go to the Versailles of
Eighth Street, a restaurant where I feast on something called Tropical Soup, the American name for
the traditional Cuban stew, ajiaco. My dessert is
also tropical, Tropical Snow, which is Miamian
for arroz con leche; and to finish off the meal,
of course, I sip some Cuban-American espresso
(don't go home without it). In this way I spend my
entire afternoon lost in translation—and loving
every minute. Translation takes you to a place*

where cultures divide to conga. My effort in this book is to show you the way to such a place. Step lightly, and enter at your own risk. Who knows, you might just end up becoming the missing link in the Desi Chain.

I-LOVE-RICKY

A few months before his death from lung cancer in 1986, Desi Arnaz remarked that he wanted to be remembered as the "I" in *I Love Lucy*. This wish was both self-assertive and self-effacing, since that "I" is fraught with ambiguity. For one thing, it refers both to Desi and to his fictional counterpart, Ricky Ricardo. Given that the program deliberately exploited the resemblances between the actors and their TV characters, it is not always easy to tell Desi and Ricky apart. For another, almost from the beginning of the show's phenomenal run, Desi's "I" was appropriated by the millions of Lucy fans, whose feelings it expressed. Indeed, the genius of the title is that it pithily describes both the subject of the show and the audience's reaction to its protagonist.

The story behind the title is well known: CBS wanted Lucille Ball to do a television version of her popular radio show *My Favorite Husband*, where her husband was played by Richard Denning. Ball agreed, but only if Desi Arnaz played Denning's part. Since the radio program was about a typical American housewife and her husband, the network balked, feeling that Arnaz would not be believable as the husband. In the radio show Lucy's husband had been a waspish banker from Minneapolis—hardly a suitable part for a conga player from Cuba. After the program's concept was modified to fit Desi's background and personality, the network finally agreed, but without much enthusiasm. Ball and Arnaz would play a show-biz couple: the husband was a struggling bandleader whose zany wife would try anything to get into his act.

The show's title remained a problem, however. Mindful of Desi's Cuban ego, Ball's first impulse was to call the show *The Desi Arnaz–*

Lucille Ball Show, but again the network balked, since she and not Desi was the drawing card for the series. In 1951 Desi Arnaz was known basically as the leader of a Latin orchestra; by contrast, Lucille Ball was "Queen of the B's," an established actress whose successful Hollywood career gave the new medium the kind of legitimacy that it needed. After much discussion, someone—it's not clear who—came up with the clever compromise, *I Love Lucy*. This title had the advantage of giving Desi top billing but without actually naming him, thus leaving the spotlight on his more famous wife.[1] The presence of Desi's "I" in the title is as evasive as it is revelatory. It does take a moment's reflection to realize to whom the pronoun actually refers. Desi's wish to be remembered as the "I" in the show reveals a desire to unmask the anonymity of that oddly impersonal pronoun.

This anonymity was enhanced by the projection of the viewer's identity into the title. Jack Gould, the TV critic for the *New York Times* during the 1950s, put it this way: "*I Love Lucy* is probably the most misleading title imaginable. For once, all available statistics are in agreement: Millions love Lucy."[2] Given Lucy's popularity, this leap from show to audience was easy to make. For Gould as for many others, the title was essentially a declaration of the audience's affection for the show's star. Back in the fifties, the Chicago department store Marshall Field's decided to close early on Monday nights because most of its customers were staying home to watch the program. The sign in the store said, "We love Lucy too, so we're closing on Monday nights." Who loves Lucy? I love Lucy, you love Lucy, we all love Lucy. Lucy's fan club was called, not unexpectedly, the We Love Lucy Fan Club. It is well to remember, further, that the series was broadcast on CBS, the network whose famous corporate logo is a giant eye, an image that was first used in September 1951, only a month before the series went on the air for the first time. In this context the title refers not to Ricky or Desi but rather to the "eye" of the beholder, whose iconographic rendering is the CBS eye.[3]

But if we are the "I," what happens to the "I" in the title? It becomes a scrambled ego. Scrambled first by the split between Ricky and Desi, and scrambled again by their absorption into the viewer's "eye." The "I" in *I Love Lucy* is less a personal than a collective pronoun, for its bearer is not an individual but a whole nation of people.

This is one reason why most of the attention bestowed on the series has focused on Lucy, whose identity does not suffer such alterations.[4] Ball or Arnaz, Lucy remains Lucy. (This was actually Desi's pet name for his wife, who was otherwise known as Lucille.) Of the two main characters in the show, Lucy is by far the more easily seen and grasped. In most of the episodes she is the instigator and Ricky the bystander, or worse, the victim. Ricky may love, but it is Lucy who *acts*. When discussed at all, Ricky is regarded as the straight man for his wife's schemes; occasionally he is also cited as an illustration of Hollywood's stereotyping of Latin characters.[5] In the first instance, he is a charming foil; in the second, he is a figure of contempt. As the owner of an "I" that nobody sees, Ricky Ricardo has been relegated to a peculiar kind of invisibility.

Nonetheless, I take the title of the show seriously: Ricky is the subject, the "I" of the show. He is neither straight enough to be a straight man nor flat enough to be a stereotype. Richer and deeper than the commonsense view of him, Ricky Ricardo lives out the dilemmas and the delights of biculturation. He is not only a central presence within *I Love Lucy*; he is also the exemplary Cuban-American subject, a significance that explains his placement at the beginning of this book. As we will see, Ricky's negotiations with North American culture, and particularly his marriage to Lucy, offer a first example of what I take to be the Cuban-American way.

I Love Lucy went on the air on October 15, 1951, and ran for nine seasons. During the first six seasons 180 half-hour episodes were filmed and broadcast. For the last three seasons the episodes were lengthened to an hour and came on either monthly or at irregular intervals. The last episode was filmed on March 2, 1960, coincidentally the day of Desi Arnaz's forty-third birthday and—not coincidentally—the day before Lucille Ball sued him for divorce.[6] During its initial run *I Love Lucy* gathered more than two hundred awards and was nominated for twenty-three Emmys, winning five times. The show has been broadcast in seventy-seven countries and translated into twenty-one languages. In the United States the original episodes have been rerun endlessly. Since its premiere in 1951, the show has *never* been off the air in southern California;[7] and by 1974 episodes from *I Love Lucy* had been shown in Washington, D.C., a total of 2,904 times, a fact which may help explain U.S. policy toward Cuba.[8]

To this day Lucy and Ricky (and Fred and Ethel) continue to be household names. Magazine stories and popular biographies about the stars appear regularly. In February 1991 CBS aired a TV movie based on Desi and Lucy's stormy marriage; two years later Lucie Arnaz put together a memorial documentary based on the couple's home movies. The success of Oscar Hijuelos's Pulitzer Prize–winning novel, *The Mambo Kings Play Songs of Love*, which has been turned into a movie, clearly has something to do with the fact that Lucy and Desi appear as characters; indeed, the climactic scene in the novel occurs when the mambo kings, César and Néstor Castillo, make a cameo appearance on the *I Love Lucy* show as Ricky's Cuban cousins. The Cuban-born *rapero* Mellow Man Ace calls himself the "Ricky Ricardo of rap," has a composition entitled "Babalú Bad Boy," and named his son Desi. *I Love Lucy* has even spawned several clever X-rated spoofs with such titles as *Lucy Has a Ball* and *Lucy Makes It Big*.

On the face of it, *I Love Lucy* is an unlikely candidate for this sort of success. Its strength has generally been considered to be its portrayal of the trials and tribulations of a typical middle-class American couple. A 1952 article put it this way: "The captivating thing about Lucy and Ricky is the fact that they hold a mirror up to every married couple in America. Not a regulation mirror that reflects truth, nor a magic mirror that portrays fantasy. But a Coney Island mirror that distorts, exaggerates, and makes vastly amusing every little incident, foible, and idiosyncrasy of married life."[9] A few years later, an unnamed "British anthropologist" reported in the *New York Times*: "Lucy and Ricky and their friends Ethel and Fred are the typical American middle class, in a typical American middle-class environment."[10] Lucy and Ricky are, nonetheless, unlikely choices as comic doubles for the folks next door. After all, the show went on the air during the Eisenhower era, a conformist age that staunchly embraced American values and sternly persecuted un-American activities. And yet the TV hit of the decade featured a couple where the husband made a living playing a conga drum—an un-American activity if there ever was one. Americans may have liked Ike, but they *loved* Lucy.[11] Strangely, the typical middle-class couple of the Eisenhower era consisted of a ditsy redhead from New York and a conga-playing crooner from Cuba with slicked-back hair and a precarious command of the English language.

The typical *I Love Lucy* episode boils down to some type of competition between the two protagonists. Even though the program's title leads the viewer to expect a loving couple, their relationship is essentially adversarial. During most of each episode, Lucy and Ricky are opponents. The battlelines are usually well drawn: on one side, Lucy and Ethel, on the other, Ricky and Fred. Usually the conflict is an example of the irreducible differences between husbands and wives, or men and women. In the episodes I find most interesting, however, the conflict emerges from a clash of cultures. Ricky is not just male, but Cuban. Lucy is not just female, but American. What puts them at loggerheads is not only gender, but culture. In these episodes the overriding theme is not the war of sexes but the "battle of the accents."

This phrase occurs in "Lucy Hires an English Tutor" (December 29, 1952), an episode from the second season that deals with Lucy's efforts to improve Ricky's broken English.[12] As the episode begins, a pregnant Lucy sits in the living room knitting something for the baby. Ricky comes in with a "papaya-juice milk shake," into which she dips a dill pickle. The conversation turns to the sex of their child. Ricky wants a boy and Lucy wants a girl. Every man wants a boy, Lucy says, "so that he can see himself running around." Every woman wants a girl, he replies, so that she can "teach her daughter how to catch a man." Ricky volunteers that his son will attend his alma mater, "Havana U," and launches into a rendition of the school anthem—"Havana U, la mejor eres tú," which he sings to the tune of the Michigan fight song. This gets them into an argument about the child's upbringing and Ricky's deficient English. After Ricky tries unsuccessfully to pronounce such words as "bough," "rough," "through," and "cough" (which he pronounces "buff," "row," "thruff," and "coo"), he concludes that, since English is a "crazy language," his son should speak Spanish instead. Lucy counters that she is going to hire a tutor for themselves and the Mertzes. Her reason: "I want anyone who is going to converse with my child to speak perfect English."

In the next scene we are back in the living room with Mr. Livermore, the English tutor (played by Hans Conried). Mr. Livermore is a stuffy, bespectacled pedant with an affected pronunciation and a hysterical aversion to slang. After a few funny scenes where Mr. Livermore tries to improve Ricky's English, the lessons come to an unexpected conclusion. Instead of changing Ricky's accent and diction, the English tutor adopts a Cuban accent and launches into a spirited rendition of "Babalú." Lucy is graceful in defeat. "It was a battle of the accents," she says, "and Mr. Livermore lost."

In a show that has often been criticized for its ethnocentrism, Lucy's acceptance of difference marks an interesting moment. Rather than persisting in her efforts to "Americanize" her Cuban husband, Lucy just gives in. The reason is that, as many episodes make clear, Lucy loves Ricky because he is *not* American. When she calls him her "Cuban dreamboat," as she sometimes does, she intends the phrase without any irony whatsoever. If anything, the phrase is a pleonasm, not a paradox. Early in their careers Lucy and Desi put together a vaudeville act where they played the parts of "Cuban Pete" and "Sally Sweet."[13] Cuban Pete is "the king of the rumba beat," Sally Sweet is "the queen of Delancy Street." At first Pete and Sweet can't get their act together; she steps on his lines and he steps on her toes. As the song progresses, however, they begin to blend and by the end of the number they are singing and dancing in unison. Cuban Pete and Sally Sweet are Ricky and Lucy in microcosm.

Another episode that turns on cultural differences is "Ricky Minds the Baby" (January 18, 1954), which culminates in a brilliant long scene during which Ricky tells his son the story of *Little Red Riding Hood*—in Spanish. Ricky's *Caperucita roja* includes just enough English to be intelligible—"Granmamá, pero what big ojos tú tienes," the *lobo* says—but otherwise the viewer is subjected to nearly five minutes of Spanish. It's an unusual scene because of its length, because of its language, and because of its location. The scene takes place in the apartment, normally Lucy's domain, but it is Ricky who occupies the spotlight. As she listens by the door with Fred and Ethel, Lucy is for once reduced to the role of passive bystander. Not only that—Ricky gets into the act by using Lucy's best resource: impersonation, for as he tells the story, he deftly assumes the identity of the various characters. Most of Ricky's monologues are either song lyrics or rapid-fire Spanish-language tirades. Combining elements of the two, the bedtime story blends the predictability of a song lyric with the spontaneity of the tirade. Ricky's *Caperucita roja* is a tender tirade, a demonstration that he can use Spanish for purposes other than romance or remonstrance.

There is no doubt that *I Love Lucy*'s portrayal of things Cuban is generally stereotypical and sometimes condescending. Ricky's thick accent and his vaunted malapropisms—"Birds of a feather smell the same"; "I'll cross that bridge when I burn it"; "You can lead a horse to water but you can't make him a drink"—provided an inexhaustible source of cheap laughs. All Lucy had to do was mimic Ricky's "dunt"s and "wunt"s and the audience's amused response was automatic. Yet episodes like "Lucy Hires an English Tutor" and "Ricky Minds the Baby" not only raise the question of the couple's biculturalism, but resolve it in Ricky's favor. The point of contention between Lucy and Ricky is what today we would call "ethnicity," a word that had not yet entered common usage in 1953.[14] Ricky wants their child to grow up "ethnic," but Lucy dissents. She doesn't want little Ricky to [speak] Spanish, or even Hispanicized English, and she certainly doesn['t want] him to attend Havana U. As she points out, why go to school in [Cuba] when there are so many fine universities right here in the U.S.A.? B[ut] when the English lessons don't succeed, Lucy gives up. To be sure, this does not mean that little Ricky will grow up to be Cuban; but it does mean that some of his father's culture and language will be passed on to him. If not an ABC, an American-born Cuban, little Ricky will be a CBA, a Cuban-bred American.

But what if Lucy had won? What if Mr. Livermore's diction lessons had succeeded? Given the importance of Ricky's speech in the overall dynamic of the show, such an outcome is almost unimaginable. I said earlier that Ricky Ricardo was something of an invisible man. Another reason for his invisibility is that his signature is not visual but aural. This is not to say that Ricky's physical appearance is not important, for it clearly is. But since *I Love Lucy* is notable for its broad slapstick comedy—disguises, pratfalls, stunts, props—it is easy to underestimate the importance of Ricky's voice. Yet without Ricky's aural presence, the program would have a different "look." Above all, Ricky is the sound of his voice, a distinguishing trait made all the more evident by the fact that he is a singer. If Lucy's a clown, Ricky's a crooner. Lucy is a genius with props; Ricky has a gift for malapropisms. Lucy mugs; Ricky goes "¡ay, ay, ay, ay, ay!" or sings "Babalú." We remember Lucy for her wonderful repertoire of "faces"—"Spider," "Puddling Up," "Foiled Again," "Umlaut." [15] What we remember most about Ricky is the sound of his voice.

One of the most touching moments in all of *I Love Lucy* occurs in "Lucy Is Enceinte" (December 8, 1952) when Lucy tells Ricky that she is pregnant. Nearly overcome with emotion, Ricky then sings "We're Having a Baby." Toward the end of the song, Ricky and Lucy adlib the following brief exchange:

> Ricky: *I bet he's gonna look just like you.*
> Lucy: *I bet he'll speak with an accent like you.*

Lucy and Ricky understand each other's distinctiveness. What defines Lucy is her "look"; what defines Ricky is his "accent."

A key element in Ricky's aural signature is his habit of launching into Spanish-language outbursts when he gets exasperated with Lucy's schemes: "Dios-mío-pero-qué-cosas-tiene-la-mujer-ésta!" Clearly these

express Ricky's "Latin" temper, and in this
ter what he says. The interesting thing, though,
ays speak gibberish. If one listens to what he
mes one hears statements that he could not
ill, for example, declare that he is fed up with
e her. At times, he will even lapse into profan-
, "Mira que jode la mujer ésta." Sometime
si did a skit for a *Bob Hope Show* where they
s. In the course of the skit Hope's character
d orders him to "lose that accent." Ricky
retaliates not only by not losing his accent but by saying: "Mira qué
tiene cosas el narizón, sinvergüenza, zoquete éste, carajo."[16]

Ricky's Cuban *descargas* allow him not only to let off steam but
to speak the unspeakable, to say things in Spanish that he could not
get away with in English. During the 1950s it was unthinkable that
someone would actually curse on TV, as Ricky does on occasion.
Although the writers and actors of the show were exceedingly cautious
in approaching sensitive subjects (the episodes having to do with Lucy's
pregnancy, for example, were vetted by a rabbi, a priest, and a minis-
ter), when it came to Ricky's Spanish, they were considerably less vigi-
lant. Their revealing but dubious assumption, of course, was that no
one would understand what Ricky was saying. Today it is doubtful that
Ricky could get away with saying to Lucy, "Tú eres la persona más
estúpida que yo he conocido," as he says in more than one episode. It
is also doubtful that Lucy's pregnant whim would be to dip pickles in a
"papaya-juice milk shake," since *papaya* is Cuban slang for the female
genital organ.

The episode entitled "Home Movies" (March 1, 1954) also plays
off the couple's biculturalism. Ricky is making a TV pilot entitled
"Ricky Ricardo Presents Tropical Rhythms," which he is filming in
the nightclub. When Lucy finds out, she decides to make her own pilot,
a "Western-musical-drama" shot entirely in the Ricardo's living room.
When a TV producer arrives to preview Ricky's effort, he is also treated
to a sampling of Lucy's film, which she has intercut into Ricky's musical so that Ricky's rendition of "Vaya con Dios" is interrupted by Lucy's
rendition of "I'm an Old Cowhand from the Rio Grande." Ricky is
furious and breaks into one of his patented tirades. The producer, however, thinks the montage is brilliant and calls Ricky a "genius." Ricky
may have *genio*, of course, but he is no genius, since it is Lucy who has
spliced together the films.

Lucy's montage, which offers yet another example of her penchant for "visual" gags, is revealing not only because it gives us a timid glimpse of bicultural cinematic art, but also because it illustrates that the cultural differences between Lucy and Ricky are often expressed as the juxtaposition of two spaces, Ricky's nightclub—where Ricky films his show—and the Ricardos' apartment—where Lucy films hers. This was already evident in the denouement of "Lucy Hires an English Tutor," since the definitive sign of the "cubanization" of Mr. Livermore is his rendition of "Babalú" in the middle of the living room. When Livermore sings "Babalú," the nightclub takes over the apartment; Ricky wins and Lucy loses.

This bicameral arrangement is crucial. The setting of *I Love Lucy* contains two discrete realms—Ricky's nightclub, the Tropicana, where Ricky reigns supreme; and the Ricardos' apartment, where Lucy puts on her best performances, many of which are intended to find her a place on the nightclub stage. The apartment serves as an informal, substitute stage, and indeed, Lucy's performances in her own living room, which include the whole gamut of theatrical tricks and devices, usually upstage anything that goes on at the Tropicana. When Lucy is asked about her show-biz experience during an audition, she replies that she has just finished an eleven-year stint at "Ricardos'," a "three-ring circus" ("Lucy Tells the Truth," November 11, 1953). The Ricardos' living room is indeed a stage, a performance arena that in most ways overshadows the real stage of the Tropicana. And it does have three rings: the kitchen, the living room, and the bedroom. At one point in this episode Lucy says to Ricky, "You're scared to death I'll steal the show." Of course stealing the show, getting into the act, is what *I Love Lucy* is all about. But in spatial terms, getting into the act means either occupying Ricky's stage or turning the living room into a stage. This is why in the pilot episode there were only two sets: nightclub and living room. They are the nuclear spaces in the show, the architectural metaphor for Lucy and Ricky's cultural and gender differences.

Living rooms are a staple of situation comedy. In the forty years since *I Love Lucy* went on the air, America's living rooms have been filled with living rooms—from the sparse, working-class furnishings of the Ralph and Alice Kramdens' apartment to the yuppie affluence of *The Cosby Show*. But no living room has seen as many marvels as that of Apartment 3-B. To describe it as a "centrally placed, nondescript but middle-class living room" hardly does it justice.[17] Most living rooms fit this description, but not Lucy and Ricky's. As the modern equivalent of the hearth, living rooms are supposed to be cozy, reassuring, stable. In the living room one retreats from the world, lets one's hair down, settles in. If all the world's a stage, the living room is a backstage. The Ricardos' living room certainly has this quality. Here is where Lucy and Ricky repair after coming home from work or finishing household chores. Many an episode or scene begins when Ricky comes through the door, takes off his overcoat, loosens his tie, announces "Lucy, I'm home," and plops himself down on the sofa with the newspaper.

But Ricky's living room is never uneventful for very long. No sooner has he opened the paper than Lucy runs out of the kitchen dragging a gigantic loaf of bread. The Ricardos' living room is also an arena for the spectacular, a wondrous protean space. One moment the Ricardos and the Mertzes are sitting on the sofa, drinking coffee and chatting; the next moment the living room has been turned into the Wild West (as in "Home Movies"), or into a classroom (as in "Lucy Hires an English Tutor"), or into Old Havana (more on this one later).

When I said above that the living room was a stage without foot-lights, I was thinking of Mikhail Bakhtin's description of carnival, for the world of the living room is very much the inverted, topsy-turvy world of carnival.[18] Recall, for example, the famous episode where Lucy and Ricky trade places: while Lucy and Ethel go find a job, Ricky and Fred, dressed as homemakers, vacuum and cook ("Job Switching," September 15, 1952). In the living room Lucy is homemaker, wife, and mother; but she is also a bellydancer, hillbilly, ballerina, circus clown, bearded lady, señorita, vamp, Tallulah Bankhead, Vivien Leigh, Ricky's mother, and one of his poker pals. In one episode she even assumes the identity of a dog that sneaks under the dinner table, fights another dog for a scrap of meat, and then licks Ricky's hand! Here Lucy and at times the other characters don one disguise after another. The Ricardos' hearth is a space of shifting identities and fluid boundaries. Less a sanc-tuary than a circus, it exposes Lucy and Ricky to pitfalls and pratfalls and all kinds of unlikely occurrences.

The characters' continual "bets" add to the circus atmosphere. Ricky bets Lucy that she cannot tell the truth; or Lucy bets Ricky that he can save money; or the men bet the women that housework is a breeze. These bets create a competitive frenzy that may remind us of carnival's jousts and contests. The living room is indeed a circus, as Lucy rec-ognizes. David Marc is right to conclude that *I Love Lucy* and other domestic comedies of the 1950s consistently oppose what he terms "role restlessness."[19] Whatever the temporary disruptions of traditional gender roles, by the end of each episode Lucy and Ricky have settled back into their assigned places—Lucy in the home, Ricky outside of it.[20] But one should not overlook the extent of the disorder that happens in the interim. For most of each episode the living room, which should be the seat of domestic tranquillity and role stability, becomes a theater of chaos.

One of the most impressive things about the show's scripts is the writers' ability to keep finding ingenious uses for this drab space. The living room's furnishings contain nothing out of the ordinary. Although the individual pieces changed throughout the years, the basic components remained the same: a sofa and chairs, a coffee table, a writing desk with a phone, a TV set, a piano, a fireplace, a coat closet, and a dining table that mysteriously appears in the center of the room when the situation requires it.[21] At different times nearly all of these pieces were used as props for Lucy's bits.

But perhaps the most important components of the living room are its three doors. The door of the apartment and the door to the kitchen are placed on the viewer's right; facing them is the door to the bedroom. This placement of entrances and exits is meaningful. The doors on the right are the passageways to the outside world. The apartment door is Ricky's path to fame—the world of agents, auditions, nightclubs, fan and trade magazines. The kitchen door is mostly for Lucy's entrances and exits; it takes her to the kitchen, where she meets Ethel each morning for coffee and hatches her schemes. The kitchen door also leads to the back door, the alternate way out of the apartment, which Ethel uses frequently. The kitchen also communicates with the living room through a pass-through window—a structural link that emphasizes the continuity between these two spaces. In some ways the apartment is a contested space; Ricky says to Lucy: "We're going to run this home like we do in Cuba, where the man is the master and the woman does what she is told" ("Equal Rights," October 26, 1953). But in most ways it is Lucy's alone. Lucy replies: "Oh yeah? I don't know how you treat your women in Cuba but this is the United States." Lucy's dominance over the living room and kitchen helps to establish the apartment as her terrain.

On the viewer's left is the door to Lucy and Ricky's bedroom, a different kind of space altogether. If the kitchen and apartment doors connect the characters to the outside world, the bedroom door takes them into seclusion. Given the constraints of fifties television, the writers had to use this space cautiously, with the result that the bedroom scenes in

I Love Lucy are both anodyne and packed with tension. The bedroom is a dangerous place, especially in a show whose title speaks of love. The furnishings in the bedroom—twin beds, dressers, a vanity, a reading chair—also were renovated periodically but without significant alterations. The one significant change had to do with the position of the twin beds. During the early episodes, the twin beds are always pushed together, the only separation being the border created by the individual blankets neatly tucked under each mattress. As best as I can determine, putting the beds together was unique for fifties television, whose rules of decorum required that the spouses sleep in separate beds (although perhaps the fact that Lucy and Desi were married in real life helped to soften this restriction). Sometime during the second season, during Lucy's pregnancy, the beds drifted apart and remained that way for the run of the series. It could be that the combination of Lucy's pregnancy and joined beds was too visible a reference to the couple's sex life. At any rate, the bedroom is another important space in the series. A good number of episodes either begin or end there; indeed, the first scene ever shot—the opening scene of the pilot—shows Lucy and Ricky in bed; likewise, the first scene of the first show in the regular series takes place in the bedroom.[22]

Having now cased the whole apartment, let us return to the living room. Its location between the realms of the public and the private endows it with a double identity. As an extension of the street, it is a public area, constantly being visited or occupied by outsiders—neighbors, salesmen, talent scouts, Lucy's bridge club, Ricky's poker pals. The "openness" of the living room is sometimes so pronounced that one time Lucy and Ricky are forced to celebrate their anniversary in the coat closet in order to get away from Fred, Ethel, and other visitors ("Sentimental Anniversary," February 1, 1954). At other times, however, the living room becomes an intimate abode, taking on something like the aura of the bedroom. Not infrequently we see Lucy and Ricky, on the sofa, cuddling or kissing; in "Don Juan and the Starlets" (February 14, 1955), when Lucy and Ricky go into a clinch on the sofa, Fred says to Ethel, "Let's go, the love birds are at it again." (Appropriately, this show was first broadcast on Valentine's Day.) Just like the characters, the living room itself has a fluid identity. Placed between the street and the bedroom, it is an interior margin, central but eccentric.

The living room is the kind of "between and betwixt" entity that Victor Turner has labeled "liminal." According to Turner, the liminal is a "gap," a "moment when individuals were liberated from normative demands, when they found themselves betwixt and between successive lodgements in jural or political systems."[23] Even if *I Love Lucy* deals with social conventions rather than jural proscriptions, this seems a fairly precise description of what happens in the Ricardos' living room: a temporary liberation from "cultural scripts" (Turner's phrase) during which almost anything can happen. The Ricardos' living room is a gap, a jubilant border or festive fringe where the spectacular and the everyday embrace.

As a border zone, it is also the logical locus for Lucy and Ricky's intercultural encounters. Their minimal expression is Lucy's mimicry of Ricky's accent, a leitmotif that regularly reminds the viewer of Ricky's status as a foreigner. Is Ricky ever really at home in the apartment? "Lucy, I'm home" is a line that he repeated innumerable times during the nine years that the series was on the air. But was the apartment really his home? For a home, it was certainly full of surprises. One day he comes through the door to find the living room emptied of furniture; once he walks in on Lucy, Fred, and Ethel in the middle of a pillow fight; on another occasion he opens the door and finds that Lucy has turned the apartment into a playground (to enter, he has to go down a slide). In English, a man's home is his castle; in Spanish, a man's home is his *casa*. But for Ricky 3-B is neither castle nor *casa*. It has neither the impregnability of the former nor the coziness of the later.

It may be that the apartment is not the place where Ricky feels most at home, which would explain why he seems to spend so little time there. Fortunately, Ricky has a home away from home—the nightclub, where he spends most of his days and nights either rehearsing or performing. The "club" (as he normally calls it) is a less complicated place than the living room. If the living room was a margin at the center, an interior margin, the nightclub is marginal in a more orthodox way, for people come here only after-hours. But the Tropicana, paradoxically, is a far more predictable place than the apartment. The nightclub's decor—some palm trees, Ricky's band, and a few tables with mostly anonymous customers—imposes a stability disrupted only on those instances when Lucy manages to get into the act. Unlike the furniture in the living room, the club's decor does not lend itself to inventive manipulation. Rather than helping to further some comic scheme, the club's furnishings set limits to how that space can be used. The countless references to Ricky's rehearsals reinforce the club's ethos of predictability. Unlike the apartment, the club is not a place for improvisation, for setting in motion zany schemes. Hardworking and conscientious,

Ricky leaves nothing to chance. Time after time we see him giving instructions to his band members, limiting their break time, asking for still another run-through. In spite of Lucy's persistent efforts, the night-club remains Ricky's space. At one point he actually buys the Tropicana and gives it his own show-business nickname, Club Babalú.[24]

As an extension of Ricky, the club has a "Cuban" or "Latin" personality. It is in the nightclub that one finds the only other Cuban character with a recurring role in the series, Marco Rizo, Desi Arnaz's longtime pianist, whose name comes up often and who occasionally has a few lines. Several other members of the band are Cuban as well. It seems to me crucial that at the club Spanish is a "normal" language rather than an unintelligible expression of anger or exasperation. Ricky's patented Spanish-language tirades against Lucy are funny because they are incongruous. When Ricky speaks Spanish at home, he is talking to himself. When he is railing at Lucy, he is talking to himself. Even when he is telling the story of *Caperucita roja* to little Ricky, he is talking to himself. But at the Tropicana Spanish is not deviant or incongruous. When Ricky sings one of his Spanish-language ballads, the setting and the song harmonize. And every once in a while, he will have a brief exchange in Spanish with one of the musicians. The Club Babalú serves to legitimize and place Ricky's Cubanness; it constitutes a kind of imagined community that embodies and enhances his identity as a Cuban male. In addition, the fact that Ricky may well be more Cuban at work than at home points up the connection between his origins and how he makes a living. As a home away from home, and as a business that will eventually bear his name, the Tropicana offers a cultural and commercial validation that Lucy cannot provide.

The two spaces that I have described—nightclub and living room—limn the two faces of Ricky's character. Like other hyphenated Americans, Ricky is blessed with a double personality. At the nightclub, he is the up-and-coming, dynamic showman who expertly commands his orchestra with a flick of his baton; at home, he is the befuddled husband who cannot control—or even keep up with—his wife's crazy schemes. These two facets of his "I"—star and husband—match up with his redundant name. At the Tropicana, he is Ricardo, the Latin lover; at the apartment, he is Ricky, the harried husband. Antic and romantic by turns, Ricky Ricardo is really two people.

Let's think for a moment about his name. Like Lucy's montage, the name is a bilingual text that contains both original and translation, since Ricky is a familiar American rendering of the Spanish Ricardo. But it is a translation that distances, a traductive translation: the Germanic Ricardo (which, incidentally, means "king") is not only anglicized but turned into a diminutive: it does not become Richard, or even Rick, but Ricky—a child's name (much as, one may add, Desiderio became Desi).[25] And, of the two given names—Ricky, Ricardo—it is the North American one that comes first. Ricardo—which in Spanish is seldom a last name and at that time was the first name of one of Hollywood's leading Latin lovers, Ricardo Montalbán—becomes the last name. It is as if Ricky had pushed Ricardo into last name position, with the consequence that Ricardo's "real" last name, say, Rodríguez, drops out of the picture entirely. In a sense, Ricky Ricardo is an orphan's name, one that reveals nothing about Ricky's parentage. Still, what matters about Ricky's ancestry is that he is Hispanic, and Ricardo functions well enough as a marker of ethnicity. Ricardo signifies that the subject is Hispanic; Ricky signifies that the Hispanic subject—the "I" in *I Love Lucy*—has been acculturated and domesticated. Ricardo is the Cuban man, Ricky is the American husband. Ricky Ricardo is the Cuban-American man and husband.

In a subtle way the contrast between Ricky and Ricardo is conveyed by the different connotations of the final letters in each name, *y* and *o*. In English, the suffix *y* is used in forming diminutives, nicknames, and terms of endearment or familiarity. By attaching a *y* to a proper name we establish an affective relation with the name's holder, we make the name contingent or dependent on us—an effect that may have to do with the other function of the suffix *y*, which is to turn a noun or verb into an adjective, as when we turn "touch" into "touchy" or "feel" into "feely." By contrast, final *o* is a marker not of familiarity but of foreignness, and not of endearment but of distance. Think, for a minute, of the words in English that end in "o." Once we get past the names of a few fruits and vegetables—potato, tomato, avocado, mango—and of some musical instruments—piano, cello—we run into psycho, wacko, weirdo, bucko, bimbo, tyro, Drano, Oreo, boffo. The fact that in Spanish *o* is a masculine ending probably also acts on our sense of the suffix in macho, mambo, Latino, and Gustavo. The story of *o* is a tale of estrangement, for the English language treats *o*-words as foreign bodies. Thus, by replacing the *o* in Ricardo with the *y* in Ricky one removes the unfamiliarity, and perhaps the threat, of the foreign body. (One might recall here that in certain quarters the politically correct spelling of "women" is "womyn," where the *y* feminizes, takes the "men" out of "women.") Replacing Ricardo with Ricky is, at the very least, an acculturating gesture, a way of turning the resident alien into a naturalized citizen. Ricky is the price that Ricardo pays for loving Lucy—the price he pays for being allowed into Lucy's bedroom and America's living rooms. Lucy and Ricky—the *y* that ends their names is not the least significant of things they have in common.

Ricky Ricardo's name alerts us, therefore, to the schisms that rend what Michael Fisher has called "the ethnic I."[26] It is certainly easy to ridicule the stereotypical elements in Ricky, who—as Desi himself used to do—ends each rendition of the Afro-Cuban song *Babalú* with an entirely un-African "olé." But it may also be possible to see Ricky Ricardo (name and character) as a moving emblem for what is both lost and gained in translation. Every time Ricky breaks into his nearly unintelligible Spanish or says "wunt" for "won't" or "splain" for "explain," his words, beyond whatever comedic value they may have, remind us of the risks and rewards of loving Lucy.

Neither Ricky nor Lucy was unaware of both risks and rewards. The most instructive episode in this regard is "Be a Pal" (October 22, 1951), the second episode of the series to be broadcast, whose premise is Lucy's fear that Ricky has become bored with her. In order to rekindle his interest, she tries a number of different tricks. First she greets him in the morning wearing a tight-fitting sequined gown, but Ricky doesn't even notice. Next she tries playing poker with Ricky and his pals, but that turns out badly when she beats the boys. Finally, following Ethel's urging, she decides that the way to get his attention is to mother him, to "treat him like a baby and surround him with things that remind him of his childhood." In the next scene the living room has become a flea-market of Cuban icons, or of items that Lucy thinks are Cuban icons, since they include two individuals with serape and sombrero, a donkey, a chicken coop, bananas, and a couple of palm trees. Since Ricky's mother was a "famous singer and dancer," Lucy herself dresses up as Carmen Miranda, fruit-hat and all. When Ricky walks in after a hard afternoon of rehearsals, Lucy launches into a rendition of "Mamãe Eu Quero," a song that Miranda made famous and that has an appropriately infantile theme.[27] As Lucy begins to sing, five children run out of the bedroom (Ricky supposedly had five brothers). In shock, Ricky pleads to know what is going on. Lucy explains: "I thought you were getting tired of me and if I reminded you of Cuba you might like me better." Ricky's response is thematic: "Lucy honey, if I wanted things Cuban I'd stayed in Havana. That's the reason I married you, 'cause you're so different from everyone I'd known before."

These two sentences are crucial. With this statement, Ricky sums up why he loves Lucy. If Lucy loves Ricky because he is Cuban, Ricky loves Lucy because she is not. Both espouse difference; that is, they seek out and prize what is different in their spouse. For Ricky this means, most pointedly, distancing himself from the maternal.

Lucy not only dresses up like his mother, but sings a song where the speaker insistently asks his mother for a pacifier. Beginning with its title, "Mamâe eu quero" (Mama, I Want) is nothing if not regressive. It is not entirely a mistranslation that the title of the song in English is "I Want My Mama."[28] A substitute for the mother's breast, the pacifier satisfies a need for maternal nurturance and security. To ask for a *chupeta*—the Portuguese term means, literally, "sucker"—is to yearn for mother. What Ricky wants, Lucy believes, is to be sheltered and protected in the way a mother would shelter and protect her infant son. If she can become the original Mrs. Ricardo, all will be well. Her motivation in this scene is no different from that which has made Cuban exiles endeavor to reproduce Cuba in Miami. Both are exercises in substitution. When Lucy redecorates the living room, she turns it into a Little Havana. But Little Havana is a pacifier, a sucker's paradise, an insufficient substitute for what was left at home.

Ricky wants no part of it. He has no interest in regression, a word that I intend in this context not only in the psychological sense, but also as the English cognate of the Spanish *regreso*, which means "return." In this scene the psychological merges with the cultural. Lucy offers Ricky the possibility of a fantasy return to his mother and his mother country. But Ricky's acceptance of Lucy's Americanness, which nicely balances Lucy's acceptance of Ricky's accent, involves precisely a rejection of both *regreso* and *regresión*. Ricky's project is nothing less than the detachment of the feminine from the maternal, which in his case involves a distancing from his culture of origin. When Lucy dresses up as the Cuban Mrs. Ricardo, she gives life to every boy's fantasy, which is to marry a girl just like the girl who married dear old dad. The Carmen Miranda costume is entirely apposite to this end. Dressed in her fruit-topped *baiana* outfit, Miranda is an avatar of Mother Nature, a comic Medusa who transfixes you with her frozen smile and gyrating hips.

When Ricky tells Lucy that he loves her because she is so different from everyone he's known before, foremost in that group is his mother. Notice how his statement plays off the song's lyrics. The speaker of the song tells the mother what he "wants"; Ricky replies to this expression of want by correcting Lucy's idea of what his wants are: "If I *wanted* things Cuban," he says, "I'd stayed in Havana." Notice also how the very title of the song echoes that of the TV series: "Mamâe eu quero" / *I Love Lucy*. The Portuguese sentence articulates a repetitive, irreflective wanting that grows out of infantile needs. The English sentence, by contrast, is a straightforward declaration of love. "Mama, I Want" is a reflex; *I Love Lucy* is a choice. Furthermore, since in both Portuguese and Spanish the verb *querer* means both "to want" and "to love," what really sets the two phrases apart are the objects of desire, "Lucy" and "mama"—four-letter words both, but separated by a world of differences.

By making up as the Cuban Mrs. Ricardo, Lucy momentarily turns the living room into a womb, or at least a maternal space. The only adult "male" in the scene other than Ricky is Ethel—dressed in drag. Fred, who certainly could have been used to comic effect (dress him up like a bullfighter!), is nowhere in sight. What Lucy fails to recognize is that, whatever else the living room may signify for Ricky, it is not a womb. That's what's right and what's wrong about it, for its openness and chanciness make it the very opposite of the secure, stable environment of the womb. The living room is a space of adventure, not retreat. When Lucy attempts to address Ricky in Spanish, Ricky does not respond in kind; instead, he responds with a quintessentially American comeback: "Lucy, have you gone off your rocker?"

Yet Ricky's rejection of the maternal, personally and culturally, is certainly not absolute. Perhaps it is better to speak of distancing rather than rejection. Ricky wants to keep his mother at a distance; he realizes that she belongs in Cuba, not in his apartment. But during those not infrequent moments when Ricky parades his ties to Cuban culture, the maternal is often in evidence. In the Little Red Riding Hood episode, for example, when Lucy questions Ricky's knowledge of this story, he answers that he learned it from his mother, who used to tell it to him when he was a "little child." Then he goes into his own child's room and tells his son the story that his mother used to tell him. By doing this, Ricky puts himself in his mother's shoes. Interestingly, the plot of *Little Red Riding Hood* itself turns on impersonation and cross-dressing—the wolf in drag pretending to be the grandmother. Yet the most significant instance of impersonation here is Ricky's emulation of his mother, which shows that even the wolfish Cuban *macho* has a nurturing, maternal side.

Although Ricky does not reject his "roots," he does not spend his life in fetishistic worship of them. More precisely, he does not seek to surround himself with sameness. I wonder to what extent the objections that are sometimes voiced to this show's portrayal of Hispanics stem from Ricky's unregressive, unnostalgic view of "things Cuban." It seems odd that Ricky does not notice the inappropriateness of sombreros, serapes, and Carmen Miranda as metonyms of his childhood.[29] That may be because for him there is a more important issue here than Lucy's warped sense of "things Cuban," an issue that has to do with being receptive to otherness, to what is different, new, or exceptional. This is why the living room is a perfectly suitable venue for Ricky's espousal of difference, for here anything is possible—even this ditsy, distorted re-creation of Ricky's Cuban childhood.

It is difficult to watch many episodes of the series without noticing that one of the not-so-hidden themes of the show is one Cuban man's fascination with Americana, and more pointedly, with *americanas*—those "glorious hunks of stuff" that Ricky tends to drool over (Ricky's phrase in "Lucy Plays Cupid"). In one sense, *I Love Lucy* is a theater of domestic war; in another, it is melodrama, or better, a mellow drama that plays out the fateful rendezvous of Cuba's scrambled ego with its no less scrambled id. Looking at the series through Ricky's eyes, that is, looking at it through the "I" in the title, the theme of the show is Ricky's romance with otherness. *I Love Lucy* showcases the advantages of what we might term "heteroculturalism," the belief that opposite cultures attract. A confirmed heterocultural, Ricky thrives on unlikeness. His cultural preferences merge with his sexual preferences. The opposite sex is the apposite sex. The opposite culture is the apposite culture. When he says "I love Lucy," Ricky liberates himself from cultural and sexual regression.

As we saw above, Lucy and Ricky's bedroom is an important element in the spatial disposition of the program. One may even venture that the twin beds themselves are material symbols for Lucy's and Ricky's differences. If this is so, the definitive metaphor for the cultural divide that separates Lucy from Ricky (and Ricky from Ricardo) is simply the distance between beds. But this distance was certainly not inviolable. The twin beds stand in apposition, not opposition. Let's remember how the typical episode ends: Lucy and Ricky make up, clinch, and kiss. After the kiss the next thing we see is a heart superimposed on rumpled satin sheets, and moments later the inscription, "I Love Lucy."[30] Stripped to its literal core, the title of the series is quite racy, for it is in the bedroom that Ricky *really* loves Lucy. In his memoirs, Desi states: "I think the audience could visualize Lucy and Ricky going to bed together and enjoying it."[31] Fred could visualize that too, since he calls Lucy and Ricky "lovebirds" who are "at it" all the time (when he says this Lucy and Ricky had been married fifteen years!). The show's logo leaves little doubt that Desi and Fred are right. This is a show not just about domestic trials and tribulations, but about physical intimacy, sexual love. *Every* word in the series title is ambiguous, for "love" also has a double referent. On the one hand, it refers to the affection that Ricky and the viewers feel toward Lucy; on the other, it names an erotic relation. There is a world of difference between *My Favorite Husband*, the title of Lucille Ball's radio program, and that of the TV series. *I Love Lucy* defines Ricky not as husband, not as father, not as entertainer, but only as lover. Ricky's is a lover's "I." The episodes of the series are fragments from a lover's discourse. Who can doubt that Lucy and Ricky spent their nights making cross-over dreams come true?

These sexual undertones make *I Love Lucy* an unusual exemplar of the fifties sitcom. The other family-centered sitcoms of the era convey a very different message, one that emphasizes domestic travails or family life rather than romance. Think, for example, of the famous beginning of Jackie Gleason's *The Honeymooners*: a splash of fireworks, followed by an urban landscape where a moon rises from behind a skyline; tondo-like, the moon serves as a frame, first, for Jackie Gleason's face, then for his name, then for the title of the show, and finally for the names of the other actors. Although the initial image of exploding fireworks is consistent with the title's romantic connotations, these connotations soon vanish. For one thing, the skyline establishes a social rather than an intimate setting for the show. We are placed not in the privacy of an apartment, and certainly not in the intimacy of a bedroom, but in the midst of skyscrapers and highrises. In addition, by using the rising moon as a tondo for Gleason's mug, the show's focus shifts from a couple of honeymooners to one star (he is the only actor thus featured). Almost imperceptibly, after only a few seconds into the opening credits, the pilot metaphor has changed from that of the "honeymoon" to that of the "man in the moon." This subtle shift revises the viewer's expectations about a program called *The Honeymooners*. Since the Kramdens are a far cry from honeymooning lovebirds, the comic reversal of the opening images prepares us for the diverting but dreary, funny but unsexy lives of Ralph and Alice.

Another example is *Make Room for Daddy*, a show directly inspired by *I Love Lucy*. The similarities between the two programs are obvious enough. Like the Ricardos, the Williams are a show-biz family living in an apartment in New York. Just as Ricky is Desi's TV twin, Danny Williams is Danny Thomas's fictional persona. If Ricky Ricardo headlines at the Tropicana, Danny Williams headlines at the Club Copa. In addition, since Danny Williams is also "ethnic" (Lebanese), his ethnic idiosyncrasies are both a recurring motif and a running gag.[32] But one fundamental difference between the two programs is that, from the title onward, *Make Room for Daddy* highlights Danny's role as devoted family man. Danny and Daddy are the same person, and practically the same word. The show's opening scene underscores this: as Danny walks in through the door, his wife comes out of one room and his two children come out of the other. They meet in the center of the living room, embrace, and fall back together onto the sofa. This makes quite a contrast with the rumpled satin sheets of *I Love Lucy*. *Make Room for Daddy* begins and ends with the whole family converging in the living room; *I Love Lucy* opens and closes in bed. This also is the Cuban-American way.

I Love Lucy is not a "family" show inasmuch as the idea of family does not play significant role in the plot. For all practical purposes, Lucy and Ricky do not have a family. The lyric of the show's familiar theme song says, "I love Lucy and she loves me. / We're as happy as two can be."[33] These words were sung only once, at the end of the second season, in the episode "Lucy's Last Birthday" (May 11, 1953). What is odd about this is that the lyric speaks of Lucy and Ricky as if they were childless—"we're as happy as *two* can be." And yet, little Ricky had been born only a few episodes earlier! Even after the birth of their son, the Ricardos remain essentially a childless couple. Little Ricky did not become a significant character until the sixth season, the last in the half-hour format. Throughout the duration of the series, there are passing references to Ricky's ample Cuban family, Ricky's mother visits once (with dire consequences), and Lucy's mother, Mrs. McGillicuddy, puts in a few appearances. But for the most part Lucy and Ricky are accompanied only by Fred and Ethel, another childless couple, who seem even more bereft of family than the Ricardos.

Lucy's mother makes her debut in the episode entitled "California Here We Come" (January 10, 1955). On first blush, the "we" in this title seems to refer to the Ricardo family, which by now includes little Ricky. But when Lucy and Ricky take off for California by car, they are accompanied not by their son and his grandmother (who take the train), but by the Mertzes. The "we" primarily refers to Lucy and Ricky and Fred and Ethel. Although Lucy and Ricky are always portrayed as attentive, loving parents, they hardly spend any time with little Ricky, who must be one of the most neglected children in the history of American television. Significantly, even in the two movies that Lucy and Desi spun off their series, *The Long, Long Trailer* and *Forever, Darling*, they play a childless couple (more on this in the next chapter).

I Love Lucy is the great Cuban-American love story. Essentially a chronicle of how a Cuban man and an American woman live together, this show is as fine an example as we have of the pleasures and perils of bicultural romance. Beginning with the title, the focus is on the Ricardos' rich, complex, and sometimes conflicted relationship—a relationship that in ways both deliberate and inadvertent mirrored Ball and Arnaz's own complicated marriage. From Ricky's perspective, the lesson is that one should embrace difference, even if it comes in the form of a beautiful but zany redhead from New York. When Ricky falls into Lucy's non-Cuban, nonmaternal arms, he loses and he finds himself. What he loses is his primitive sense of self as his mother's son; there is no denying that by loving Lucy Ricky distances himself from his native language and culture; in this respect he becomes "less" Cuban. Perhaps biculturation always entails some degree of deculturation. What Ricky gets in return, though, is a renewed self compacted from his Cuban past and his Cuban-American present. New and old selves relate as childhood and adulthood, or infancy and maturity. Being half Cuban, Ricky becomes a whole man. This Cuban-American self is certainly not an easy or stable achievement, and it requires constant struggle against encroachments from both sides. Regression remains a constant temptation, as does assimilation. It is not always easy for Ricky to give Ricardo his due, and vice versa.

Another way to say it is that the bicultured "I" is always an interim self, by which I mean both a temporary, provisional self—a self with an expiration date—and one that exists in the gap or interim between cultures. Little Ricky's occasional appearances in the show make clear that, his father's bedtime stories notwithstanding, the bicultural identity is *papi*'s alone. Little Ricky couldn't speak accented English even if he tried. There is a healthy continuity between father and son, but there is also a healthy distance. When Ricky gets old enough to play an instrument, he follows in his father's steps by choosing drums. But instead of the Afro-Cuban *tumbadora*, little Ricky plays the American trap drums.

(The same held true, by the way, for Desi, Jr., who started his show-biz career as a drummer in a rock band.)

The bicultural placement, the bicultural fix, is Ricky's alone. As a one-and-a-halfer, he is too young to be Cuban and too old to be American. But he is exactly the right age to be Cuban American, and exactly the right age to make the best of loving Lucy. Cuban-American culture begins in bed, on those rumpled satin sheets that by now have become an enduring American icon. Lucy and Ricky enjoin what they enjoyed: life on the hyphen, the Cuban-American way. Desi Arnaz once remarked that "history is made at night." He must have been thinking of the Ricardos. Lucy and Ricky—when they made love they made history.

I will make no attempt to hide my bicultural bias. I love Ricky because he loves Lucy. In the Cuban-American tradition, one calls this a Desi Chain.

Spic'n Spanish

MAMBO NO. 2 *Miami Spanish includes a term that, so far as I know, is unique to the city of sun and solecisms:* nilingüe. *Just as a* bilingüe *is someone who speaks two languages (say, Spanish and English), a* nilingüe *is someone who doesn't speak either: "ni español, ni inglés." Such a person is a no-lingual, a nulli-glot. My example of nilingualism is Ricky Ricardo. Ricky's occasional Spanish utterances are shot through with anglicisms:* falta *for* culpa, introducir *for* presentar, parientes *for* padres, *and so on. Sometimes the anglicisms seem deliberate (so that the monolingual viewers understand what he is saying), but at other times they're plain mistakes. A curious thing: as Ricky got older, his English didn't get any better, but his Spanish kept getting worse. Equally curious: the same thing happened to Desi Arnaz. In 1983 Arnaz was picked "king" of the Cuban carnival in Miami, Open House Eight. By then, his Spanish was as frail as his health. He now had an accent in* two *languages.*

In Spanish to know a language well is to "dominate" it. But my mother tongue has it backward: people don't dominate languages, languages dominate people. By reversing the power relation, English comes closer to the truth. When someone speaks English better than Spanish, we say that he or she

is "English-dominant," an expression in which the
language, and not the speaker, has the upper hand.
But in Ricky no language achieved dominance;
English and Spanish battled each other to a tie (a
tongue-tie). A nilingüe treats his mother tongue
like a foreign language and treats the foreign language like his other tongue. T. W. Adorno once
said: "Only he who is not truly at home inside
a language can use it as an instrument." Ricky
Ricardo is a multi-instrumentalist. He is homeless
in two languages.

Two

THE-MAN-WHO-LOVED-LUCY

One more chorus of "Babalú," and out you go.
BOB HOPE TO DESI ARNAZ [1]

When the nine-year run of *I Love Lucy* ended in April 1961, one of its stars went on to other successful TV series, remaining in the public (and the CBS) eye for the rest of her life. Her co-star, by contrast, retired to Palm Springs, bought a ranch, and devoted much of his time to breeding race horses. Aside from sporadic guest shots on talk shows and a couple of one-time roles on television series, he all but disappeared from view. Desi Arnaz's one return to the spotlight took place in 1976 upon the publication of his memoirs, which he called simply *A Book.*[2] Timed to coincide with the twenty-fifth anniversary of *I Love Lucy,* *A Book* was greeted with mixed reviews, but it sold well, thanks in large part to Desi's willingness to promote it on talk shows. Today, however, *A Book* is out of print and difficult to find.

The front and back covers of *A Book* are studies in contrasts. The front cover (Fig. 3) shows Desi as he looked in the mid-seventies— jowls, creases on his neck, thinning gray hair, a weathered complexion unretouched by makeup or photography. He is standing on a dimly lit stage; in his right hand he is holding a long, thin microphone; in his left he has a half-smoked cigar that the stark shadows have reduced to a sliver of light. He is wearing street clothes—a sport jacket over a rumpled light-colored shirt, no tie. As he talks to the audience, Desi looks away from the camera. The stage is dark. His expression is serious, even somber.

This Desi is certainly different from his show-business image.

Although he is on a stage, instead of singing or dancing he is talking, perhaps explaining something. Since the photograph is taken from an angle, the message is not only that this is a "candid" shot, and perhaps revelatory of facets of his life or personality that we may not have seen before, but also that the individual in the pages of this book is someone other than the funny, upbeat, somewhat bumbling bandleader of the TV series. Whoever this man may be, it is not Ricky Ricardo or Mr. Babalú.

The back cover is nearly identical to the front. Instead of endorsements or information about the book or its author, again we find the title, the name of the author, and the same brief blurb. Because the layout is the same, when one picks up *A Book* it's impossible to tell which is the front of the book. What is different, and strikingly so, is the photograph. On the back it's Desi again, but now forty years younger, since the photograph is his typical publicity shot from the 1940s (Fig. 4). This time it's a brightly lit, frontal shot. His complexion is perfect, the teeth are white and glistening, the abundant shiny black hair is attractively tousled, he has a glint in his eye and a big cheesy smile on his face. A white rumba shirt opens in the middle to reveal a medal hanging from his neck. A conga drum is slung around his right shoulder, and the photographer has caught his subject as he is about to strike the drum skin.

Considered together, the two photographs compose an allegory on the transience of youth and beauty. But the theme of the diptych is not only the ravages of time; the contrast between the two portraits also suggests the ambiguous relation between life and art, living and performing, an ambiguity that *I Love Lucy* exploited with abandon.[3] More to the point, the diptych suggests the difficulty of sustaining this distinction in an autobiography, which is always performance parading as life. At first blush, it would seem that whereas the back cover exhibits Desi's performing self, the front cover gives us a glimpse of the man behind the mask. Yet the "real" Desi is *also* on a stage. He's in street clothes, there's not a drum skin in sight, but still he's there with a microphone in his hand. The ambiguity is made more poignant by the blurb that appears on both front and back. Placed immediately below the book's title and author, in smaller lettering, it says: "The outspoken memoirs of 'Ricky Ricardo'—the man who loved Lucy." Ricky Ricardo? The man who loved Lucy? Just like the TV series, the blurb jumbles the identity of the "I" in *I Love Lucy*, for it seems that Desi's "book" is also Ricky's "memoirs." The enclosure in quotations of

A BOOK

by Desi Arnaz

The outspoken memoirs of "Ricky Ricardo"
—the man who loved Lucy

FIGURE 3   *Desi Arnaz,* A Book *(front cover). Photograph used by permission of William Morrow & Company, Inc.*

A BOOK

by Desi Arnaz

The outspoken memoirs of "Ricky Ricardo"
—the man who loved Lucy

FIGURE 4   *Desi Arnaz,* A Book *(back cover). Photograph used by permission of William Morrow & Company, Inc.*

Ricky's name lessens the equivocation only slightly, given the equivocal phrase that follows: "the man who loved Lucy." Which "man"—Ricky or Desi? And which "Lucy"—Ball or Ricardo? One cannot tell *A Book* by its cover.

What is puzzling, also, is that in spite of the mention of Ricky Ricardo neither of the photographs captures Desi during the years when he played this part. As if to give the lie to the blurb's conflation of Desi and Ricky, they portray him the way he looked before and after the heyday of *I Love Lucy* in the 1950s. Even if the blurb conflates Desi and Ricky, the photographs seem to say that Desi has other faces and facets, that he is more than the sum of his TV part. Again the "I" question arises, this time with special urgency, given that *A Book* is an extended first-person account. Who is this "I" who opens the account of his life by saying, "I was born in Santiago de Cuba, on March 2, 1917. (I had to start someplace.)"?[4] And does "start" refer to the book or to his life?

The more or less prevalent view of Desi Arnaz is that he owed his success to his talented wife. As one recent critic put it, "Every viewer knows that Desi Arnaz's success in show business was primarily the result of his marriage to Lucille Ball."[5] The truth is somewhat more complex, however. While no one can deny that the success of *I Love Lucy* was due in large measure to the comedic talents of Lucille Ball, Desi Arnaz was not simply Lucille Ball's husband. For years before the TV series went on the air, Arnaz enjoyed a lucrative career fronting his own orchestra. By the late 1940s, he was netting well over $100,000 from his band tours—a not inconsiderable sum for the time. According to the jazz historian Will Friedwald, "Arnaz had virtually the only success story of any new band launched after the war."[6] In addition, during the forties Arnaz had acted in half a dozen movies, generally to good reviews. And once the TV series became a hit, he was smart enough to make the best of it, artistically and commercially. Never a great actor, he understood his limitations and worked effectively within a limited range; never a great singer or musician, he was nonetheless a first-rate showman. His business acumen in parlaying Desilu into a major studio is well documented, as are his contributions to the staging and filming of *I Love Lucy*, many of whose episodes he directed.

In many ways Desi is a consummate example of the Cuban type of the *vivo*, the term for someone who lives and prospers by virtue of his wit, his *viveza*. What the *vivo* lacks in formal education or native talent, he makes up in plain smarts. His intelligence is a species of ingenuity, his wit a species of cleverness.[7] Throughout his career Desi repeatedly showed these qualities. He was smart, resourceful, and realistic. The other side of the *vivo* is that he tends to be a *vividor*, a bon vivant, and by all accounts Desi was certainly an inveterate *vividor*, one major reason for the collapse of his marriage. After all, this was a man who, according to one admiring female acquaintance, "could rumba standing up and lying down."[8] This was also a man who was once picked up by the Los Angeles police department for taking off his clothes in front of a high-class brothel and launching into a rousing (or arousing) rendition of "Babalú." In fact, Desi should be no more invisible than Ricky.

The only son of a prominent family from Santiago de Cuba, Arnaz came to this country in 1934, as a result of the fall from power of dictator Gerardo Machado, whom his father—the mayor of Santiago—had supported. Like many other Cubans since, the Arnaz family settled in Miami, where Desi attended Saint Patrick's High, played on the football team, and befriended Al Capone's son. After graduating he worked at several odd jobs, including cleaning bird cages, until he got a job singing at a small Miami Beach nightclub. A few months later he was spotted by Xavier Cugat, who hired him to sing and play for his band.[9] Always a quick study, Arnaz soon formed his own band, began doing the conga, and became an instant success on the nightclub circuit. In New York he met Broadway director George Abbott, who liked Desi's conga act and cast him in *Too Many Girls*, a Rodgers and Hart musical that became a Broadway hit. (Years later Lucille Ball suggested that *Too Many Girls* should have been the title of Desi's autobiography.)

When the show was turned into a motion picture, a young Desi stayed on (he was twenty-three at the time). Like other Latin-flavored musicals of that era, *Too Many Girls* (RKO, 1940) exhibited a rather peculiar idea of Spanish-American culture. Desi plays the part of Manuelito Lynch, a young man from the provinces—of Argentina. So far so good, although "Manuelito" should probably have been "Manolito." The incongruities really begin with Manuelito's talents, for it turns out that he plays football—not soccer, but American football. Indeed, Manuelito is nothing less than "the greatest prep school flash in fifty years," which explains why he has been offered scholarships to Princeton, Harvard, and Yale, but doesn't quite explain how he became an accomplished conga drummer.

In fairness to Rodgers and Hart, in the original play Manuelito did not do the conga, a sidelight added by Abbott in order to exploit Desi's nightclub popularity. In the Broadway version the conga came at the end of the first act; according to Arnaz and others, it never failed to stop the show. In the film version the conga sets the stage for the jubilant finale. This scene by itself is worth the price of a video rental. After the big football victory, Manuelito leads his classmates into a large plaza where a big bonfire is burning. With the flames spiraling around him, he pounds out a spirited conga as he mouths Afro-Cuban vocables, "Oh-Eh, Oh-Eh." The students pick up the chant and form conga lines. Some are carrying torches, other bear *farolas*, the lanterns typical of carnival celebrations. Soon the whole plaza is full of screaming, swirling bodies. The scene cuts to a professor in a lab; when he looks through his microscope, he sees that even the paramecia on the slide are doing the conga!

The picture of an Argentine Desi, dressed in a football uniform, with a *tumbadora* slung around his neck, leading a conga in the New Mexico desert is the kind of mishmash that makes Lucy's Carmen Miranda seem authentic by comparison. (One wonders what the conga would have been like if Desi's understudy, Van Johnson, had played the scene.) But this is not all. While Desi thumps and grinds, Ann Miller taps (Fig. 5)! Never mind that she plays a Mexican girl with the unlikely name of Pepe. Never mind also that a close-up of Desi's conga drum shows that it is decorated with Indian motifs. Hyperbolic even in its title, *Too Many Girls* meshes too many cultures.

The movie's ignorance is so utterly blissful that I find its mindless agglutinating energy difficult to resist. To be sure, *Too Many Girls* is a multiculturalist's nightmare. All of the principal American cultures are there—black, white, Indian, Hispanic; but every one is caricatured and distorted. Yet perhaps here lies the film's achievement. Jitterbugging to a conga, as some of the dancers do, is to treat the Afro-American jitter-bug with no more respect than is bestowed on Cuban music or Amerin-dian art. In the throes of conga-fever, feeling the heat of the bonfire, the celebrants fuse into one swirling mass. The town plaza becomes a melt-ing pot. As the camera moves hectically from one group of revelers to another, the impression is of a boiling, moiling, multicultural mass of humanity that moves in unison. Everyone is stepping to the beat of the same conga drummer, Desi, who looks about to be swallowed by the flames.

Over the next several years scenes of this type were to be replayed over and over in Hollywood musicals. The conga, which originated in Cuban carnival celebrations, was ideal for big production numbers. It was a group dance, it was simple to do, and it had the requisite foreign, festive air to it. A partial listing of the Hollywood conga roll would

include "The La Conga," with Mickey Rooney and Judy Garland dancing in a high school auditorium, from *Strike Up the Band* (1940); "Cali-
Conga" from *A Night at Earl Carroll's* (1940); "Doing the Conga" from
Down Argentine Way (1940); "Doing the Conga" (same title, different
song) from *Up in the Air* (1941); "Kindergarten Conga" from *Moon
over Miami* (1941); "Ora O Conga," a lusophone entry, from *Rio Rita*
(1942); "Conga from Honga," the third-world contribution, from *The
Fleet's In* (1942); and "Congaroo" and "Conga Beso" from *Hellzapop-
pin'* (1941). There was also a low-budget movie called *La Conga Nights*
(Universal, 1940), about a "music moron" (as he's called) who opens
a nightclub in the Spanish section of New York. Were one to include
nonconga numbers set to a conga rhythm (like Miranda's "Mamâe eu
quero"), this list would be much, much longer. But the conga backlash
was not long in coming: "I Hate the Conga," from *Born to Sing* (1942).

Desi's performance in *Too Many Girls* was to set the tone for his
subsequent roles, including that of Ricky Ricardo. The conga, which

had been his nightclub trademark, became his filmic signature as well. But for the *I Love Lucy* aficionado, the movie is memorable primarily because it contains the first on-screen encounter between Desi and Lucy. Lucy plays Connie Casey, a billionaire's daughter and "international showoff" whose father thinks she needs protecting. He hires four young football stars (including Manuelito) as her bodyguards. Since Manuelito's love interest is Ann Miller's character, he and Connie don't have much to do with each other. But when Manuelito first runs into Connie/Lucy, he takes one look at her and faints. In real life Desi had met Lucy only a few days before and had fallen instantly in love with her. Sometimes life imitates RKO.

Too Many Girls received generally good notices. An RKO publicity release touted Arnaz as the new Latin heartthrob: "If Desi Arnaz, handsome, olive-tinted, black hair, smoldering eyes, Cuban chap whom Abbott saw at La Conga, cast him in *Too Many Girls* and became a matinee idol, can now repeat on the screen, he may well cause movie producers to search for Latins as they did following Valentino's rise. . . . Desi Arnaz, the newcomer, may be just what the doctor ordered for the revival of the Latin craze following Valentino's success, the blade to carve out such a revival." [10] Along the same lines, the reviewer for *Time* called him "a terpsichorean Rudolph Valentino" who left you wishing for more dancing. [11] But not everyone agreed. Bosley Crowther, the influential movie critic of the *New York Times*, was less flattering: "Mr. Arnaz is a noisy, black-haired Latin whose face, unfortunately, lacks expression and whose performance is devoid of grace." [12]

Still, as a result of his work in *Too Many Girls*, RKO gave Arnaz a three-picture contract, though none of the movies that followed matched the success of the Rodgers and Hart musical. In *Four Jacks and a Jill* (1941) and *Father Takes a Wife* (1941), Desi reprised his role as "terpsichorean Valentino." *Four Jacks and a Jill*, a negligible movie with few redeeming moments, had him in another unlikely part. Instead of an Argentine football star, he played a South American king. The plot of the movie turns on a case of mistaken identity (will the real king please stand up and conga?), and is too silly to summarize. Desi's best, brief moment is his rendition of "The Boogie Woogie Conga," which he does in the backseat of a cab.

Considerably more accomplished is *Father Takes a Wife* (1941), where Desi gets fourth billing as Carlos Valdés, a refugee from an unnamed Latin American country (from prep flash, to king, to expatriate!). Carlos, who has a fine operatic voice, arrives in the United States as a stowaway. He becomes the protegé of a famous stage actress, Leslie Collier (Gloria Swanson), much to the chagrin of Frederick Osborne (Adolphe Menjou), a rich shipping magnate and her recently acquired husband. In his most important scene Desi sings the lovely bolero "Perfidia," which was part of Desi's nightclub act and has been recently revived (in English translation) by Linda Ronstadt for the movie *Mambo Kings*. But as Hollywood logic would have it, since Carlos was an opera singer, "Perfidia" was dubbed by an Italian tenor. The movie does have a conga scene, but curiously Desi is not in it. To the other characters what seems most remarkable about Carlos is not his singing but his face. Leslie's Aunt Julie remarks, "When you have a face like that all you need is a face like that." Apparently the director felt the same way, for Arnaz was not given much to do besides strut around and look good.

Because *Father Takes a Wife* represented Gloria Swanson's return to the screen after a seven-year absence, RKO released it with much fanfare. The ads proclaimed, "There's glamour on the screen again because Gloria's back." Even so, the film was a flop, grossing less than $100,000. One of the problems may have been that Arnaz was actually prettier than Swanson. Sic transit Gloria.

His last picture under the RKO contract was *The Navy Comes Through* (1942), about which one reviewer remarked, I think unfairly, "The navy comes through but the movie doesn't." [13] Desi plays a "Cuban hotfoot" who enlists in the Navy; in between skirmishes with German subs, he finds time to sing the Cuban *son* "Masabí" and to recite, in Spanish, some lines from the Cuban national anthem. Much better received was his other war movie, *Bataan* (1943), the first picture he did for MGM and also the first in which he had a nonsinging part. Probably the best, if not the most interesting, movie Desi had acted in up to this point, *Bataan* recounts the heroic last stand of an American platoon in Manila. As private Félix Ramírez, the "kid" in the platoon, Arnaz has two important scenes. In the first he fixes a radio and gushes over Tommy Dorsey: "That's Tommy Dorsey! From Hollywood! Oh, he sends me, sarge; he makes me lace up my boots. Oh, brother. Keep growing, Tommy, keep growing. Oh, he's tall tonight, he's tall tonight. Give me some of that trombone, Tommy." Not even in Manila does Desi escape typecasting, for although he doesn't play a musician, he plays a musician's groupie. In the other scene he becomes delirious with malaria, calls out for his "mamacita," recites an act of contrition in Latin (which Desi remembered from his Jesuit schooling in Cuba), and dies. His agony prompts Robert Taylor, the leader of the group, to speak the only good line in the movie: "Jitterbug kid, he's shaking himself to death." His well-acted death scene did earn Arnaz the Photoplay Award for the best performance of the month, about which he remarked years later, "It wasn't the Academy Award but damn good enough for me."[14]

During World War II, Arnaz interrupted his career to serve in the army. (But he did not end up in Manila; apparently he spent most of his stint touring with the USO and fooling around with the nurses.) After the war he went back to MGM, where he was still under contract, but by then the studio had a new Latin heartthrob, Ricardo Montalbán. Seeing no future for him at MGM, Desi went back to the band business. It was around this time that he began to sing "Babalú." After a few months the band's popularity got him back into the movies. *Cuban Pete* (Universal, 1946), a low-budget musical that was filmed in all of twelve days, gave Desi his first starring role. Billed as "The Rhumba Rhythm King," he plays a Cuban bandleader who goes to New York to headline in a radio show. With a running time of barely an hour, *Cuban Pete* is little more than a musical review. Arnaz has four songs, including two renditions of the title song, which became part of his nightclub act and was later featured in one of the first *I Love Lucy* episodes ("The Diet," October 29, 1951). Desi himself considered *Cuban Pete* a "B-minus picture" whose principal value was to drum up business for the band, which it did.[15] *Variety* agreed: "This light-budgeted musical programmer from Universal is also lightweight entertainment. It hangs eight tunes on implausible plotting, features dull pace and few chuckles." And even though "Arnaz tries hard and his music and songs are an aid," he can't save this "haphazard affair."[16]

Arnaz's last movie before *I Love Lucy* followed in the rumba steps of *Cuban Pete*, but with considerably more polish.[17] Although *Holiday in Havana* (Columbia, 1949) is all but forgotten today (even by Arnaz himself, who does not mention it in *A Book*), it is an enjoyable picture, with excellent music, plausible characters, an unobtrusive plot, and vintage footage of the Cuban carnivals. This time *Variety* was far more encomiastic: "Here's a rhythmic programmer which skyrockets above the average medium-budgeter, an entertaining musical which will garner hefty response by virtue of its haunting rumbas."[18] Desi reprises his usual role of Latin-lover-cum-conga-drum, with the advantage that here he doesn't have to dance wearing cleats, shoulder pads, and a helmet. As Carlos Estrada, a busboy and budding composer, he chances upon the direction of a rumba orchestra when its director runs off after the Brazilian bombshell, Pepita. ("I'm going back to Brazil," Pepita says, "where men not only make love to you, they marry you.") His love interest is Lolita Valdés (Mary Hatcher), "the greatest entertainer in all of Cuba," who coincidentally needs a band to back her up at the carnival competitions in Havana. Carlos and Lolita meet and fall in love, but are driven apart by a series of misadventures and misunderstandings. In the end everything is cleared up, and Cuban boy gets Cuban girl just in time for carnival. Dancing off with the first prize in the competition, they rumba happily ever after. Carlos sums up the movie this way: "How about that, I looked for a girl all over and she was right here under my maracas."

Like *Too Many Girls, Holiday in Havana* culminates with an apocalyptic conga scene. For once, however, the conga takes place in an appropriate setting, the Cuban carnival. In the midst of the celebrations, with streamers piercing the Cuban night and confetti showering down, Desi performs the title song, a conga with an English lyric:

> *Holiday in Havana,*
> *the thrill of romance*
> *as you dance*
> *with a lovely* cubana.
>
> *Holiday in Havana,*
> *dance the night away,*
> *that's the Cuban way*
> *in Havana's holiday.*

Intercut with his singing is footage of real carnival floats and dances, as well as a brief close-up of a black dancer in a *rumbero* outfit who does wonderful twists and turns. The deft editing creates the impression that everybody in Havana is gyrating to the rhythm of Desi's English-only conga. As often happens in the best musicals from this period, the music makes the movie. The other musical numbers, which are equally well done, offer something for every taste: Latin-tinged ballads by Oscar Hammerstein ("I'll Take Romance") and René Touzet ("Made for Each Other");[19] an English version of "Rumba rumbero," a composition by Miguelito Valdés, the original "Mr. Babalú";[20] and two songs written by Arnaz himself—"Holiday in Havana" and the "Arnaz Jam." Enhancing the quality of the music is Arnaz's band, which stands around in almost every scene waiting for Desi to give a downbeat.

As a Cuban-motion picture, *Holiday in Havana* offers a typical example of the "maraca musicals" of the 1940s, with their picturesque locales, inconsequential plots, and "latunes" (as Latin-influenced songs were sometimes called).[21] Perhaps the best examples of the genre are *You Were Never Lovelier* (1942), with Fred Astaire, Rita Hayworth, and Xavier Cugat, and *Down Argentine Way* (1940), with Betty Grable, Carmen Miranda, and Don Ameche (in a part that was originally offered to Arnaz). Havana locales were not scarce either, as witnessed by *Girl from Havana* (1940), *Moonlight in Havana* (1942), *Club Havana* (1946), and *Havana Rose* (1951).[22] Especially reminiscent of *Holiday in Havana* are two MGM productions, *Weekend in Havana* (1941), with Carmen Miranda, and *Holiday in Mexico* (1946), with Jane Powell and Xavier Cugat. In *Weekend in Havana*, Miranda's second American film, Alice Faye is a Macy's salesgirl on vacation in Cuba, where she finds romance in the person of John Payne; in *Holiday in Mexico* Xavier Cugat provides the rumbas, while Jane Powell plays the daughter of the retired ambassador who falls for a much older musician (José Iturbi).[23]

Compared to other movies in this genre, *Holiday in Havana* stands out for its smooth blend of script and score. This time Desi is just right for the part, and since he provides most of the music, the transitions in and out of the musical numbers are effortless. Effecting such transitions was perhaps the major structural problem of the maraca musical. In movies with Xavier Cugat, who usually only had a bit part, it is fun to observe the contortions that the writers had to go through in order to set up his rumbas; and when American song-and-dance men played Latin parts, the Spanish-language singing was either dubbed or nearly unintelligible. No one has yet figured out the lyric of the Spanish-language bolero that Don Ameche sings in *Down Argentine Way*.

Where *Holiday in Havana* does push credibility is in the casting of Lolita, Desi's love interest. With her demure blonde prettiness, Mary Hatcher looks every bit like the Hollywood starlet that she was. Carlos even remarks that she dances "like an American tourist" (he's right). Since Lolita could just as easily have been an American singer, it's not clear why she was given a Cuban identity. As in many other maraca musicals, the real and not-so-hidden subject of *Holiday in Havana* is intercultural romance. This is evident even in the lyric of the title song, which encourages American men to come to Havana and dance "with a lovely *cubana*." Like its two immediate predecessors, *Holiday in Havana* rehearses the standard story of the American girl who goes south and finds romance. It would not have taken much to substitute "*linda americana*" for "lovely *cubana*" in the title song.[24]

Carlos Estrada, Desi's most convincing role before Ricky Ricardo, shows how Arnaz modified the Latin lover type. Although Desi is normally considered a second-string Valentino, his characters really don't fit this mold. As disciples of Valentino, Manuelito Lynch and Carlos Estrada just don't make it, for they lack intensity as well as polish, savagery as well as suaveness.[25] A "sex menace," as Valentino was labeled, they certainly are not. The impression they make is one of safety, not threat.[26] The romantic highpoint of *Holiday in Havana* occurs when Carlos and Lolita find themselves in Carlos's parents' house. Thinking that Carlos and Lolita are newlyweds, his parents escort them to the bedroom. Since Carlos doesn't dare reveal that he and Lolita aren't married (such a confession would get him arrested for abduction), he reluctantly carries Lolita over the threshold. Once in the bedroom, though, he treats Lolita with a respect bordering on fecklessness. When Carlos asks Lolita to turn the light off, she thinks he's getting romantic, but no, he's only being gentlemanly: he doesn't want to be tempted by her beauty. He does manage to sing a tender bolero, "Made for Each Other," but once the song is over he says goodnight, grabs a blanket, and goes out to sleep on the porch—which promptly collapses under him. This scene deftly plays on two rather different Latin types, the lover and the caballero.[27] This time around, the lover doesn't stand a chance.

Anticipating Ricky Ricardo, Desi's screen persona has an offbeat, slightly ludicrous edge. He is a comic caballero, a somewhat ridiculous Don Juan. The classical Latin lover is aggressive to the point of violence. Valentino swept women off their feet and carried them off on his white steed; but Carlos has to be forced to carry Lolita over the threshold, and when he "abducts" her it's in the broken-down band bus. In *The Sheik*, the movie to which I just alluded, Valentino spends most of his time stalking a fearful but titillated Agnes Ayres. In *Holiday in Havana*, when Carlos is mistakenly accused of abducting Lolita, he marries her, reasoning that "you cannot abduct your bride." Desi is the Latin-lover-next-door, the one who won't abduct you unless he marries you first. No wonder Lolita's implacable mother calls him "a corny Casanova."

Desi's Cuban nationality may have had something to do with his softening or domestication of the Latin-lover type. As an unofficial (and at times official) protectorate of the United States during most of the first half of this century, Cuba was not a mysterious country. In the popular mind it was an accessible paradise, foreign and familiar at the same time. A 1928 tourist guide carried the reassuring title *When It's Cocktail Time in Cuba*; its first chapter was called "Have One in Havana."[28] This nearby garden of earthly delights, whose very name seemed to contain an American greeting ("see you" in "C-U-B-A," as in Irving Berlin's "I'm on My Way to Cuba"), was not the sort of place that was likely to spawn sex menaces. It's not surprising, therefore, that a Cuban bandleader who made his name leading conga lines in U.S. nightclubs was not exotic or mysterious enough to play a Valentino type. There is nothing mysterious about Carlos Estrada. We see him with his parents, with his little sister, and in the house where he grew up. The fact that Carlos and Lolita spend their first night together in his parents' house only confirms that he is very much a homebody, a *muchacho de su casa*, in the Spanish phrase.

Besides, the notion of the Cuban Latin lover had already been hilariously exploded by Helen Lawrenson in a notorious 1936 piece in *Esquire*, "Latins Are Lousy Lovers." The lead-in to the essay states, "Patriotic American beauty dares all to prove that the composite Cuban is not so hot as he's cracked up to be."[29] Basing herself on a "special course" she took during a stay in Havana, Lawrenson has this to say about Cuban men (36):

> *They are convinced that all American women worship them; and they love American women because they're so free and easy. With their money, they forget to add. There are very few who object to acting as amiable escorts to American girls who foot the bills. In fact, some of them can be said really to live only during the tourist season, when they emerge like butterflies to meet all incoming ships. The rest of the year, they just languish around, recounting their exploits and saving their strengths.*

On the crucial subject of sex, Lawrenson reassures the American man (the typical reader of *Esquire*) that he has little to fear from Cubans (37):

> *God knows, the Cuban man spends enough time on the subject of sex. He devotes his life to it. He talks it, dreams it, reads it, sings, dances it, eats it, sleeps it—does everything but do it. That last is not literally true, but it is a fact that they spend far more time*

in words than in action. Sitting in their offices, rock-
ing on the sidewalk in front of their clubs, drinking at
cafés, they talk hour after hour about sex. . . . A
smart American who makes an appointment with a
Cuban at a café always makes the Cuban sit with his
back to the street; because if he does not, the Cuban
will eye every woman who passes, and, like as not,
at a crucial point in the business transaction, will
interrupt to make anatomical comments on some
pretty who is just going by. They telephone each
other at their offices during business hours to describe
in minute detail a new conquest. According to them,
they always had their first affair at the age of two.
This may account for their being worn out at twenty-
three.

So much for Cuban Valentinos. But in fact the screen Latin lover was Mediterranean rather than Cuban or Latin American. Valentino, who created the type, was Italian; when he played a Spanish American, he was a gaucho, from the mysterious and vast pampas of distant Argentina (there may be a residue of this in Manuelito Lynch's Argentine nationality), not from nearby Havana.[30] It is no surprise, then, that when Desi returned to Hollywood after World War II he found that the leading-man parts were going to Ricardo Montalbán, for Montalbán's screen presence—enigmatic, dashing, romantic—matched the conventional definition of the type more closely. (The mysterious Mr. Roarke that Montalbán played for many years on *Fantasy Island* clearly descended from his Latin lover roles.) Desi's Don Juans are nearly a tongue-in-cheek or *choteo* version of their model. Cuban Pete, "the king of the rumba beat," is equal parts lover, rogue, and clown. He certainly has sex appeal, but it is based as much on tropical charm as on animal magnetism. Then also, a rumba is not a tango. Playful rather than passionate, smooth rather than sultry, the rumba is a dance of elegant courtship, not of violent possession.[31] Valentino's steamy sexuality would have been out of place in "a little rumba numba."[32] Unlike the tango, where the man often seems to drag the woman across the floor, the rumba is consensual. It really does take two to rumba.

Desi's screen image was of a piece with Hollywood's efforts to promote Roosevelt's Good Neighbor policy toward Latin America. Desi was the Latin Lover as Good Neighbor, the Latin-lover-next-door—a role that he would of course perfect a few years later in Ricky Ricardo. It has not been remarked, I think, that when *I Love Lucy* went on the air in 1951 Desi had already been playing a big-screen version of Ricky Ricardo for over a decade. Even his Spanish outbursts had been previewed in his movies. In *Holiday in Havana* Carlos has a Ricky-like tantrum when he thinks that Lolita doesn't like his songs: "¡Quédese Ud. con sus compositores, señora, que no la voy a molestar más con mi música!"

The difference is that Ricky drew out even more the homebody tendencies of characters like Carlos Estrada. As the first husband that Desi played, Ricky Ricardo emphasized the "domestic" and "comic" side of his screen persona. In an early analysis of *I Love Lucy*, Jack Gould remarked that Ricky's "awkwardness" was one of the most appealing facets of his character.[33] The reason is that it mitigated the supposed sexual threat of the Latin leading man. Ricky's awkwardness made him safe for demographics. Although the TV scripts contained many references to his popularity with women, and although Lucy's jealousy toward her live-in lothario was a recurring motif, there never was any real suggestion of infidelity. Every time Lucy got worried about an old flame or a new girl singer, her fears turned out to be baseless. The only time Ricky cheats is in one of Lucy's nightmares, where he leaves his wife and son for a Spanish dancer ("Ricky's Old Girlfriend," December 21, 1953). But Lucy's worst nightmare is only that. Even if Ricky went to Hollywood to play the part of Don Juan, womanizing was not his style. For a Latin lover, Ricky is safely domestic. Appropriately, the Don Juan movie was never made.

The basic formula of *Holiday in Havana* and similar movies—Cuban boy gets American girl—did become one of the premises of *I Love Lucy*. What is more, the sitcom's recreation of how Lucy and Ricky fell in love was lifted right out of a maraca musical. Almost ten years after *Holiday in Havana*, Desi would find himself again in the same type of story, this time as Ricky Ricardo. The first hour-long *I Love Lucy*, "Lucy Takes a Cruise to Havana" (November 6, 1957), borrows heavily from Desi's maraca musicals. Vacationing in Cuba, Lucy and her friend Susie MacNamara (Ann Sothern) meet two locals who run a sightseeing service, Ricky Ricardo and Carlos García (César Romero). It's love at first sight. Ricky and Lucy go to a Havana nightclub, El Tambor (Spanish for drum), where they declare their love for each other. After discovering that Ricky's dream is to have a musical career in the United States, Lucy gets jobs for Ricky and Carlos with Rudy Vallee's orchestra. The plotline is right out of *Cuban Pete*, with an older and more portly Desi resurrecting the part of "terpsichorean Valentino" that he had played throughout his Hollywood career.

After *Holiday in Havana* Desi did not act in another movie for several years. He made his return in two films that tried to capitalize on the popularity of *I Love Lucy, The Long, Long Trailer* (MGM, 1954) and *Forever, Darling* (MGM-Zanra, 1956). By the time he made the first of the movies, Desi was no longer the Cuban Pete of the 1940s. But he wasn't quite Ricky Ricardo either. Even if Ricky served as the inspiration, the characters he now plays deliberately diverge from his television role. In these two films Ricky has become a corporate man. His Latin lover days are definitively behind him, and there is little of the *vivo* in his personality. In *I Love Lucy*, when Ricky buys the Tropicana, he also becomes a businessman, but he keeps on performing with the band and retains his highstrung temperament. The film Ricky is different. He doesn't rant and rave, and he seldom lapses into Spanish. On occasion he still loses his temper, but for the most part his anger is genuine and unfunny. This is an older, more serious, more mature Ricky Ricardo, one who spends his time building bridges rather than banging on a drum skin.

This is also a more American Ricky. In the translation to motion pictures, Ricky all but loses his accent. I don't mean that Desi no longer says "dunt" or "wunt," but that his Cuban inflections are not accompanied by consonant gestures or behavior. Desi's Cuban background does not figure in the scripts. Rather than from cultural differences, the tension between Lucy's and Desi's characters now emerges solely from gender and personality conflicts. The relative dullness of the results demonstrates in striking fashion how important the cultural dimension was to the appeal of *I Love Lucy*. Take away Ricky's conga drum, downplay his and Lucy's diverse backgrounds, and what you have left is indeed a typical middle-class American couple with typical middle-class American problems. This is a valid subject for cinematic treatment, to be sure, but one that lacks the edge and charm of the sitcom.

Based on an autobiographical novel by Clinton Twiss, *The Long, Long Trailer* marked only the second time that Lucy and Desi had acted together in a movie. The first time, in *Too Many Girls*, Desi had fainted at the sight of Lucy, but it was Richard Carlson who got the girl. In *The Long, Long Trailer*, which became the most successful comedy

MGM had ever done up to that time, Lucy and Desi are newlyweds who have decided to spend their honeymoon traveling across the country in a three-ton trailer. With the long, long trailer in tow, the trip becomes a series of comic catastrophes: the trailer gets stuck in the mud, it almost goes off a cliff, it backs into a house. Making things even worse, the trailer parks are full of nosy busybodies who prevent the honeymooning couple from consummating the marriage.[34]

Little effort is made to conceal the movie's debt to *I Love Lucy*. The parentage is written into the movie's very title: a "trailer" in its theatrical sense is a short filmstrip that follows the main feature. This particular Arnaz-Ball "vehicle" is a long, long trailer to the TV series. Thus, the characters' names are only slight variations on Lucy and Ricky: Ricky becomes Nicky; Lucy becomes Tacy (in Twiss's autobiographical novel, the characters' names are different of course). Although there are no references to Nicky's foreign origins (his last name is Collini), at one point he does launch into a Ricky-like tirade (the movie does not explain how it is that a "Collini" speaks Cuban-accented Spanish). For her part, Lucy does her usual sight gags. In what is perhaps the funniest scene in the movie, she tries to prepare dinner inside the moving trailer. Utter pandemonium ensues: pots and pans and glasses slide to the floor as Lucy frantically attempts to keep the food on the table.

Other than the attenuation of Ricky's Cubanness, the crucial difference between the TV show and the movie is their tone. Even though some scenes in *The Long, Long Trailer* could have been written for the sitcom, the movie as a whole has a somberness that is foreign to *I Love Lucy*. This becomes evident in the opening scene, which shows Nicky in the middle of a rainstorm, desperately seeking Tacy, who has abandoned him and made off with the trailer. He finds the trailer but cannot get inside. At the trailer park office, he meets a man who is about to buy the trailer from Tacy. This prompts Nicky to advise the man not to do it, for it will surely ruin the man's marriage. In Nicky's case what began as a "a great big joke" has turned into a "nightmare." This cues a retrospective account of the events leading up to this moment.

The initial scene sets the tone of the movie, whose plot takes shape as the explanation not of a joke but of a nightmare. The pitch-black night and the violent rainstorm serve as atmospheric echoes of the couple's troubled relationship. Tacy is nowhere to be found; Nicky has lost both wife and home. As he puts it, with only a slight trace of humor, "It's a fine thin' when you come home to your home and your home is gone."

Even during the film's funniest moments, the viewer cannot forget that all of this leads up to that desolate night. The couple's funny misadventures with the trailer are framed by the viewer's knowledge of how badly things have turned out. In the end, of course, everything comes out alright. Once the flashback catches up to the present and the scene gets back to the trailer park office, Tacy runs into Nicky and they make up. But the happy ending does not quite erase the somber mood created by the opening scene and sustained for most of the movie's duration.

The Long, Long Trailer is a parable of mobile homelessness. This sets it apart from the television show. Whatever else may happen inside Apartment 3-B, at least Ricky knows it does not move. The apartment was an unpredictable space, but only because of Lucy's schemes. Just as she tries to manipulate Ricky, Lucy manipulates her living room. But in the movie it is the trailer that manipulates its owners. Neither Nicky nor Tacy can entirely control its movement. A monstrous, uncontrollable version of the myriad props that appear in the sitcom, the trailer is the movie's real protagonist. This time the characters are subordinate to the props, which is why the title refers to it rather than to the human protagonists. Nicky and Tacy's anger at each other is ancillary to their frustration with the trailer. The war of the sexes takes a back seat to the struggle between man and machine.

The audience's reaction to Nicky and Tacy's predicament is not simply laughter. Their helplessness makes us grimace rather than laugh, for it just doesn't seem like a fair fight. The scene where Nicky, trying to park the trailer, wrecks Tacy's aunt's house is as excruciating as it is hilarious. Time after time he tries, slowly, deliberately, to back the trailer into the driveway. Time after time he fails, and with each attempt some new havoc is wreaked. First he runs over the flowerbeds, then he smashes a trellis with roses, and finally he rams the house. The demolition is witnessed by Tacy's whole family, which cringes along with the viewer. It's as if the trailer had a will of its own. Nicky cannot stop it from getting into the act.

Because the trailer steals the show here, Desi and Lucy play their parts with a restraint that is absent from their TV roles. Lucy is never clownish, Desi is never shrill. When Tacy spills the salad, she's funny without being ludicrous. When Nicky loses his temper, his anger contains genuine pathos. Less a foil for Tacy than a victim of the trailer, Nicky shows a quality of emotion unknown to Ricky. Since Nicky is an engineer, there's little opportunity for a song-and-dance. The only reminder of Desi's musical roles is a song that he and Tacy sing as they ride along, a scene reminiscent of the "California Here We Come" episode of *I Love Lucy*.

Not really an "*I Love Lucy* on wheels," as one wag remarked,[35] *The Long, Long Trailer* is actually an accomplished black comedy that was a critical and commercial success. Even if the initial motivation was essentially to cash in on Lucy and Desi's popularity, *The Long, Long Trailer* is coherent and convincing in its own terms. By exploiting its relation to *I Love Lucy* without being fatally hitched to it, this particular star vehicle acquires a life of its own. The quotations from *I Love Lucy* only help to establish the ways the movie deviates from the television series. What the movie lacks is the sitcom's bicultural brio. Nicky Collini gives little sign of having ties to Hispanic culture. His is an accidental accent, a sound effect without visible cause. Likewise, his name *sounds* like Ricky's, even in its alliterations, but that's where the similarity stops. Although "Collini" suggests Italian rather than Hispanic ancestry, nothing is made of this either. The point, I think, is that Nicky is a melting-pot alumnus, a second or third generation immigrant. His cultural heritage, whatever it may be, has ceased to signify; it remains only as a quirk, a residual mannerism that has little impact on his behavior or his values.

No more "Latin" than its predecessor, *Forever, Darling* was far less successful in establishing its autonomy from the series. Once again Desi is cast against type. Here he plays a brilliant chemist, Larry Vegas, who has invented a crack new insecticide. His wife, Susie (Lucy), is a social butterfly who could care less about insects. The movie begins at the Vegas's wedding reception, and then fastforwards through the next several years, which show the once happy newlyweds becoming bored and disaffected. By the fifth anniversary, they have settled down to a drab, if affluent, existence. As co-owner of Finlay-Vegas Chemicals (an inside joke: Carlos Finlay was a Cuban physician who helped discover a cure for yellow fever), Larry has done well enough to afford a beautiful home, a maid, and sumptuous furnishings. But now that the fires of passion have subsided, Larry and Susie have little in common. Larry cares only about his research, Susie cares only about the social register.

As in *The Long, Long Trailer*, these characters are derivative of, but different from, their sitcom counterparts. Susie is Lucy as blue-blood—snooty and frivolous. Larry is Ricky with a Ph.D.—successful, upwardly mobile, and assimilated. His last name is Hispanic, but no attempt is made to portray his cultural heritage. Just as Vegas is a Spanish name that has become an American city, Larry is a Hispanic man who has become a dyed-in-the-wool American. The movie takes pains, in fact, to distance Larry from Ricky. At the wedding reception, Larry and Susie dance in front of an orchestra, an image familiar to viewers of *I Love Lucy*. The difference is that the orchestra is a string quartet, and it is playing the movie's theme song, a waltz. A bit later Latin Larry will sing this song, accompanying himself on a concertina! Ricky and Larry are as different as a rumba band and a string quartet, a *tumbadora* and a concertina, a conga and a waltz.

Although these recastings signal the movie's commendable desire to get away from *I Love Lucy*, ultimately they are ludicrous. Desi is hardly believable as a "Latin Louis Pasteur," as Susie calls him. One of the few unintentionally comic moments in the film occurs when he tries to tell Susie about "larvae" and "pupae." He can barely get the words out of his mouth. The movie endeavors to make Larry look scholarly and distinguished. He is portly, his temples are gray, and his clothes are elegantly conservative. But he lacks Ricky's vivacity, his energy and passion. Larry's interest in his research cannot match Ricky's enthusiasm for his music. Larry in the lab is a far less compelling sight than Ricky at the Tropicana.

But the fundamental problem with *Forever, Darling* is that it does not have the courage of its convictions. During a particularly bitter quarrel, Larry tells Susie that she is becoming like her airhead cousin, who spends her life harboring "secret crushes on movie stars." "I'm telling you Susan, that's the way you're headed." That same night Larry's prophecy comes true when Susie is visited by none other than James Mason in the form of an angel. This is the crucial moment in the movie, and the point at which both movie and character lose their nerve. An upright *deus ex machina* with a British twang, Mason dissuades Susie from cheating on Larry; his instrument of dissuasion is a fable about a woman who thought her husband had the face of a mountain goat, but who realized that "the man with the face of a mountain goat had the heart of an Abraham Lincoln." This is all Susie needs to hear: Larry is the man with the face of a mountain goat! Forget that Larry looks like anything but a mountain goat. Forget that the movie gives no hint of his big-heartedness. Susie desists from her romantic daydreams and joins her husband for a field test of the new insecticide. *Forever, Darling* then becomes a rerun of the "Camping Trip" episode from *I Love Lucy*.[36]

In some ways this turn of events is a pity, for this movie broaches a dangerous and interesting subject, one that could never have been explored on the sitcom: Lucy's desire for other men. Perhaps because they could draw on their own experiences, Lucy and Desi are quite convincing in their portrayal of estranged spouses. Unlike Lucy Ricardo, Susie is genuinely unhappy in her marriage. The bedroom quarrel contrasts sharply with the countless inconsequential spats in the bedroom of Apartment 3-B. This is no a silly fight that will lead to a quick resolution. When Larry says to Susie, "I'm sick and tired of the whole thing," his words are not a setup for a joke. Had Ricky said this in the sitcom, Lucy surely would have gone for a laugh by repeating the sentence mimicking Ricky's accent, "So you're sick and tired of the whole thin', huh?" In the movie Susie replies, "You're just sick of me; you just don't like our whole marriage."[37] Saying "Maybe I don't," Larry picks up his pillow and spends the night in his study.

After *Forever, Darling* Arnaz made one more screen appearance, fifteen years later. Billed as Desiderio Arnaz, he had a small part in *The Escape Artist* (Zoetrope, 1982), a weird and at times unintelligible comedy about a child magician. What is most striking about this role is simply Desi's appearance. He's overweight, wrinkled, and shorter than during his Ricky Ricardo days. His hair has turned white and his voice has been reduced to a gravelly croak. The one thing he has salvaged is the accent, which if anything is even thicker. But it's difficult to believe that he is the same man who babalú'd his way to fame and fortune. The *vivo*'s vivacity is gone. So are the music and the humor. By 1982 Desi had suffered several major illnesses and was in poor health. He looks every bit like a man desperately and unsuccessfully trying to hold on to life. He would die of lung cancer only four years later at the age of sixty-nine.

Nonetheless, his infirmity made him just right for the part of Quiñones, the decrepit major of a city in California. His longest scene pits him against Raul Julia, who plays his estranged son. The scene ends when Julia overturns the chair where Mayor Quiñones is sitting. Desi falls to the floor, mumbling unintelligibly. He has to be helped to his feet. The pathos of the scene extends beyond its significance in the movie, for Arnaz and Julia are members of the same clan in ways that escape *The Escape Artist*. As Raul Julia's performance in *Havana* (1990) illustrates, Julia is himself a contemporary version of the dashing, romantic Latin. But since Desi's modest heyday in the 1940s, Latin lovers have changed considerably. For one thing, they have gotten caught up in history. For another, they have lost some of their veneer of sophistication. Bullying rather than ebullient, the contemporary Latin lovers have turned suaveness into a form of cynicism. When Desi tumbles to the floor, Cuban Pete and Ricky Ricardo go down with him.

I would prefer to remember Desi for a different, and somewhat more upbeat, farewell performance. I am referring to his autobiography, *A Book* (1976); and I say "performance" advisedly, because *A Book* is far from being an innocent act of self-disclosure. As we have already seen, the covers signal that this is indeed a performance, an act, though an equivocal one. Even when he is dressed in street clothes, Desi is up on a stage with a microphone in his hand. Someone looking for intimate details or meditative introspection will not find much of that here. Desi is interested in conveying a certain image of himself as bandleader, actor, lover, husband, and entrepreneur. It's not that what he says is untrue—other sources confirm the veracity of his claims—but that all we are allowed is a partial portrait of the Cuban-American artist. For the most part, this is Cuban Pete as *auteur*.

As an immigrant autobiography, *A Book* bears comparison (if not in quality in intent) to such works as Richard Rodriguez's *Hunger of Memory* (1982), Oscar Hijuelos's *Our House in the Last World* (1983), or Edward Rivera's *Family Installments* (1982). Like these, Desi's bio recounts the story of a young Hispanic man's adaptation to life in the United States. Moreover, like *Hunger of Memory, A Book* is a success story told from the point of view of a semi-assimilated, "mainstreamed" Hispanic-American. But that's where the resemblance with Rodriguez ends. The tortuous, introspective traumas of Rodriguez or Hijuelos are foreign to Arnaz. One reason for this is, of course, that Arnaz doesn't have Rodriguez's quality of mind. Ricky is no Richard. He does not seem introspective enough to agonize over the dilemmas and paradoxes of biculturation. Nor does he write elegant literary prose. As a reviewer pointed out, Arnaz "offers no felicitous phrases and few insights"; what he offers, instead, is "the force of his presence."[38]

The best way to understand *A Book* is to read it as a *vivo*'s bio, a picaresque tale that recounts its protagonist's rise in the world. A rogue in two languages, Desi recounts how, by dint of native resourcefulness and persistence, he becomes a big shot, a television star, and the co-owner of Desilu, which at one time was the largest film and television facility in the world. If *A Book* were a maraca musical, its theme song could well be "I Came, I Saw, I Conga'd," for the theme of the book is how Desi cons and congas his way to the top. Unlike other ethnic autobiographies of recent years, *A Book* does not portray its protagonist as the victim of prejudice and exploitation. The *vivo* is victor, not victim. Desi sees himself as a canny manipulator who knows how to make the best of the opportunities America affords him. His is an old-fashioned, rags-to-riches Cuban-American success story.

Desi's *viveza* is demonstrated time and again. Without any musical training, he gets Cugat to hire him for the band. After less than a year with Cugat, he's learned enough to form his own band, which becomes a hit on the nightclub circuit. In Hollywood, seeing that his movie career is going nowhere, he tricks MGM into releasing him from his contract. He returns to his lucrative band business and makes a mint. Years later he is astute enough to get CBS to give him ownership of *I Love Lucy*, only to sell the show back to the network for millions of dollars. Then, in the midst of filming an *I Love Lucy* episode, he negotiates the purchase of RKO, the same studio that had fired him fifteen years earlier. When Philip Morris, the sponsor of the series, was giving Desi a hard time with Lucy's pregnancy, Desi went to the head of the company, Alfred Lyons. After hearing Desi out, Lyons sent this memo to his staff: "Don't fuck around with the Cuban."

Desi's business acumen is complemented by his amorous conquests. Although reticent when it comes to names (as any Cuban caballero would be), he leaves little doubt of his interest in and success with the opposite sex. This *vivo* is very much a *vividor*. Witness the following scene, where Desi is auditioning for the legendary Louis B. Mayer. Mayer calls in some of his female stars to test with Desi:

> He then pressed a button and said, "Have Lana come in."
> As soon as Miss Turner arrived, he said, "Will you stand next to her, then turn her around and look at her, up and down, then turn her around again, hold her in your arms and kiss her?"
> What a sweet job this was going to be!
> I did what he told me and then he said to Lana, "Go back to the set."
> I escorted her to the door and said, "Thank you." She said, "My pleasure," and left.
> The button again. "Have Judy come in."

> *Judy Garland came in and he made me go through*
> *the same thing with her. By this time my bird really*
> *wanted to fly.*
>
> *He then said, "You know this is the best studio in*
> *the world, and we make stars here, a lot of stars. I*
> *think you have a chance to be a star."* (A Book,
> *141)*

Of course, Desi never did become a star, though this doesn't disturb him too much. Ever the *vividor*, he seems less interested in stardom than in getting the chance to kiss the likes of Lana Turner and Judy Garland. Like Ricky and like most of the characters he played during his career, Desi does not hide his fascination with women, especially American women. His "bird's" fondness for flying American fills many pages of *A Book*, a feature that caused some reviewers to label it "raunchy" and others to complain of its "not-so-funny sexual jokes."[39]

Today Arnaz's autobiography would not win much favor among opponents of "heterosexism" (not to say heterosexuality), and it is certain that Desi's Cuban bluster would offend many readers. Another example: from his wise old grandfather Desi imbibed the following wisdom, "Ponga el corazón con Dios, y el rabo tieso," which he translates as "Keep your heart in God, and a stiff prick" (10). Not surprisingly, this anecdote is followed by the story of Desi's deflowering at a brothel in Santiago de Cuba.

Ethnic autobiographies tend to subordinate gender to culture. In Rodriguez's *Hunger of Memory*, to name an obvious example, the reserve about things sexual is very nearly alarming. But remaining silent about sex may be impossible for Desi, not just because he is Cuban (Lawrenson dixit), but also because he is a one-and-a-halfer. For Arnaz, who came to this country as an adolescent, sexual maturation and cultural adaptation are so tightly wound together that it may be impossible to pry them apart. Gender identity merges with cultural identity, as sex becomes a way of finding and defining one's place in the new world. It may not be too much of an exaggeration to say that Desi's womanizing was one way—perhaps his dominant way—of conversing with American culture. The *americana* incarnates Americana; she is America in its most graspable form. In her wonderful memoir, *Lost in Translation*, Eva Hoffman remarks, "When I fall in love with my first American, I fall in love with otherness."[40] Something of this love for otherness comes across in Desi's attraction to American women. If he is more explicit about sex than other ethnic autobiographers, it's partially because for him sex is a form of cultural insertion.[41]

But there is a further dimension to the erotic agenda of *A Book*, a dimension that adds depth and pathos to Desi's dialogue with otherness. It has always seemed to me that *A Book*'s generic title is a joke that doesn't quite work. As author, Desi also tries to behave like a *vivo*. Eschewing a ghost writer, he undertakes to compose his own life in spite of his "not too good knowledge of the English language" (322). The awkward syntax of this confession already tells us that this is an author who can't write, but writes nonetheless. The existence of *A Book* becomes another example of Desi's Cuban *chutzpah*, one more in his string of successful performances. In this context his title functions both as an admission of imaginative poverty (he couldn't think of anything better) and as a *vivo*'s way of saying that he does not have to play by the rules. Not giving *A Book* a conventional title is an act of both modesty and insolence.

Although I understand the logic of this, I can't help reading the gesture in another way. For me the title is primarily a blank, a void. As such, it refers to material that the autobiography leaves out or plays down because the author did not find a way of coming to terms with it. This material of course has to do with Lucy. If on a general plane *A Book* is about Desi's fascination with *americanas*, the concrete embodiment of that fascination is Lucy, who for Desi is not just a pair-of-legs but a paradigm, not just a *tipa* but an *arquetipa*. The central subject of *A Book* is Desi's lifelong attachment to Lucy and his pain and remorse at the marriage's dissolution. *A Book* is both a chronicle of conquest and a litany of loss. Like other autobiographies, it is simultaneously picaresque and elegiac.[42] What is unusual is that the elegiac strain has not to do, as one might expect, with Desi's departure from Cuba, but with his separation from Lucy.

Howard Cady, his editor at William Morrow, has told one of the couple's biographers that when Arnaz was trying to write *A Book*, anytime the subject of the divorce came up, he would fall apart.

> *It was apparent that he still loved her very much.*
> *He would get very emotional as he realized that he'd*
> *been a rotten husband and had not treated her very*
> *well. Desi became extremely tense and increasingly*
> *nutty, in the sense that he would get desperate for a*

> *drink or female companionship. When he imported*
> *a floozy from Baja California [they were working*
> *in a motel in Del Mar, California] and installed her*
> *in the same motel, everything sort of fell to pieces.*[43]

In the final editing, one-third of the original manuscript, dealing with Desi's life after Lucy, had to be edited out because it was too "depressing and sad." Although the deleted part of *A Book* apparently has not survived, Desi's papers do contain fragments that give an idea of what Cady was talking about. In a letter from 1974 addressed to his second wife, Edie, Arnaz details how far his fortunes (and his fortune) had fallen in the years since *I Love Lucy*. As he puts it, he has gone from the plushest office in show business to a closet at Universal, and from the penthouse suite of the Chateau Marmont to the basement of his sister-in-law's house.

Rather than going on to describe Arnaz's apparently unhappy life without Lucy, *A Book* ends with an account of the filming of the last *I Love Lucy* episode on March 2, 1960. By then the marriage had been on the skids for several years, and Desi and Lucy no longer lived together. The final scene of the final episode called for Lucy and Ricky to kiss and make up.

> *Doing the last Lucy-Desi Comedy Hour was*
> *not easy. We knew it was the last time we would be*
> *Lucy and Ricky. As fate would have it, the very last*
> *scene in that story called for a long clinch and a kiss-*
> *and-make-up ending. As we got to it, we looked at*
> *each other, embraced and kissed. This was not just an*
> *ordinary kiss for a scene in a show. It was a kiss that*
> *would wrap up twenty years of love and friendship,*
> *triumphs and failures, ecstasy and sex, jealousy and*
> *regrets, heartbreaks and laughter . . . and tears. The*
> *only thing we were not able to hide was the tears.*
>
> *After the kiss we just stood there looking at each*
> *other and licking the salt.*
>
> *Then Lucy said, "You're supposed to say 'cut.'"*
> *"I know. Cut, goddamn it!"*
> *I Love Lucy was never just a title.* (317)

A sensibility different than mine may find this mawkish, but I find it moving. If Desi could not find a title for his memoirs, it's because the appropriate title, *I Love Lucy*, had already been taken. By conflating the last scene of the series, the conclusion to his autobiography, and the end of his marriage, he makes it seem as if both his life and his career ended with the divorce. Two years later both Lucy and Desi had remarried and the name of her new TV series was *The Lucy Show*. *I Love Lucy* was no longer even a title.

To my mind, *A Book* is a significant contribution to Cuban-American culture. Love, lust, loss, language, identity, authenticity—these are the large themes of Desi Arnaz's biography and autobiography, and the reasons why he is a crucial presence in Cuban America. Arnaz exemplifies a legacy of achievement based on acceptance, not refusal. In his negotiations with North American culture, he is receptive and resourceful, not resistant. Ethnic purists and recalcitrant Cubans may find Desi "inauthentic"; they may regard him as a tropical fish caught inside an aquarium, someone who traduces his culture by collaborating in its caricature. I find this view predictable and simple minded. I prefer to stress Arnaz's verve and nerve, his generous gestures of accommodation, and his enduring romance with otherness. One could do worse than build a career and make a life out of loving Lucy—even if at the end all you're left with is *A Book*.

Desi Does It

MAMBO NO. 3 *Going through her father's house after his death, Lucie Arnaz found a box of papers and memorabilia that she donated to the Love Library at San Diego State University, where Desi had lectured several times. The Desi Arnaz Collection contains a few home movies, an old film short entitled* Jitter-humba, *several drafts of* A Book, *and assorted notes that Arnaz took when he was working on his autobiography. Originally intending to write either a sequel to* A Book *(to be called* Another Book*) or a novel (probably to be called* A Novel*), Arnaz marked some of these jottings "Other Book" or "Novel." The notes contain not only many self-revealing moments and juicy gossip (like a list of Lucille Ball's alleged lovers), but also some of Desi's best quips.*

Seeing Gary Morton, Lucy's second husband, on a TV talk show, he writes: "About Gary on TV with Lucy: Seems to be suffering from a massive inferiority complex to which he is fully entitled." To his children, Lucie and Desi, Jr., he once remarked: "The only reason you are here is because I woke up one night and couldn't think of anything else to do." About his famous quarrels with Lucy, he says: "Lucy and I had some great battles but at times when someone asked me why we fought, I had to

answer, 'I don't know. She wouldn't tell me.'"
Most pertinent, perhaps, are his thoughts on being a writer: "Writing a book is, I discovered, not an easy thing to do. It also proves that the brain is a wonderful thing. It starts up when you are born and stops when you sit down at the typewriter."

But my favorite is the simple aphorism "History is made at night." It seems appropriate that the box ended up at a place called the Love Library.

Three   # A-BRIEF-HISTORY-OF-MAMBO-TIME

Some months ago my 11-year old son, knowing that I had been reading *The Mambo Kings Play Songs of Love*, came home with a Simpsons' poster that bore the legend "Let's Mambo!" A few days later he showed me a booklet that revealed that dancing the mambo was one of Homer Simpson's favorite pastimes—along with bowling, playing catch with Bart, and eating Pork Rinds Lite. The mambo's filtering down into a children's cartoon demonstrates the extent to which this music has become an enduring part of American folklore. The critical and commercial success of Hijuelos' *The Mambo Kings Play Songs of Love*, along with its adaptation into a successful motion picture, *Mambo Kings* (1991), provides further evidence of its continuing appeal.

In fact the mambo revival has been underway for several years. In the movie *Dirty Dancing* (1987), set in the Catskills during the 1950s, Patrick Swayze plays a dance instructor who teaches Jennifer Grey how to do "Johnny's Mambo." A year earlier the theme song of another popular movie, Jonathan Demme's *Something Wild* (1986), had been a mambo called "Loco de amor," composed by David Byrne and Johnny Pacheco and sung by Byrne along with Celia Cruz. Even Barry Manilow and Kid Creole have jumped on the mambo bandwagon.[1] In the last few years the word, if not the music, has been cropping up everywhere: in John Leguizamo's one-man Broadway show, *Mambo Mouth*; in the southern rock group Little Feat's *Representing the Mambo* (1990); in Campbell Armstrong's spy thriller, *Mambo* (1990); and in Sandra María Esteves's book of poems, *Bluestown Mockingbird Mambo* (1990). There is a Mambo Café in Los Angeles, a Mambo Club in Miami, a Mambo Records in New York, and a porn actress whose name is the euphonic Myrle Mambo.

There is even a super-gravity fowl named the Great Mambo Chicken.[2] Just last week in Chapel Hill, North Carolina, where I live, a local journalist entitled his column (about biorhythms!) "Radio Mambo."

If Ricky Ricardo is one of the great icons of Cuban-American culture, the mambo is the other. Like Ricky, the mambo is no less American than Cuban, and it was never as popular in Cuba as it has been in the United States. The mambo is a one-and-a-halfer, born in Cuba but made in the U.S.A. Unlike the conga or the rumba, the mambo is not a Latin American "import." Less an exotic melody than a native *son*, the mambo's distinctive form grew out of the combination of Cuban and American music. As a bicultural creation with divided roots and multiple allegiances, the mambo has always been Cuban American.

In a brief essay written in 1971, the Cuban novelist Alejo Carpentier described Cuban popular music as "resistance music"—"a music that resists all the foreign influences that could have dislodged it from its proper place [*ámbito propio*]."[3] Carpentier's definition is difficult to apply to a hybrid like the mambo. Receptive rather than resistant, the mambo tends to confound the distinction between the foreign and the homegrown. Which is the "foreign" strain in mambo—the Afro-Cuban percussion or the big-band orchestration? Both are equally responsible for the music's distinctive sound. And where is the mambo's "proper place"—Havana, Mexico City, or New York? Although some of its roots are Cuban, the mambo's sound emerged only in contact with North American music; moreover, it spread to Latin America and the United States from recordings made in Mexico City. The mambo's oddity, its breathless tempo, its convulsive choreography, its stridencies and dissonances, are symptomatic of a taut agglutination of diverse musical traditions. It is no coincidence that the English-language title of the first mambo is "Mambo Jambo," for the mambo is indeed a jumble, a forum for foreignness and a haven for the heterogeneous. The great Cuban ethnologist Fernando Ortiz aptly described it as an "estofado de sonoridades," a stew of sounds.[4] Since for Ortiz the essence of Cuban culture was also its nourishing combination of foreign ingredients, the mambo's impurities did not make it any less Cuban. If the mambo was a stew, Cuba was one also. And who's to say that an *estofado* is any less Cuban than an *ajiaco*?

When Carpentier speaks of popular music as resistant to "dislodgement," his choice of a territorial metaphor supposes a view different from Ortiz's. Carpentier speaks as if Cuban culture had a fixed habitation, a permanent address, an *ámbito propio* from which it should not be removed. For Carpentier, dislodgement entails denaturalization. To dislodge is to unsettle, to wrench something from its proper place and by so doing to denature it. Of course, this "proper place" is none other than Cuba as a geographical entity. But we already know that Cuba is one of the least insular islands on the face of the earth. Written in 1971, after a decade of an exodus unprecedented in the island's history, Carpentier's affirmation of the significance of staying in place sounds almost quaint. Conceived in Cuba, nurtured in Mexico, and brought to maturity in the United States, the mambo is a child of the Cuban *monte* that spent most of its life away from the island. From Carpentier's perspective the mambo would be nothing if not unsettling, in both the psychological and topographical senses: unsettling psychologically because it is such a jumble of sounds, and unsettling topographically because it dislodges native rhythms. There's always been a certain petulance to the mambo, a kind of music that does not know its place. The name connotes excess, outrageousness, lack of decorum. A mambo mouth is a loud mouth, someone with a loose tongue, someone who doesn't abide by rules of propriety. The mambo is nothing if not uncouth, improper, its musical improprieties sometimes even bordering on the *improperio*, the vulgar or offensive outburst.

This book upholds a view of Cuban culture that stresses its itinerant impulses rather than its homing instincts. I find no contradiction or incompatibility between the Cuban condition and the Cuban-American way. The passage from Cuban to Cuban American may not be an easy trip, but it is not beset by insurmountable roadblocks. Since for Cubans the hyphen is not a minus sign but a plus, a Cuban American is not less Cuban but more American. Because there are no natives in Cuba, Cubans have *always* been hyphenated Americans, in the larger sense of the toponym. I realize there are many "ethnics" in this country who wail and worry about the danger of assimilation, of losing their roots. But Cuban culture, like the mambo itself, has little to do with roots. We Cubans have a strange relationship with our roots: we *eat* them. We don't worship them. We don't enshrine them. We consume them. The mambo is not a root, it's an anchor. It places, but it does not ground. Let's mambo!

Even though the mambo craze is a 1950s phenomenon, the origins of the music go back several decades before then. The word derives from the Congo religion, where it referred to the concluding section of a ceremony to take possession of the spirit of the dead. After the priest makes contact with the spirit, the act of possession is reinforced by chants called "mambo" or "mambu." The word's original meaning, thus, is "conversation" or "message." As Fernando Ortiz describes it, the mambo was a "final agudo," an emphatic liturgical flourish that sealed the compact between the living and the dead.[5] By the 1930s the word had acquired a secular meaning. Around this time the *danzón*, an instrumental genre that had been invented (or at least codified) in 1879 by Miguel Failde, developed an improvised final section that gave musicians and dancers a chance to strut their stuff. Probably suggested by the *montuno* or refrain of the *son*, this section came to be called "mambo." Although it's not clear who first used the word in this new sense, when Orestes López composed a *danzón* entitled "Mambo" in 1938, the term's secular sense was already firmly in place.[6]

Orestes and his brother Israel (a legendary bassist known as "Cachao") both belonged to Arcaño y Sus Maravillas (Arcaño and His Marvels), a popular orchestra whose motto was "un as en cada instrumento y una maravilla en conjunto" (an ace in each instrument and marvelous as a group). Arcaño, who had expanded the traditional *charanga* format of strings, flute, and timbales by adding a conga drum and cowbell, called López's "Mambo" and other similar compositions "danzones de nuevo ritmo." Other bands, notably Arsenio Rodríguez's, soon began playing the expanded *danzón*, and the term "mambo" became increasingly widespread. According to the singer Rolando Laserie, who began his career as percussionist with Rodriguez's orchestra, Arsenio used to cue his trumpet section by yelling, "¡Mambo! ¡mambo!"[7]

For years after Arcaño popularized the new *danzón*, "mambo" remained the name for the last part of these compositions. This was true as late as 1948, when *Bohemia* published a long article by Manuel Cuéllar Vizcaíno entitled "La revolución del mambo," perhaps the earliest serious discussion of the genre.[8] Described only as a novel way of playing and dancing a *danzón*, the mambo here is still subordinated to the older genre. According to Cuéllar Vizcaíno, what sets the mambo apart is improvisation: "All the musicians, except for the bassist and conga player, have the liberty to do whatever they please, inspiring themselves and improvising airs at their whim, so that the result is what we'd call a capricious and informal conversation among piano, flute, violin, *güiro, timbal,* and cowbell, while the bass and the conga

drum scold them rhythmically so as to put the house in order" (20).[9]
Although the resulting improvisation lacks the "elegance" and "grace"
of the rest of the *danzón*, it enjoys great acceptance among dancers and
musicians alike (21).

Writing that same year, the musicologist Odilio Urfé also stresses the
spontaneous polyrhythms of the mambo. According to Urfé, since the
mambo is characterized by "anarquía dentro del Tempo," "anarchy in
Tempo," mambos traditionally have not been written down.[10] With the
advent of the jazz-band format, however, arrangers have begun scoring the mambo section, although in these instances the result is less a
mambo than a "mambo atmosphere" (12). He concludes that the true
mambo demands free improvisation: "For the mambo to occur, it is
fundamental that everyone, absolutely everyone who participates in
its formation, play something different from what has been written
down. What is more, everyone needs to play what has been left unwrit-
ten within what has been written. To obtain a genuine mambo the
musicians should apply rhythmic effects only in the 'climax' or 'knot.'
Rhythm against rhythm. No tunes or definite melodies. No instrument
should have a fixed rhythm" (12).[11]

I have quoted these two little-known essays at some length because
they help to fill in some of the gaps in the early history of the mambo.
Several points need to be made. First, they establish the link between
the sacred and the profane mambo. In both contexts, mambo designates
an emphatic finale; moreover, both sacred and profane mambos involve
a dialogue or conversation, but in the latter not among spirits but
among instruments. As Ortiz put it, a mambo is "a typical musical
effect produced by the crossing of the rhythms of various instruments,
that is to say, a *palabre* or conversation of rhythms."[12]

Both authors also stress the mambo's freedom. Cuéllar Vizcaíno calls
attention in no uncertain terms to the importance of devil-may-care
improvisation. The musicians must improvise freely, even capriciously—
"a la diabla" (*diablo* was in fact an early synonym of mambo). The ensu-
ing free-for-all is controlled only by the steadying bass riffs and conga
figures. Everything else is left up to the orchestra's daring and discre-
tion. The Cuban phrase "relajo con orden," which designates a chao-
tic coherence or a ruled unruliness, describes precisely what Cuéllar
Vizcaíno has in mind. Urfé's nice formulation of this notion is "anarchy
in Tempo." His intriguing idea is that the mambo teases out unheard
melodies, "lo que no está escrito dentro de lo que está escrito." This
may be a further reminder of the music's religious origins: just as the

sacred mambo established contact between the visible and the invisible, the profane mambo establishes a dialogue between the heard and the unheard. The mambo is a musical séance.

The two essays are equally significant for what they do *not* say. Musicologists interested in establishing the "Cubanness" of the mambo like to call attention to Arcaño's role in its evolution. His importance, like that of Arsenio Rodríguez and the López brothers, is undeniable. Still, it seems clear that neither Arcaño nor Arsenio (both of whom are quoted in *Bohemia*) initially treated the mambo as an autonomous musical genre. Arcaño's definition was simply "a syncopated *montuno*."[13] In 1948, at least ten years after the word had acquired its musical sense, the mambo had not yet become an autonomous form.[14] Yet the defining moment in the mambo's evolution surely has to be the point at which it was detached from the matrix of the *danzón*. The man responsible for this feat was Dámaso Pérez Prado, the original *rey del mambo*.

Although the mambo certainly has had its share of noteworthy exponents, Pérez Prado stands out as the one most responsible for both its musical shape and its commercial success. Dubbed king of mambo by his contemporaries, Pérez Prado exerted an influence and reached an audience that far surpassed those of the other great Latin bandleaders of the 1950s—Tito Puente, Machito, and Tito Rodríguez. If in the thirties and forties Desi Arnaz had been the "conquistador of conga," during the fifties Pérez Prado became the undisputed "mambo king." As Natalio Galán has noted, the mambo as we know it was essentially an individual "excogitación," Pérez Prado's bright idea.[15] It is crucial to realize that, unlike the *son* or the rumba, the mambo did not arise from a long-standing popular tradition. The first rumbas were danced on the street; the first mambos were danced in dancehalls. Galán goes on to compare the mambo to sugarcane juice served up in a plastic container—not a bad analogy, even if he intends it as a putdown, for the mixed metaphor calls attention to the mambo's artificiality, to the fact that it is a "learned" rather than a "popular" genre. Although many musicians contributed to this concoction, it was Pérez Prado who added the final ingredients, distilled it, and packaged it for consumption.

Born in the Cuban province of Matanzas in 1916, Pérez Prado moved to Havana in 1942, where he began playing in small clubs like the Kursal and the Pennsylvania.[16] He later joined the orchestra Casino de la Playa, for which he played the piano and arranged until 1949, when he left Cuba and settled in Mexico. Although by 1948 Pérez Prado was a well-known figure in Havana's musical circles, neither Cuéllar Vizcaíno nor Urfé so much as even mentions him, which would indicate that, even at this relatively late date, he was not strongly associated with the incipient genre. Yet only two years later his name would be synonymous with the mambo.

Although Pérez Prado began experimenting with the mixture of a big-band sound and Afro-Cuban rhythms as far back as 1942 or 1943, the blend came together only several years later. In 1946 Pérez Prado spent several months in New York, where he did some arranging for Desi Arnaz, Miguelito Valdés, and Xavier Cugat. On his return to Cuba, he was interviewed by Enrique C. Betancourt for *Radio Magazine*, a Havana publication. At the end of the interview Pérez Prado states: "I am preparing a new musical style that I think is going to be well liked: the *son mambo*. The first number is called 'Pavolla.' All it needs is a piano transcription and perhaps some corrections. The firm of Vda. de Humara y Lastra is eager to have it in order to record it and distribute it. Let's see what happens."[17] Although it is unclear what effect the visit to New York had on Pérez Prado's musical thinking, one thing is certain: his "son mambo" is, at least, a forerunner of what he was later to call simply "mambo." Although the recording he mentions probably was never made, his words are prophetic indeed. Accompanying the text was a photograph of Pérez Prado at the piano holding a piece of sheet music on which he has written, in large letters, "son mambo."

In spite of Pérez Prado's optimism in 1946, Cuban record companies did not exhibit much interest in his music, which was considered weird and highbrow.[18] It was not until 1949, after he had left Cuba and settled in Mexico City, that he got the opportunity to record. Herman Díaz, who was in charge of RCA-Victor's international division at the time, recalls that the date of the first recording session was March 30, 1949.[19] If one wanted to celebrate the mambo's birthday, this would be the day, for it was in this session that Pérez Prado recorded "Qué rico el mambo," the song that started the mambo craze. "Qué rico el mambo" (sometimes written "Qué rico mambo") took the music world by storm, becoming a hit in Mexico and in the rest of Latin America. Over the next several years Pérez Prado was to record dozens and dozens of mambos, his press agent claiming in 1952 that Pérez Prado had sold over six million records.[20] Even if this is hype, there is no doubt that his success was phenomenal. When he left Cuba, Pérez Prado was making $50 a week as pianist and arranger; a couple of years later he was reportedly pulling down $5,000 a week. His popularity in Mexico was such that he required a police escort wherever he went.

Robert Farris Thompson, who happened to be in Mexico in 1950, provides a memorable description of the beginning of mambo madness:

> *I was in Mexico City in March 1950, mere weeks after Perez Prado's version of the New York–born, Bop-flavored Mambo had conquered the land. At the Hotel del Prado I observed a Mambo fiesta which threatened to demolish the building. No one at the party had even danced the Mambo before, but the new music shrieked an insistent "come hither." Those dancers made up their minds that, unlike other dances, Mambo could be done by anyone. Some tried to Fox Trot. Others laughingly attempted Samba. A tall, beautiful woman commented, "En serio, mi vida, pero qué ritmo más raro."* [21]

What made Pérez Prado's mambos seem so strange, as Thompson suggests, was their combination of Bop flavor and Cuban *sabor*. Some of the antecedents of this stew certainly go back to Arcaño's "danzón de nuevo ritmo," but others come right out of North American jazz. Before Pérez Prado came along, the mambo was linked to the *charanga*, with its characteristic complement of flute, violins, bass, and timbales. Patterned after North American bands, Pérez Prado's orchestra, with its large reed and brass section, diverged sharply from the Cuban model. [22] Even Arsenio Rodríguez's *conjunto*, with its small trumpet section, did not provide a strong precedent for this. A great admirer of Stan Kenton and other American musicians of the day, Pérez Prado used his frontline of four saxes and five trumpets in ways unheard of in Cuba. His trumpet voicings, with their dissonances and piercing high notes, and the contrapuntal scoring for brass and reeds, introduced a new sound into "Cuban" music. [23] Orestes López's "Mambo," lively but subdued, sounded nothing like this. To Cuban ears, the mambo was indeed mumbo jumbo.

The modern mambos were strange also in that they lacked the two- or three-part structure of other Cuban forms. Because the mambo began its life only as a type of improvised refrain, when it achieved independence it became a free-standing fragment, a part that has escaped the whole. Thus, as John Storm Roberts points out, it lacks "formal and internal complexity."[24] A composition like "Qué rico el mambo" is a brief, brash outburst of sound, complex in its internal harmonies and dissonances, but disquietingly uniform in texture.

Their uniformity makes Pérez Prado's compositions rather disconcerting. If one comes upon a piece *in medias res*, it's difficult to tell whether the song is at the beginning or near the end. The words do not help. When they exist, they are minimalist to the point of absurdity. Pérez Prado uses lyrics in the manner of scat words, with single syllables repeated like piano or trumpet stabs. The entire lyric of "Qué rico el mambo" runs, "Mambo, qué rico el mambo, mambo qué rico é, é, é, é," where even the apocope of "es" to "é" betrays Pérez Prado's penchant for minimalism. The lyric of another famous mambo, "La niña Popoff," limits itself to repeating the girl's name over and over. The title of some of the best-known mambos is only a number—"Mambo No. 5," "Mambo No. 8"—a gesture that reveals not only their author's artistic pretensions (his favorite composer was Stravinsky) but also his indifference toward language. Another famous mambo is entitled "Ni hablar."

Laconic rather than lyrical, iterative rather than narrative, the mambo does not believe in stories. In its purest form it cannot be vocalized. Most vocal mambos, like those that Beny Moré recorded with Pérez Prado's orchestra, are usually *sones* or *guarachas* with mamboid flourishes. When music and words meet, the result is often logoclassia, the disarticulation or fragmentation of language. As logoclastic music, the mambo exploits language for its onomatopoetic or phonic qualities, not for its meaning-bearing capacity. Words are valued for their sound, not their sense. For the most part, Pérez Prado seems downright hostile to normal lyrics. His musical phrasings leave little room for verbal accompaniment.

It is in this context that one needs to understand Pérez Prado's most famous mannerism, the emphatic grunts with which he punctuated the music and egged his orchestra on. Shortly after his arrival in the United States in 1951, *Newsweek* commented, "Pérez's performances are trademarked by peculiar kinds of burp-like noises which he produces vocally to induce his orchestra to 'give.'" At about the same time *Ebony* remarked, "Uttering strange, guttural sounds as he conducts, Prado drives his musicians to a furious musical intensity." Others compared his grunts to "the cries of an excited muledriver" or to the barks of Sharkey the Seal.[25] Pérez Prado's grunts, however, were simply vestigial words. As he explained on several occasions, the sounds he made were slurred enunciations of the word *dilo*, with which he urged his musicians to give it their all (Fig. 6).[26] Pérez Prado's disarticulation of *¡dilo!* into "ugh!" makes evident the mambo's logoclassia, its tendency to reduce speech to sound, communication to expression. The fact that *dilo*, say or state, is the word that is submitted to this reduction makes the gesture all the more powerful. The act of *decir* makes stories possible in the first place; without the *dicendi* verb there is no narration. Yet here the very idea of saying is rendered insignificant, meaningless. Saying becomes nonsaying. One grunt is worth a thousand words.

From a practical standpoint, the mambo's laconism only aided its international diffusion. Since there was no need for translation of lyrics, diverse nationalities could be reached by the same recordings. (A decade earlier the conga also had owed some of its popularity in the United States to its basically instrumental character.) The mambo's hybridness remained more "pure," as it were, for not having to pick a language. The mambo is a balancing act. Articulate lyrics in Spanish would have tipped the scale toward the Hispanic strain; extended lyrics in English would have done the same in the opposite direction. Inarticulateness left it in the middle, with its Cuban and American components in precarious, taut balance.

The contrast between the mambo and "latunes" of the 1940s is instructive. Most of these songs, like Irving Berlin's "I'm on My Way to Cuba" or Desi Arnaz's "Cuban Pete," were rumbas with an English lyric.[27] The bicultural balance emerged from the contrast between musical and verbal phrasings. These songs are monolingual, monomusical, and multicultural. The rhythm is Cuban, the lyric is American, and the whole is Cuban American. Many latunes were simply awful, but the best of them achieve a mellow matching of musical and verbal idioms that constitutes a characteristic form of bicultural wit. In the case of the mambo, biculturation is woven into the music itself. Rather than from the play of words and music, the wit here emerges from the counterpoint of dissimilar sounds and rhythms.

Perez Prado's large output from the mambo era breaks down into three broad categories. The first includes the core mambos, classic pieces like "Qué rico el mambo," "Caballo negro," "Mambo No. 5," "Mambo No. 8," "La niña Popoff," and a few others. These compositions contain Pérez Prado's sonorous stew in its spiciest, least diluted form. The second group comprises pieces that, while not mambos through and through, include mambo passages or quotations. Structur-

FIGURE 6

Dámaso Pérez Prado goes "Ugh!" Photograph from The Bettmann Archive; UPI/Bettmann.

ally this group is reminiscent of Arcaño's *danzón de nuevo ritmo*, for in these compositions the mambo is part of a larger whole. Here one would include Pérez Prado's two biggest hits, both million sellers, "Cherry Pink and Apple Blossom White" (actually a *chachachá* version of a French popular song) and "Patricia" (a swing).[28] "Cherry Pink" enjoys the distinction of having stayed on the Billboard charts for twenty-six weeks, a tenure surpassed only by Elvis Presley's "Don't Be Cruel." The second group also includes many of the vocalized mambos that Pérez Prado recorded with Beny Moré in the early 1950s, songs like "Pachito E'Ché" and "Bonito y sabroso," whose subject is Mexicans' ability to dance the mambo as well as Cubans. The biggest irony of Pérez Prado's career is that *el rey del mambo* achieved his greatest successes with compositions that weren't really mambos. Indeed, by the time "Cherry Pink" became a hit in 1955, the mambo wave had begun to recede; and when "Patricia" became a hit in 1958, the mambo lived on only in Latin strongholds like the Palladium in New York.

The last category in Pérez Prado's mambo *oeuvre* comprises mamboid versions of standards like Agustín Lara's "Granada," the old Cuban *danzón* "Almendra," or Moisés Simons's "The Peanut Vendor," the song that had initiated the fashion of Cuban music in the United States back in the 1930s. Pérez Prado's innovative arrangement of a shopworn standard like "Granada," from his *Havana 3 A.M.* album (1956) or his recasting of classic boleros in *Latin Satin* (1958) is indeed music for tired ears. His witty, sometimes wild versions of ballads like "Bésame mucho" or "Ojos verdes" include some of his best work. The word for these arrangements is fresh, in both senses of the adjective: original as well as outrageous. Often writing against the mood and tempo of the music, Pérez Prado's version of something like "Bésame mucho," where the shrieking, aggressive trumpets all but debunk the sappy melody, amounts to a good-natured parody or *choteo* of the original. The strict musical dissonance is underscored by what one might call a tonal dissonance: those screeching horns are completely out of place in such a setting. In Pérez Prado's hands, the *trompeta* sometimes becomes a *trompetilla*, Cuba's version of the Bronx cheer. Those who question his "Cubanness" would do well to ponder whether this demystifying humor does not go back to the Cuban *choteo*. Carpentier once remarked that Pérez Prado used "the verbal non sequitur with a brashness [*desparpajo*] that confers upon him, at least, the merit of being a humorist."[29] What needs to be added is that the *desparpajo* surfaces not only in the minimalist lyrics but also in his offbeat arranging.

There are two schools of mambo thought. The first, which I will call the "Havana" school, underscores the mambo's roots in the *danzón* and holds up Bebo Valdés, the composer of "Güempa," "Mambo Caliente," and many others, as the standardbearer of the "genuine" Cuban mambo. According to one historian of Cuban music, for example, Valdés's mambos are "much better elaborated and more Cuban than those by Pérez Prado."[30] The other school, which I will call the "New York" school, rightly calls attention to the fusion of Afro-Cuban and jazz music that took place in New York in the 1940s. According to the New York school, the central figures in the evolution of the mambo are New York musicians like Machito, Tito Puente, Tito Rodríguez, and Justi Barreto. Pérez Prado does not quite fit within either school. Although he was of course very familiar with the Afro-Cuban pedigree of the mambo, and although he may well have picked up some ideas from his stay in New York in 1946, his spectacularly successful career tends to skew both accounts. For the Cuban school Pérez Prado is too American; for the New York school he is too commercial. Besides, he rarely performed in New York, where Tito Puente occupied the throne of the mambo king.

Pérez Prado is a misfit because he exists in translation. As one more representative of the great Cuban tradition of dislodgement, he is another of those Cubans for whom unhousedness and misplacement seem to be conditions of creation. John Storm Roberts has criticized Pérez Prado's mambos for being "extremely, if misplacedly, ingenious."[31] But misplacement is the boon and the bane of the mambo, as it is of Cuban-American culture in general. Because of its ostentatious hybridness, the mambo forfeits any fixed cultural niche. Located somewhere between Havana and New York, it is unsettled and unsettling. Natalio Galán called it "a neurotic rhythmic disequilibrium," but one man's neurosis is another man's genius.[32] Tense, intense, and intrepid, Pérez Prado's mambo mix bears witness to the disquieting power of bicultural syntheses.

Before April 1951, when Pérez Prado first played before American audiences, the mambo was scarcely known in the United States. Its diffusion occurred in two stages. Beginning in the late forties, Cuban music had been popular with the Latin population in New York, which had just increased substantially as a result of the large Puerto Rican influx after World War II. Already in 1947 Tito Puente headed an orchestra called the Mambo Devils, and as early as 1946 the Cuban José Curbelo made a recording entitled "Los reyes del mambo."[33] In all probability, however, the word was used here in its *danzón*-related sense; that is, it did not refer to a discrete, autonomous composition but to the up-tempo jamming at the end of a *guaracha* or a *danzón*. Significantly, "Los reyes del mambo" is not a mambo but a *guaracha*.

Then, early in 1951, Pérez Prado was "discovered" by American audiences. Bandleader Sonny Burke, on vacation in Mexico in 1950, heard "Qué rico el mambo," liked it, and recorded it under the title "Mambo Jambo." The following year Decca released an album of Burke's mambos (most of them covers that followed Pérez Prado's arrangements very closely), and one of Burke's own compositions, "Mambo Man," was featured in the musical *Painting the Clouds With Sunshine* (1951). Encouraged by Burke's success, RCA Victor switched Pérez Prado from its international to its pop label, and the story of his Latin-American success was repeated in this country. "Qué rico el mambo" became a hit, selling upward of 600,000 copies, and from this point on the mambo became identified with the diminutive bandleader from Cuba who wore zoot suits, jumped wildly onstage, and uttered strange guttural sounds.

(Pérez Prado's American fame had a price, though. Something is always lost in translation, and what Pérez Prado lost was his first name, Dámaso. For Americans his full name became "Perez Prado," with "Perez"—or "Prez"—treated as his given name, a custom that persists to this day.)

The Americanization of the mambo, the translation of "Pérez" into "Prez," offers a striking demonstration of the United States' own romance with otherness, a romance characterized by equal doses of fascination and fear. In April 1951, on the eve of his first tour, *Time* warned that a new dance craze was about to "assault" the country. Led by "the emperor of mambo," the assault turned out to be a smash, with Pérez Prado playing to packed houses wherever he went. Reviews of the performances were usually glowing, with reviewers praising both the music and the showmanship. In August 1951, with Pérez Prado back for more appearances, *Variety* predicted that he was "a cinch bet to clean up in a series of bookings around the country," adding that he was as effective "on a concert date as he is on a terpery." A couple of months later *Down Beat* reported that Pérez Prado's West Coast tour was proving a huge success, having packed 3,500 dancing mamboniks into Oakland's Sweet's Ballroom, the first time in many years that this had happened.[34]

By the end of 1951 mambomania was going strong. Over the next few years almost every major American publication would run cover stories on the new Latin dance craze. The *New York Times Magazine, Collier's, Life, American Mercury, Ebony, Saturday Review*—all greeted the mambo with a mixture of fascination and puzzlement. No one seemed quite sure what the mambo was. Writing in 1954, the jazz historian Nat Hentoff asserted that the mambo had become "a puzzling national enthusiasm—wildly popular but difficult to define."[35] The name itself was mysterious, and different authorities had different theories: some thought it was onomatopoetic, others traced it back to Afro-Cuban rituals, some even ventured that it was a word that Cuban peasants used when cutting sugarcane ("¡mambo!" the *guajiros* would scream out, as the stalks fell to the ground).

The reputation as an uninhibited, libidinal dance increased interest in the mambo. A recurring theme in the press coverage is the mambo's "primitive" or "barbaric" dimension, what one writer called its "high sex quotient" and another termed its "lid's off demonic quality."[36] *Ebony* began its mambo exposé: "Its impulses are primitive, its rhythms are frenetic, its pace is frantic, and it is called the mambo." In a pretentious essay entitled "The Mambo and the Mood," Barbara Squier Adler concluded, "The mambo may well be the dance-floor counterpart of psychoanalysis. Both leave, or seem to leave, the individual free of tensions acquired in trying to make a normal life in an abnormal time."[37] Pérez Prado himself was dubbed "a modern pleasure god" and "a little demon"[38]—a not inappropriate description if we remember that *diablo* had originally been a synonym for mambo.

The mambo was both a threat and a temptation. Ballroom dance teachers tried to ease the threat by assuring their pupils that there were two varieties of mambo, "smooth" and "hectic."[39] Taught at uptown dance academies like Arthur Murray's, the smooth mambo was a society dance of "subtle reasonableness." While Mrs. Arthur Murray assured the American people that the mambo was nothing more than "rhumba—with a jitterbug accent," a supercilious Arthur Murray bragged on his television show that he could teach the basic step in under a minute.[40] The "hectic" mambo was a darker, ruder sibling. On display in venues like New York's Palladium, the Home of the Mambo, the hectic mambo was a dance of "uninhibited exhibitionism" characterized by wild contortions and suggestive movements.[41] Reading over the literature almost forty years later, it seems clear that no one knew exactly what the mambo was or how it should be danced. There are nearly as many ways to dance the mambo as there are dance instruction books. As late as 1958 *Dance Magazine* was publishing a debate on the proper way to mambo.[42]

To be sure, some of this apprehension was justified, for the mambo is indeed, as someone remarked disparagingly, "a mockery of normal sex."[43] Once detached from the matrix of the *danzón* by Pérez Prado, the mambo retained its intense, paroxysmal quality. But unlike the *rumba*, the *son*, or the *danzón* itself, the mambo does not build up slowly to a rousing climax. It has none of that gradual *crescendo* and *accelerando*, none of that "parabolic enthusiasm" typical of other forms of Cuban music.[44] The mambo occurs only at the apex of the parabola, at its climactic moment. In the mambo there is no warming up or cooling down, no foreplay or afterplay. The mambo begins and ends with paroxysm. The mambo is not a "mating" or a "courtship" dance because mating is a staged, multipart ritual—a play with several acts or a symphony with several movements. The mambo knows only one act and one movement: Wham-bam, thank you, mambo. If the rumba (in the American sense) is courtship, the mambo is orgasm. *Life* put it this way: "Faster and less classy than the rumba, the mambo permits its practitioners to go hog-wild with improvised solo steps while wearing an expression of ineluctable bliss."[45] The mambo is indeed a music of bliss: orgasmic rather than seductive. The fast, frenetic tempo of the music, the jerky, contortive bodily movements, the minimal lyrics, the screeching trumpets, even Pérez Prado's famous ejaculations—all contribute to the mambo's paroxysmal pitch. No wonder that the ur-mambo states, "Mambo, qué rico el mambo."

Along with repeated references to the mambo's eroticism, bizarre stories circulated about dire effects on its practitioners. It was widely reported in the American press that in Lima, in January 1951, Cardinal Juan Gualberto Guevara threatened to withhold the Holy Sacraments from anyone who attended Pérez Prado's shows. A few years later, the Colombian bishop Miguel Angel Builes issued an edict condemning mixed bathing, sex education, motion pictures, and mambo.[46] Also in 1951 a mambo-crazed man was said to have killed several people in Mexico City. And the then-president of the Philippines, Ramón Magsaysay, was quoted in American newspapers as having declared the mambo a "national calamity." Filipinos don't want to work, Magsaysay said, all they want to do is mambo. My favorite mambo anecdote, however, has to do with a Cuban bullfighter (this is already strange enough) who claimed to have been gored by a bull because officials at Mexico City's Plaza de Toros refused to permit the playing of mambo while he was fighting the animal!

It did not take long for Tin Pan Alley to jump on the mambo band-wagon. As had happened with the conga and the rumba, American tunesmiths began churning out dozens of "mamboids," that is, songs that weren't mambos though they alluded to them, either musically or in their lyrics. Most of what I call mamboids were in fact "meta-mambos," amused commentaries on mambo madness.

> *Papa loves mambo.*
> *Mama loves mambo.*
> *Look at him sway with it.*
> *Guess he's okay with it.*
> *Shouting olé with it, now—ugh!*

This comes from "Papa Loves Mambo," a typical mamboid that was a big hit for Perry Como. Rather than a mambo, it's an up-tempo, Latin-inflected swing. The mambo elements in the song are citational: some Afro-Cuban percussion, a few screeching trumpet riffs, and above all the imitation of Pérez Prado's inimitable grunts. The mambo purists of the day, of course, fulminated against mamboids. Ernest Borneman, a columnist for *Melody Maker*, called them "a wretched lot—poorly invented, poorly played, and in poor taste."[47] No matter: during just one week in October 1954 American record companies released no less than ten "mambo-styled platters."[48]

Besides "Papa Loves Mambo," the most successful mamboids were Vaughn Monroe's "They Were Doing the Mambo (But I Just Sat Around)," which started the genre, and Rosemary Clooney's "Mambo Italiano," temporarily banned from radio play for allegedly defaming Italian Americans (sample slur: "you calabrasi do the mambo like a-crazy"). Some other mamboids: "Middle Aged Mambo," "Mambo Rock," "Mambo Baby," "Loop-de-Loop Mambo," and "Mardi Gras Mambo." Christmas of 1954 saw the advent of still another weird hybrid: mambo Christmas carols like "Jingle Bells Mambo," "We Wanna See Santa Do the Mambo," "Rudolph the Red-Nosed Mambo," and Jimmy Boyd's "I Saw Mommy Doing the Mambo (With You Know Who)," about a boy who spies his mother mamboing with

Santa. Finally, as proof that the mambo was nonsectarian, Mickey Katz recorded "My Yiddishe Mambo," inspired by a Jewish mambonik who's "baking her *challes* for Noro Morales." The last words of this song raise the congenital hybridity of the mambo to new heights: "Olé! Olé! Oy vay!"

Pérez Prado's first New York booking was at the chic Starlight Roof of the Waldorf Astoria. In its early years the mambo was seen as a working-class, and more specifically a Latin and black, phenomenon; the Home of the Mambo was the Palladium, which catered to a black and Hispanic clientele. But from the Latin enclaves of New York the mambo spread to middle America and, finally, to the high-society types of the Waldorf. When Pérez Prado opened at the Waldorf on July 27, 1954, it was a sign that the mambo had definitely penetrated the upper echelons of American society. His fifteen-piece orchestra came into town primed to blow the roof off the Starlight Roof. And blow they did. His may not have been the best band ever to play the Starlight, but it was certainly the loudest. Until then the Waldorf's idea of a Latin orchestra had been Xavier Cugat, with his Mexican serapes, his chihuahuas, and his tame and lame rumbas. Even if Cugat, ever the opportunist, had already released a record called *Mambo at the Waldorf*, this was the first time that the Waldorf's well-heeled patrons got an earful of the real thing.

The reviews were positive but wary. Praising Prez's virtuosity, they lodged reservations about the appropriateness of his music for the Starlight Roof. To say that they were scandalized would be an overstatement, but they did remark on Pérez Prado's "startling" stage antics, on the "variegated clothes" of the "frantic horde" of mamboniks, and on the numerous "fems who shrieked in ecstasy" upon hearing the vamp for "Qué rico el mambo." "No question about his prowess," one reviewer mused, "but there's such a thing as overdoing your strength." [49] During its run of several weeks the show did good but not spectacular business. To my knowledge, the mambo king did not play the Waldorf again.

In July 1954 in New York the Waldorf was only one of several mambo venues. Those who found the pricey Starlight Roof out of their budget had other outlets for their mambomania. On Wednesday nights the Palladium had Mamboscope, the weekly "ballroom bacchanals" where one could dance all night with Tito Puente, compete in a mambo contest for amateurs, and get mambo classes from "Killer Joe" Piro (who was Italian) and "Cuban Pete" Aguilar (who was actually Puerto Rican). All for only $1.75.[50] Or one could go to Roseland, where Tito Rodríguez was playing, or to the Arcadia, which featured Machito, or to several other smaller clubs that also purveyed mambo. Other cities had their own mambo shrines—Chicago had Mambo City, Los Angeles had Ciro's, San Francisco had the Macumba Club.

In the fall of 1954 Tico Records organized "Mambo USA," a 56-city tour that took the mambo to America's heartland. The forty-strong mambo contingent included Machito, Joe Loco, Facundo Rivero, and many other well-known Latin musicians (in *The Mambo Kings Play Songs of Love* Hijuelos recreates this tour, though he places it in 1956). In December 1954 the stores were full of mambo-motivated gifts: mambo dolls, mambo nighties, and mambo "kits" (a mambo record, maracas, and a big plastic sheet with the mambo steps on it). And that same month Paramount released *Mambo*, with Silvana Mangano in the role of a dancer who has to choose between marriage and the title of the movie. A couple of months later Pérez Prado himself appeared in *Underwater!*—a very successful RKO film whose main attraction, in addition to the music, was Jane Russell mamboing in a bathing suit.

In 1954 Cuba was all over America. On television *I Love Lucy* was number 1 in the ratings; Ernest Hemingway had just been awarded the Nobel Prize for *The Old Man and the Sea*; and in ballrooms all over the country mambomania had reached a fever pitch. By the fall of 1954 the whole country was awash in a sea of mambo.

But unlike demons, mambo is not forever, and after 1954 the mambomania quickly subsided, to be replaced by a new Cuban dance, the *chachachá* (although as late as 1958 Doris Day and Gig Young were dancing mambo in the movie *Teacher's Pet*). Trying to keep in step, Pérez Prado also changed his tune, though not for the better. He retained the jazz-inspired brass but used Afro-Cuban percussion less often. By the time he recorded "Patricia" in 1958, he had added an organ and traded in his bongos and congas for trap drums and a tambourine. The result was what was sometimes derisively called "música de caballitos"—jingle rather than jungle music, a music that was upbeat, bouncy, and wearily monotonous. Without the Afro-Cuban backbone, Pérez Prado's music lost its hard, driving edge. At its worst, this new mix sounded like the score from a bad Italian movie.

To hear what a difference a drum makes, it is enough to compare his original recording of "Qué rico el mambo" in 1949 with the version he made a decade later.[51] In its original arrangement the song is aggressive, nervous, with the trumpets reaching what one critic called "alarming tonalities."[52] But in the later arrangement the tempo has slowed down, the trumpets are mellower, and gone are the conga and bongo figures. In their place the steady thumping of the trap drums and tambourine exerts a kind of "normalizing" rhythmic control that prevents the rest of the orchestra from getting out of hand. The lyric of "Caballo negro," one of Pérez Prado's early mambos, simply said, "Caballo negro que tienes la cola blanca" (Black horse with your white tail). This lyric was a metaphor that captured the Afro-Cuban-American hybridness, the mulattoness, of the mambo (it may also have been a reference to the slang term for cocaine, *caballo*). But in the late fifties the white tail began to wag the black horse. Although the early mambos had been paroxysmal, ever on the verge of excess, the later Pérez Prado seemed determined not to go overboard.

His mellowing is reminiscent of Desi Arnaz's. Like Desi in his 1950s movies, Pérez Prado began to lose his accent, becoming less and less "Cuban." If in *Forever, Darling* Desi gives up his conga for a concertina, Prado gives it up for an organ and tambourine. Ricky Ricardo, who once composed a "Nurtz to the Mertz Mambo," had some of the vivacity and energy of the early Pérez Prado. A mambo mouth before its time, Ricky was unafraid of dissonance, of sticking out, of parading his eccentricity. He knew that his talent was his tantrums. But when Ricky became Larry in *Forever, Darling*, he lost his aggressiveness, his rough edges. Something similar happened to Pérez Prado. His early mambos exhibit a youthful exuberance that still makes them exciting after forty years. Listening to them one often gets the feeling that their author has gotten carried away, that his penchant for the dissonant phrase or quirky voicing has gone too far. These outbursts are the musical equivalents of Ricky's tantrums. As time went on, however, stridencies were smoothed out, dissonances were softened, and excess became something to be spurned, not flirted with. The mambo king also became a sort of Larry Vegas, insipid, inoffensive, and dull. He even stopped grunting! It seemed that the more he used the organ, the less he grunted. The mambo was mambo-mouthed no more.

Although Pérez Prado evolved toward a "sweet" sound in response to the popularity of the *chachachá*, his problem was that the two genres were hardly compatible. The *chachachá* was a music of containment, not revelry. Directly descended from the *danzón*, its pedigree was untainted by "foreign" influences. More importantly, the *chachachá* was articulate, with the lyrics playing a central role. This is why there are few things more anodyne than the instrumental "chachas" with which American schools still teach this dance. Much of the interest of a *chachachá* resides in its picturesque, "newsy" subject matter—a curvy girl who wears falsies, a dentist who pulls teeth while drunk, a bald man who likes to go to the barbershop, Martians who dance. The *chachachá* imparts news or spreads gossip; it's a rumor mill, an example of what Cubans call *radio bemba*. All this was foreign to the mambo. Although popular wisdom has it that the name of the *chachachá* comes from the sound of shuffling feet, I find it plausible that it may bear some connection to *cháchara*, a slang term for conversation or gossip. The mambo is also conversation, we know, except that the instruments do all the talking. Pérez Prado's yawps are a far cry from the *chachachá*'s chatter.

The first *chachachá*, composed by Enrique Jorrín in 1948 but not recorded until 1951, was "La engañadora" (The Deceiver), one of the most famous songs in Cuban popular music (interestingly, Jorrín's original term for his new rhythm was "mambo-rumba"). "La engañadora" tells the story of a *chiquita* (Cuban for babe) who likes to parade herself up and down a busy intersection in Havana, Prado and Neptuno. Now this young woman is a Cuban man's dream—plump (*gordita*), curvy (*bien formadita*), and cute (*graciosita*). In sum, she is awesome, *colosal*. The men on the street can't keep their eyes off her.

The problem, however, is that the girl's eye-catching curves turn out to be spurious, the result of padding or *rellenos*. Once she is found out, the retribution is swift and brutal. Now the men don't give her a second look. Nobody is interested in admiring her "little cushions." The moral of the story is that women are fools for trying to deceive men. Sooner or later, the plain (not to say flat) truth will out.

> *Pero todo en esta vida se sabe,*
> *sin siquiera averiguar,*
> *y se ha sabido que en sus formas*
> *rellenos tan sólo hay.*
> *Qué bobas son las mujeres*
> *que nos tratan de engañar.*
> *¡Me dijiste!*

(But everything in this life is found out / without even having to inquire, / and it's been discovered that in her curves / there is only padding. / How silly of women to try to deceive us. / You can say that again!)

"La engañadora" is a typical *chachachá* in both content and structure. Progressing from illusion to reality, from *engaño* to *desengaño*, the garrulous lyric unfolds like an *auto sacramental* or morality play whose theme is the deceptiveness of appearances, *el engaño de los ojos*. Containment is indeed the subject of "La engañadora," as it is of many another *chachachá*. Measured and moralistic, this music has a disciplinary quality about it, which may explain why it became popular during the Batista dictatorship. *Chachachá* lyrics are full of male authority figures—cops, doctors, judges. Lacking a free-form *montuno* section with its call-and-response pattern and its attendant *inspiraciones*, this type of music does not tolerate improvisation. That is why the girl with falsies, the girl who improvises her curves, must be unmasked and punished. As anyone who has tried it quickly realizes, the *chachachá* is a prison with musical bars: one-two-cha-cha-chá, one-two-cha-cha-chá. The exuberant choreographic improvisations of mamboniks have no place in this rhythmic setting.

Let me venture an admittedly speculative suggestion. Isn't it possible to view the impostor of Jorrín's song as none other than the mambo itself? In musical terms, the *chachachá's* strategy of containment may be aimed straight at the mambo, which padded its musical forms with foreign or extraneous material. In 1951, the same year that "La engañadora" became a hit, Ortiz described the mambo using language identical to that of the song. According to Ortiz, the mambo also results from padding, from "*remplissage* o relleno."[53] Since the author of *Cuban Counterpoint* was a firm believer in mixing it up, he did not find anything wrong with this, but in Cuba generally there was a fair amount of hostility toward the mambo, which was seen as a bastard child of the *danzón*. Worse still, Pérez Prado made his name outside Cuba, where no one had wanted to record him. Thus, when the *chachachá* superseded the mambo, Cubans seemed to breathe an audible sigh of relief. Beny Moré, who had been the voice of the mambo, greeted the new dance with a song that proclaimed, "Ya los pollos no bailan mambo, ahora bailan chachachá" (The chicks no longer dance mambo, now they dance *chachachá*). As a defense of a certain type of authenticity, "La engañadora" strikes at the hybrid heart of the mambo. It may not be entirely a coincidence that the girl parades her inauthentic forms along a street called "Prado."[54]

Decir is the master verb of *chachachá*. In Jorrín's song, when the girl's deception is revealed, the chorus responds, "¡Me dijiste!" (You can say that again!). This exclamation gets to the root of the genre, which is to circulate information or gossip, what Cubans may call *chismografía*. After all, what is "La engañadora" if not a rather malicious *chisme*? Another famous *chachachá* summarizes its own news flash with the question, "¿Quién te lo dijo, nené?" (Who told you, babe?). To which the answer comes back, "Me lo dijo Adela" (Adela told me). The *chachachá's* emphasis on *decir*, word and deed, counters the mambo's laconism. Logophilia rebuts logoclassia. If the mambo is expressive rather than communicative, the *chachachá* values communication above all. The mambo's lovely inarticulateness reduces sentences to words, words to syllables, and syllables to grunts. The *chachachá* builds it all back up again. As a music of bliss, the mambo tends to the inarticulate, the interdicted: ugh!! But the *chachachá* is about amplification, not reduction. A cha-cha-mouth is not loud, merely voluble.

Just as it displaced the mambo in Cuba, the *chachachá* (with a helping hand from the Dominican merengue) conquered it in the U.S.A. In March 1954 death knells were already pealing. Herman Díaz, the same man who had originally signed Pérez Prado for RCA Victor, was quoted in *Variety* as preferring the *chachachá* since it was "musically less vulgar than the mambo."[55] Pérez Prado challenged this statement by offering the then-considerable sum of $5,000 to anyone who could demonstrate that the *chachachá* was substantially different from the mambo.[56] To no avail: early in 1955 the trade press began to carry items with such titles as "To Heck with the Mambo" and "After the Mambo, What?"[57] Adding a violin section to his orchestra (and thus making it more compatible with the Cuban *charanga*), Pérez Prado came up with a new dance, *la culeta*, similar to the *chachachá*, but it did not catch on. Later he invented the *suby*, the *pau-pau*, and the *dengue*, but also without much success. In 1956 the mambo king himself succumbed to the new vogue in a low-budget musical called *Cha-Cha-Boom* (1956), which some reviews thought should have been called instead "Cha-Cha-Bomb." The mambo was king no more.[58]

Although recently the mambo has come back strong, the current surge of interest is sure to fade also, for the true mambo is too quirky to hold the public attention for very long.[59] Like many other Cuban-

American creations, the mambo is a novelty, and novelties don't last. Still, this music remains a powerful example of bicultural boldness and hybrid wit. Pérez Prado's trumpets blow for freedom; his barbaric yawps are declarations of independence. The lyric of another famous mambo says, "A la cachi-cachi-porra-porra, a la cachi-cachi-porra-porra," which could be loosely translated, "Go to heck, to heck, to heck." Because of its fresh and refreshing willingness to go to extremes, to mix it up, the mambo occupies an important place in Cuban America's cultural landscape. The mambo is the one-and-a-halfer's dream music; it celebrates fractions and sings of parts that refuse the whole. Were it not for the mambo, we would not know the greatness in a grunt. Mambo: qué rico é, é, é, é.

The Barber of
Little Havana

MAMBO NO. 4 *When I first became interested in the mambo some years ago, I was puzzled to find that a well-respected British reference work,* The Faber Companion to 20th-Century Popular Music, *gave Pérez Prado's first name as Pantaleón rather than Dámaso. More puzzling still, after describing Pérez Prado's career in accurate detail, the entry concluded, "His elder brother Damos [sic] was also a bandleader and composer who specialized in the mambo." Later I discovered that Pérez Prado actually had a brother named Pantaleón, who was also a musician. Still later, while going through some music magazines from the 1950s, I found that Pantaleón had actually toured Europe claiming to be the* Mambo King, *an imposture that ended only when Dámaso threatened to take legal, rather than musical, steps.*

For many years there has been a barbershop on Eighth Street in Miami called Barbería Pérez Prado. Its elderly owner bears a striking resemblance to Dámaso; some say he is Pérez Prado's brother, Pantaleón. But when questioned by visitors, the barber of Little Havana disclaims any connection. Will the real mambo king please stand up and grunt?

Four

SALSA-FOR-ALL-SEASONS

W hen I was growing up in Miami in the early 1960s, we heard resistance music. What we were resisting was the reality of exile. At once reticent and self-indulgent, this music had a dual purpose, for it allowed one to vent the affect of exile—the nostalgia and the disorientation and the sorrow—without directly confronting its specific circumstances. Like exile itself, these songs were both escapist and adaptive, a "flight response" to the unpleasantness of life. One of the most popular was "El son se fue de Cuba" (The *Son* Has Left Cuba), whose author, Billo Frometá, ironically, was not Cuban but Dominican. It was performed and recorded by many artists, but I remember it best in the voices of the Duo Cabrisas-Farach, probably because Irene Farach's son went to school with me. The song tells the story of a Cuban peasant, a *guajiro*, who arrives in Havana to find that the *son*, the musical soul of Cuba, has left the country. Gone are the national anthem, "La Bayamesa," as well as Cuban classics like Moisés Simons's "El manicero." With Cuba's music gone into exile, a ubiquitous mute sadness has descended over the island.

"El son se fue de Cuba" enacts an exile ritual, which is to elevate the predicament of a segment of the population into a national malaise. Obviously its subject is not the exile of the island's music but that of its native sons, with Cuba's dark night of the *son* serving as an emblem for the distress of some of its people. When the speaker enumerates the different tunes that one no longer hears in Havana, the list oozes nostalgia. Yet it is not "La Bayamesa," the title of the Cuban national anthem, but the speaker who has left "crying from sadness"; it is not in Havana but wherever he happens to be that Cuban music is hard to find. But about his location the speaker is strangely reticent. When he says, "El son se fue de allá," he tacitly acknowledges that he is not "there," in Cuba, but nowhere does he identify himself as an exile—nor does he say anything about the reasons for his departure. All we know is that the *son* is gone, leaving the island bereft of music.

This kind of equivocation will recur in early Cuban-exile music. Listening to these songs now, I am struck by how seldom they mention any historical person or event. It is not just Fidel Castro's name that is anathema, but history itself. Even the name of Cuba is treated with reticence, as in Nazario López's "He perdido una perla" (I Have Lost a Pearl). Since Cuba is the Pearl of the Antilles, everybody knew what López was referring to, but not until the last line does the lyric actually name Cuba. These plain, plaintive tunes portray a condition of diffuse, unanchored suffering. Even as they detail the distress of exile, they abstain from giving it a habitation and a name. In Roberto Torres's "Un caminante," another hymn to homelessness, he limits himself to saying, "Yo nací en una tierra lejos de aquí" (I was born in a land far from here). Like a geological instrument that registers shock waves rather than faults, they record emotional effects but not historical causes. Indeed, if anything these songs invert the sequence of cause and effect, attributing to Cuba conditions that apply most directly to its exiled citizens. Cuba is not lost at sea, but many Cubans have been.

If truth be told, for most of the sixties there wasn't much *son* in Miami. What there was had been carried over from pre-Castro Cuba. The albums in stores were for the most part compilations of old Cuban music bearing titles like *La Cuba de ayer, Nostalgia de Cuba,* and *Añoranza cubana.* Since many performers still remained in the island, these records sometimes skipped back one generation or more, exhuming music by such old-time artists as Los Matamoros, Cheo Belén Puig, and José Antonio María Romeu. Curiously, the *chachachá* and the mambo seemed to be less represented than the *danzón.* The contemporary artists were only those who had already gone into exile—Blanca Rosa Gil, Fernando Albuerne, Roberto Ledesma, Rosendo Rosell, Eduardo Davidson, the Duo Cabrisas-Farach, and a few others. As the years went by, and many others also left, the exile musical canon swelled. Conspicuous by his absence was the greatest *sonero* of the time, Beny Moré, a problematic figure since he stayed in Cuba until his death in 1963. It would be several years before one could find records by or in homage to "el Beny."

Nostalgia ruled Cuban-exile music for over a decade. It was *la Cuba de ayer* (yesterday's Cuba) and yesterday's music. Every few months, at the Dade County Auditorium, local entrepreneurs put together variety shows with names like "Cuba canta y baila" (Cuba sings and dances). No one ever seemed to reflect on how strange it was to have Cuba dancing and singing in the middle of Miami. But an exile's talent for self-deception is matched only by his or her tolerance for pain. Featuring artists who had been more or less famous in Cuba, these spectacles would begin with the Cuban national anthem; by the time the show ended, several hours later, someone was sure to have sung "El son se fue de Cuba," "He perdido una perla," or Luis Aguilé's "Cuando salí de Cuba," another tearjerker (composed by a Chilean!) whose speaker announces that he cannot die because his heart is buried in Cuba.

I do not mean to mock the emotions or the music, both of which seemed inevitable at the time. But in retrospect one cannot overlook how much these songs leave out, how incompletely they chronicle everyday life in Miami. In this music Cuba is everywhere, but Miami is out of sight. Although the speaker in Frometá's lyric locates Cuba as being "allá," he refrains from specifying any "aquí." For all practical purposes, "aquí" doesn't exist; there is no here here. When mentioned at all, Miami appears as a term of comparison and contrast for Havana. A *chachachá* entitled "Flagler Street," the original hub of Little Havana, made the point that the presence of beautiful Cuban girls strolling along this street made Flagler seem just like San Rafael, an Old Havana landmark.[1] The substitutive gesture kept the past alive, but only at the expense of the present.

In this type of music, adaptation to American society was either not countenanced or countenanced only to be derided. As late as 1974 a song called "El bilingüe" likened bilingualism to homosexuality. The song's protagonist is Abelardo, or "Abe" for short (*pájaro* or *ave* is Cuban slang for homosexual), who avers with a lisp:

> *No ha sido la culpa mía*
> *haber nacido varón.*
> *Pero de que yo sea bilingüe*
> *de eso no hay discusión.*[2]

> *I can't be blamed / for being born male. / But that I am bilingual / there is no doubt.*

By using bilingualism as a metaphor for homosexuality, the song identifies acculturation with effeminacy. Notice that the target of derision is not someone who has forgotten Spanish but rather someone who has also learned English. Speaking English should not make Abe a renegade Cuban, a *cubano arrepentido*, though this is what the metaphor implies. But since Abe's homosexuality makes him "mono" rather than "bi," the conceit is inconsistent. Nonetheless, in the world of Los Jóvenes del Hierro (The Young Men of Iron) distinctions between homosexuality and bisexuality do not come easily. Just as homosexuals and bisexuals are birds of a feather, renegade Cubans are one with English speakers. This is a Spanish-only world. Bilingualism is a crime against Cuban nature. A Cuban *macho* is not only strong and stoic, but monolingual.

Not until the seventies did the tide of nostalgia begin to swell with other currents. As we will see, the initial exile themes never disappeared altogether, but they were complicated and enriched by other concerns. By the beginning of the seventies a younger generation of exiles had begun to form its own bands and make its own music. Most of the members of these bands were one-and-a-halfers, Cuban baby boomers who would grow up to become YUCAs. Unlike Los Jóvenes del Hierro (no longer so *joven*), very few of them were old enough to have started their careers in Cuba. The one-and-a-halfers' music was by turns nostalgic, assimilationist, and something in between. Side by side on the same album one could find songs about royal palms and designer clothes. The dominant language, musically and verbally, was Spanish; but English appeared with some regularity. Cuban and American culture began to blend in curious ways. One song talked about a man who goes to see a *santero* because he has lost his Rolex watch; another song was a *guaguancó* version of Barry White's "Can't Get Enough of Your Love." These hybrids at first seemed bizarre, but eventually they would become a way of life.

The first intimations that exile music was changing came from local party bands with names like Coke or the Antiques. All but forgotten today, these bands served an important linking function. On the one hand, they acted as a bridge to what was going on musically in the rest of the country. Coke covered Joe Cuba's boogaloo hit "Bang, Bang," and the Antiques recorded several songs by Carlos Santana. On the other hand, these same groups began to take a fresh look at the Cuban musical tradition. In the late sixties, when I was in high school, it was a revelation to hear Coke's version of "Sabor a mí," a classic bolero from the fifties that had first been made popular in the syrupy, sinusy whine of Los Tres Ases, a Mexican trio. These were the same songs that my parents had listened to in Cuba, but now they were being played by a rock band with an organ, electric guitars, and tambourines. The fact that the complicated lyrics were occasionally garbled only added to the charm and specificity of the rendition. This was appropriation by mangling. By today's standards, the music of Coke and the Antiques is unpolished and crude, and the quality of the recordings is very poor. But by developing a sound that was both nostalgic and contemporary, they helped to open the way for the more artful mixes that soon followed.

Alongside these rock bands, traditional Cuban orchestras still thrived. Untainted by rock or other American influences, these musicians continued to play "pure" Cuban music. Sometimes they composed their own songs, but their repertoire was rather heavily weighted toward old standards (an excellent example is the *sonero* Roberto Torres, who is still going strong). At its best this music was reiterative, helping to promote the continuance of Cuban culture outside Cuba. At its worst, it was self-indulgent and regressive, fostering escapism rather than adjustment.

By the mid-seventies these reiterative groups had been all but replaced by younger musicians, whose music and message were rather different. Willie Chirino began recording in 1974, at about the same time as Carlos Oliva; two years later Hansel y Raúl cut their first record, as did the Miami Sound Machine, which had its first hit in 1977 with "Renacer" (Rebirth). And in 1979 Clouds burst on the scene with the aptly titled *¡Llegamos!*. As the titles of their records suggest, these artists created a sense that things were changing, that the dark night of the *son* was coming to an end. In the music of these artists, the preoccupation with the *illo tempore* of Cuba begins to recede before the Miamian here and now. When Gloria Estefan sings in "Renacer" that a new love has made up for the loss of the old one, it is difficult not to put a broader cultural slant on her words. The cover of *¡Llegamos!* shows the members of the band getting off a train, a boat, and a plane (Fig. 7). The provocative reference to Cubans' repatriation is unmistakable—except that here the stress falls not on the departure but on the arrival. It's no longer "When I Left Cuba" but rather, "We're Here!" Leaving Cuba has become a point of departure.

This is not to say that arrival entails amnesia. As they climb down from the boat and plane, the members of Clouds are carrying with them all sorts of baggage, including a conga drum, and one of the cuts in the album is "Cha Cha Party." This is not a pristine, adamic

FIGURE 7   *Clouds, ¡Llegamos! Photograph used by permission of Crossover Enterprises.*

beginning, for the rebirth has not erased the memories of the previous life. Cuba has not vanished into the thin air; the Miami sound carries echoes of the Cuban *son*. By the same token, the uncertainties of exile do not evaporate either. One can sense this in the tension between the band's name and the photographs on the cover. How is it possible for "Clouds" to come down to earth, to set foot on the ground? What we call "landing" does not seem a cloud's prerogative. Clouds float and drift, they do not land or arrive. The point of the paradox is that the condition of exile does not go away, that in some sense one remains disconnected, out of touch, up in the air. One way to say "make the best of it" in Spanish is, *hacer de tripas corazón*, to turn worthless tripe into a life-sustaining heart. Tampering with the proverb a bit, one could say that the lesson of ¡Llegamos! is "hacer the *trips* corazón," where displacement becomes a springboard for renewed muscular achievement.

A major factor in the development of the Miami sound was an FM radio station that called itself Super Q (WQBA FM). Going on the air in March 1979, just as Cuban-American music was beginning to hit its stride, Super Q became an important vehicle for its diffusion. By 1979 Chirino, Hansel y Raúl, Los Sobrinos del Juez, Clouds, the Miami Sound Machine, and others had already been around for several years. Before Super Q, however, these artists did not have an adequate radio outlet. Their music was popular in discotheques and parties, but it got little air play. During this time the Spanish-language stations on the AM band were dominated by political talk shows, soap operas, and traditional Cuban music; the American pop and rock stations did not play anything with a Spanish lyric. Super Q was the first station to tap the younger Cuban (and later Latin American) constituency that was not being served by hispanophone or anglophone stations.

Ironically, Super Q's sister station on the AM band was none other than La Cubanísima, the paradigm of Cuban radio programming in Miami, which was ridiculed some years ago with the slogan "Más música y menos bla-bla-blá" (More music and less talk). If WQBA was the *cubanísima*, the station more Cuban than which none can be conceived, its FM twin was nothing less than Super Q, Super Cuba. Hyperbole against hyperbole, hype against hype, Super Q countered the bombast (not to mention the *bombas*) of its sister station by proclaiming itself super-Cuban in spite of the hybridity of its programming. Although the disc jockeys spoke Spanish (in one notorious case someone was fired because his Spanish was not good enough), the music was distributed evenly among rock, disco, ballads and boleros, and salsa.[3] Miami artists helped to promote the station and got a lot of air play in return. The station's bilingual jingle, which was sung by the Miami Sound Machine, ingeniously and succinctly defined the station and its audience:

> *Super Q, we love you,*
> *la mejor música la tocas tú.*
>
> *(Super Q, te quiero a ti.*
> *You play the best music for me.)*

By personifying the station and addressing it as both a *you* and a *tú*, this odd but heroic couplet says: look, we are as Cuban as *tú* and as American as you. Like us, because we are like you. Even phonically the slogan conveys the station's hybrid identity. The gist of the jingle is the triple rhyme between *tú* and *you* and Q, which stands for Cuba. But in which language does one make the rhyme? Is it "Super Qú" or "Super Qiú?" Given that the sentence contains both Spanish and English, does one say it with an American or with a Cuban intonation? When one says it in English, one tends to distort the sound of *tú* by pronouncing it something like "tiú." And when one says it in Spanish, one tends to hispanicize *you*, which then is pronounced something like "yú."[4] Spanish and English are both broken and spoken here. By bundling together *you, tú* and Q, the jingle establishes the bicultural compact that defines its audience. There is one other rhyming word in the poem, but one that is never mentioned: the numeral "two." Since we are *tú* as well as *you*, we are double; since we love in English ("I love you"), but we play in Spanish ("la mejor música la tocas tú"), we are double. In sum: we are two, we are *tú*, we are you. And to top it off, we are Super-Cuban, so there's no question about assimilation. The mockery of bilingualism present in Los Jóvenes del Hierro has disappeared altogether.

This jingle offers an example of what I will call a "cultural oxymoron," a term I will use to designate both the paradoxes of clouds that land and the mixing of cultures that these types of paradox engender. Like the mambo, the Miami sound is a stew, an *ajiaco* that feeds on odd couplings and curious (or Q-rious) cohabitations. There is a Miami version of "Good Loving" by Miguel, Oscar y La Fantasía that turns this rock-and-roll standard into a six-minute *son* where even the *manicero* makes an appearance.[5] Like the mambo, this song pairs Cuban and American cultures and has them enter into dialogue. The Cuban-American "Good Loving" culminates in a *montuno* where the traditional *charanga* flute weaves playful intricate figures around the unvarying English-language refrain. This magic *montuno*, with its bewitching call-and-response figures, is a mating song, the musical equivalent of bicultural romance. Good loving is good playing. Good playing is mixing it up. What the doctor in the song orders is a little mambo jambo. Cuban Pete never had it this good!

Cultural oxymora are affirmative—they do not shy away from the risk of contradiction. Back in the mid-eighties there was a popular Latin discotheque in Miami called the Banana Boat. "El platanito de Kendall," as it was sometimes called, featured live music by many of the exponents of the Miami sound. One night I was there to hear Willie Chirino, the Billy Joel of the YUCAs, about whom I'll say more later. In addition to going through his repertoire of hits, he played a traditional Cuban *son* by Miguel Matamoros called "El son de la loma." Now this song is really an inquiry into the essence of *cubanía*, an inquiry that takes the form of a question about the birthplace of the members of the Matamoros Trio. In the opening lines a young girl asks her mother where the singers, *los cantantes*, come from: "Mamá, yo quiero saber, de dónde son los cantantes." The punning answer is that the singers hail from the hills but sing on the plain, "son de la loma y canta en llano." *Llano* means both "plain" and a way of singing and *son* means both "they are" and the name of the music in which the reply is framed.

Apparently unbeknownst to Chirino, one of the people in the audience that night was José Fajardo, a gifted flutist who in the fifties led Fajardo y Sus Estrellas, a Cuban *charanga* second only to the Orquesta Aragón in quality and acclaim. When Chirino began to play, Fajardo went up on the stage, took out his wooden flute, and—*sin estrellas pero brillante*—joined in the *son*. What then followed was a "Son de la loma" memorable for the extended counterpoint between Chirino's American keyboard and Fajardo's Cuban flute. Given that this musical mix was taking place only a few blocks from a strip mall called Loehmann's Plaza, in my mind the "Son de la loma" became the "Song of Loehmann's," and as such a moving, melodious emblem of the cultural oxymora that make up Cuban-American culture. It was remarkable enough to hear the "Son de la loma" in a Banana Boat; but to hear it played in tandem by Chirino and Fajardo seemed downright marvelous. That night I realized where the *son* headed when it left Cuba: to Kendall.

Cultural oxymora: *son* and song; *loma* and Loehmann's; Havana beats and Banana Boats. Cultural oxymora: Cuban lyrics and American melodies; American words and Cuban rhythms; *alma de rock* and *corazón de bolero*. Cultural oxymora: one of Clouds' albums is *Me gusta hablar español* (1990), whose title song defies the English Only movement; but this spirited defense of Spanish occurs in a musical context that is hardly Cuban. Whatever the lyrics may say, musically the song speaks English. The hip-hop rhythm and the electronic, synthesizer-based sound have little to do with Cuban music. Cultural oxymora: at a recent New Year's party in a Miami Beach hotel, Clouds shared the stage with Chubby Checker (salsa with a twist).

At its best and most typical, the sound of Miami feasts on contradictions. Like Super Q, it flaunts its roots only to consume them. But there is no contradiction without conflict, and another meaning of consumption is to shrivel up. As we will see a bit later, the Miami sound retains a conflicted, cacophonous strain. Cultural oxymora celebrate what they cannot avert. But the effort of translation cannot but remind one how out of place Los Matamoros really are in Kendall. The Song of Loehmann's is both a panegyric and a dirge. The joy of arrival is clouded by somber recollection.

      A list of the most notable exponents of the Miami sound would include Alma, Willie Chirino, Clouds, Conjunto Impacto, Hansel y Raúl, Carlos Oliva y Los Sobrinos del Juez (also known by their English-language name, the Judge's Nephews), the Miami Sound Machine, Orquesta Inmensidad, and Miguel, Oscar y La Fantasía.[6] Most of these groups came upon the local scene in the seventies; many are still going strong today. Rather than attempting to do each of them justice, I will focus instead on the three that best illustrate the dominant features of this kind of music: Hansel y Raúl, Willie Chirino, and the Miami Sound Machine.

      Hansel y Raúl (Hansel Martínez and Raúl Alfonso), who are both now in their forties, got their start in New York as the lead singers of Charanga 76. Their first hit was "Soy," a Willie Chirino composition that I will discuss a bit later. When they moved to Miami, the group became Hansel y Raúl y la Charanga and later simply Hansel y Raúl. Between 1976 and 1989 they recorded a dozen albums and played constantly in local clubs.[7] In 1989 Raúl was busted for drug-related activities and the duo split up, with Hansel continuing a successful career on his own. Raúl is now out of jail and once again recording, but apparently the two have no plans to join up again.

      Hansel and Raúl typify the more traditional vein of the Miami sound. In some ways they continue the tradition of Roberto Torres, Los Jóvenes del Hierro, and similar groups, for their music is firmly entrenched in the old Cuban values. Musically their band at times sounds like a clone of fifties' *charangas* like the Orquesta Aragón or Fajardo y Sus Estrellas. Indeed, for several years their bassist was none other than Orestes López's brother, Cachao, one of the "fathers" of the mambo and a member of Arcaño y Sus Maravillas. (But roots can only reach so far: the band's original flutist was a Jewish woman from Brooklyn!) Even Hansel y Raúl's nickname, "Los gallos de la salsa," bespeaks their Cuban pedigree, since *gallo*, rooster, was a label given to Cuban *rumberos*.

Their lyrics tend to stay with the staples of Cuban folklore: cuckolds, big-assed women, bastard children, homosexuals, society snobs, and so on. But their adherence to tradition at times produces startling anachronisms. "Ponme la mano, Caridad" (1984) tells the story of Caridad, a girl from a rich family, who elopes with the son of the milkman. Set in Miami and in 1984, this tale is nothing short of fantastic. To write a song in Miami in the mid-eighties that draws on the old stereotype of the lecherous *lechero* is to inhabit a world that no longer exists. When was the last time you saw the milkman? Caridad lives in a time capsule. In a typical gesture of exile substitution, the song turns today's Miami into the Cuba *de ayer*. The song's title evokes a pre-Castro tune, "Ponme la mano aquí, Macorina," and even the girl's nickname, Cachita, goes back to a classic *chachachá* "Oyeme, Cachita" (not to mention that it is also the nickname of Cuba's patroness, Our Lady of Charity). The one concession to reality may be that Caridad elopes with the milkman's *son*, rather than with the milkman.

But Hansel y Raúl are not always so out of touch. Although musically they never stray far from Cuban formulas, their most interesting lyrics do reflect the new realities of life in America. Still, even in these instances they remain quite traditional in outlook. When they address contemporary subjects, Hansel y Raúl give voice to the values and worries of an unassimilated, hispanophone, Cuban-exile working class. Theirs is a kind of blue-collar salsa that speaks for those who work in factories or department stores. Their music's "proper place," to return to Carpentier's phrase, may well be the working-class neighborhood of Hialeah, in West Miami. Hansel y Raúl's compositions discuss such subjects as alimony, the Florida lottery, intercultural romance, Japanese imports, drugs, women's lib, or the drudgery of getting up every morning to go to work—but always from a "Cuban" point of view. In Hansel's "Latinoamericano" (1992), the speaker tells his American girlfriend that if she really wants to make him happy, instead of "honey" she should call him *papi*.

What comes through in these songs, often in a humorous way, is how difficult it is to be Cuban in America. The general impression is of a world gone slightly haywire, where the old values no longer hold. Husbands do not support their wives, wives run around on their husbands, and the children are strange long-haired creatures that speak an unintelligible language. One of their biggest hits was "María Teresa y Danilo" (1985), a spoof of Cuban-American high society that takes off from the *Dallas* television program. Danilo is worried because his daughter is about to marry a young man who is actually his illegitimate son. Not to worry, says María Teresa, his wife: you're not the only one who's been sleeping around, your daughter is illegitimate too. But in the end the whole thing turns out to have been a bad dream.

Since they are *gallos*, Hansel y Raúl are cocky, aggressive, sometimes crude. Sex and women's anatomies are a constant preoccupation. A song by Hansel called "El carro y la mujer" (1989) resorts to the cliché of women as cars, except that now the old jalopy of a wife is being traded in for a little Japanese number with cruise control. In "Esa mujer me gusta" (1982), a man compliments a woman because her ample behind doesn't fit inside a plane seat. This bicultural battle of the seats— buttock against *butaca*—may be taken as typical of Hansel y Raúl's subject and style. Their subject is the clash of cultures; their style is to talk about it in coarse, anatomical terms. "Esa mujer me gusta" is built on an extended pun on *corazón*, heart, and *culo*, ass. Hansel y Raúl are not always as vulgar as this, but they sure would not win the sensitive-male sweepstakes. Their music tends toward a kind of *salsa cruda* that reflects, and reflects upon, the dislocations of Cuban ways in a foreign culture.

More diverse musically and culturally is Willie Chirino, who has been called the "pop king of Cuban-American Miami."[8] Born in Cuba in 1947, Chirino arrived in the United States as a young teenager and finished high school in Miami. After a stint in New York, he came back to Miami, where he put together a rock band, Willie Chirino and the Windjammers, which played local clubs like the Sonesta on Key Biscayne and the Papá Grande (the Cuban Big Daddy) in Coral Gables. The Windjammers blew away after a couple years, but Chirino continued performing, eventually developing a large and loyal following. Although his music has had some success outside of Miami (particularly in Puerto Rico and Cuba, where pirated copies of his records abound), he remains essentially a local artist. For years now he has been announcing plans to record in English, but so far this hasn't happened, perhaps because his music is too firmly anchored in Little Havana.[9] Chirino is the musical guru of the one-and-a-half generation.

A gifted composer and multi-instrumentalist, Chirino put these talents to good use in his first album, *One Man Alone* (1974), where he plays all the instruments. Since then he has released a dozen albums, including *Acuarela del Caribe* (1989) and *Oxígeno* (1991). Rather than sticking to one tried and true sound like Hansel y Raúl, Chirino—a consummate translator—has experimented with different musical genres and orchestral formats. When his music takes on an overtly nostalgic or iterative bent, the emphasis falls on recasting rather than repeating. I have heard him do "Hava Nagila" in a *guaguancó* rhythm and the *merengue* "El negro" as a bolero. From his earliest to his most recent work, his albums run the gamut of musical styles and subjects. Cultural oxymora proliferate. His recording of "Can't Get Enough of Your Love" concludes with an Afro-Cuban doo-wop chorus.

In the liner notes to his second album (*Chirino*, 1975), Chirino states that he plays "an elastic music." This is as good a sobriquet as any to describe his songs—and perhaps to describe Cuban-American culture as well. As Chirino uses the term, "elasticity" is the opposite of resistance. Elastic music accommodates otherness. More than one older Cuban musician has told me that Chirino does not play "Cuban" music. His is certainly not a music that shields itself from foreign influence. If anything, his early recordings are weighted toward American sounds, with songs carrying titles like "We Just Want to Rock and Roll." The best of these are competent imitations of American rock, but it is curious to hear Chirino, who speaks fluent but accented English, singing a falsetto chorus à la Brian Wilson.

Chirino's first album did contain one song that has become his signature. Even though it's been almost twenty years since "Soy" was first recorded, it remains to this day an obligatory and central part of every Chirino performance. It is one of those songs that, without being startlingly original musically or lyrically, seems to render precisely a community's deepest feelings and convictions at a particular moment in its history. If "El son se fue de Cuba" captured the nostalgia of the early exile years, "Soy" puts its finger on the disorientation that followed. The first song belongs to the world of exilic substitution, for its assertion that the *son* has left the island paves the way for its recreation abroad. "Soy" belongs to the second moment, to the world of exilic destitution, for it gives voice to feelings of rootlessness.

Bearing the title "I Am," the song promises a self-definition, perhaps a portrait of the Cuban-American artist as a young man, but what it actually delivers is far from definitive. The lyric consists of a long list of equivalences. It begins:

Soy la más pequeña aldea
en un distante lugar.
Soy el ruido y la marea
del inmenso mar.
No soy cadenas ni rejas.
Soy azúcar y soy sal.
Si me quieres o me dejas
me da igual.

(I'm the smallest village / in a distant place. / I'm
the noise and the tide / of the immense sea. / I'm not
chains or prison bars. / I'm sugar and I'm salt. / If
you love me or you leave me / it's the same to me.)

The most noticeable thing here is the reduction of person to place. The speaker does not say that he comes from a small town (Chirino in fact does: Consolación del Sur, in the province of Pinar del Río), but that he *is* a small town. He does not say that he is not in jail, but that he is not a jail. He does not say he has a sweet tooth or a salty mouth, but that he is sugar and salt. The metaphors are both direct and evasive, making the speaker difficult to situate. Who or what speaks in these words? Perhaps the speaker is not a person but a place, and the whole lyric is an extended prosopopoeia. The insistent geographical references give one the feeling that the subject may not be Chirino but Cuba, the land of sugar and salt and jail cells. But this is never actually said, and Cuba's name goes unmentioned. Instead, the lyric's reticence feeds into its overt theme, which is the speaker's lack of essence or identity. He does not stay put long enough for us to class him as one thing or another.

Merging personal identity with national destiny, "Soy" sets them both adrift, as if Cuba itself were a moving island, floating aimlessly at sea. As happened in early exile lyrics, dislocation is transformed into a national characteristic. In "Son de la loma," the question about identity was answered by rooting the singers in the Cuban earth, in its hills and its plains.[10] But the dominant imagery in "Soy" has to do with the sea, with tides, with salt. Aquatic rather than chthonic, these images suggest itinerancy, nomadism, displacement. They limn a network of routes, not roots. The "immense ocean" has no "ground," in both the physical and metaphysical senses. You can perhaps drop anchor there, but you cannot dig in.

This cluster of images will recur with some regularity in Miami music. Another of Chirino's songs is called, "Yo soy un barco" (I Am a Ship, 1979); Clouds has one entitled "Amor velero" (Love with Sails, 1980); Hansel y Raúl recorded "Alma de marinero" (Soul of a Sailor, 1982); and Gustavo Rojas "Soy como el viento" (I'm Like the Wind, 1980). In all of these songs the self is portrayed as unmoored, homeless, lacking direction and definition. Clouds, breezes, boats, ocean spray—these are the metaphors of choice for the itinerant self. Yet all of these songs also attempt to make the best of it—"hacer de *trips* corazón"—by teasing out of homelessness a lesson in life-affirming freedom. As Chirino puts it in "Soy," since he is "a bit of a vagabond," he is content coming or going.

Rather than a definition, "Soy" is a riddle, an *adivinanza*. There is in Spanish, as in English, a type of conundrum where one is asked to guess the identity of an object from its characteristics. If the riddle is a good one, the distinguishing traits are both misleading and right on the mark.

> *Soy al revés y al derecho*
> *el mismo nombre y valor;*
> *en la tierra está mi lecho*
> *y amarillo es mi color.*
> *¿Quién soy?*
>
> (I am the same name and worth backward and for-
> ward. I come from the earth and yellow is my color.
> Who am I?)

The answer is gold, "oro," a palindrome which is yellow and comes out of the earth. "Soy" is structured like an *adivinanza*. Its puzzling catalogue of traits encourages the listener into trying to unite all the unrelated traits under one name or label. But it can't be done. In this musical puzzle dispersion does not lead to unity because dispersion is the point. By joining consciousness of self with consciousness of locality, "Soy" dramatizes the physical dispersion of the island and the attendant psychological dispersion of its people. Not to know your place is not to know yourself. "Who am I?" can only be answered by "I am nowhere."

Musically the song is equally difficult to place. In the original version, "Soy" is soft-rock ballad with Spanish words. Parsimoniously accompanied by organ, acoustic guitar, and American drums, Chirino moans his way through the lyric. Some years later he recorded the song again in a more brassy and upbeat arrangement that is perhaps less faithful to the spirit of the *letra* (*Amándote*, 1988). But either version is a far cry from the *típico* sound of the Matamoros Trio. One reason why the song works is that its music does not correct or compensate for the homelessness expressed in the lyric. A Cuban rhythm would have grounded the lyric, would have made the song familiar in a way that countered the speaker's disorientation. In music and words, "Soy" remains adrift, unanchored.

After *One Man Alone*, Chirino produced several albums that are interesting mostly for their experiments with different sounds and styles. These recordings show him trying to *colocar la voz* (place his voice), the Spanish phrase for locating a suitable vocal register and style. But it is not until his fourth album, the appropriately titled *Evolución* (1978), that he achieves a comfortable musical and cultural collocation. The title cut is an "elastic" *danzón* that combines the standard flute and strings of a *charanga* with a piano, synthesizers, and a saxophone. Halfway through the piece, the *cinquillo* rhythm of the *danzón* is abandoned and the lyric announces that this is "a new version of yesterday's rhythm" (*ritmo de ayer en su nueva versión*). Because the phrase *ritmo de ayer* echoes the exile mantra *Cuba de ayer*, Chirino's new *danzón* represents an attempt to take distance from the reiterative music of the early years. Striving to renew rather than repeat, he inserts the *danzón* in a different instrumental setting and adds a *montuno* section in chachachá rhythm.

But his evolutionary, recasting impulse surfaces most audibly in a "Salsa Medley" of several Cuban *rumbas*. At the beginning of the medley Chirino states that since other parts of Miami now have their songs, it is time that the southwest area also had its own anthem, "a *guaguancó* for the *sagües*" (*sagües* is Spanglish for southwest). A couple of years earlier another Miami musician, Luis Santí, had composed "La Norgüesera," a paean to the northwest area of Miami; now it's the *sagüesera*'s turn to be memorialized in song. Like "Danzón evolución," "Salsa Medley" updates and relocalizes a traditional Cuban rhythm.

With "Salsa Medley" the dispersion of "Soy" gives way to a concrete act of nomination rooted in a specific time and place. The vagabond singer of "Soy" reappears here as a genius loci. Notice the complicated topography of the song. The English-language title, with its reference to "salsa" (a term not then widely used in Miami), alludes to the Latin music of New York in the sixties and seventies. By offering this medley as *la sagüesera*'s theme song, Chirino moves salsa to Miami; and by weaving the theme song from classic *rumbas* like "Amalia Batista," he perhaps suggests the Cuban provenance of New York music. The streets of *la sagüesera* are haunted by other streets, other cities; Miami is a kind of arrangement, a certain way of orchestrating the past. Chirino's term "elastic" is an accurate label for the multilayered sense of place evident in these songs. Miami is an "elastic" place—one inhabited by other places like Cuba or New York.

The very name *la sagüesera* exhibits a consciousness of difference that distances this song from "El son se fue de Cuba" and similar compositions. Most important here is the act of nomination, the mere act of saying *sagüés*. This name is another cultural oxymoron, one that opens the way for institution, for emplacement. A sense of self requires a sense of place. Self: being in place. Indicating where you are may seem like a simple thing, but for many years the substitutive impulse among Cuban exiles was so strong that acts of emplacement like this one were few and far between. In 1974 it seemed both strange and liberating to realize the streets where you lived belonged to a neighborhood with its own name, one that blended Spanish and English. One had to be a part of this particular community to understand how deeply ingrained was its aversion to the here and now. By the time Chirino recorded this song the term *sagüesera* had been in use for a long time. But it took a while for it to enter songs and books. Even then, the gesture was unusual, for the music has always seemed to lag behind the times. Making a living was one thing; music and literature were another.[11] Even if one conducted everyday affairs with full awareness of locality (the economic success of Cuban Americans reflects this), popular songs continued to offer a retreat into a comforting world of imaginary substitutions.

Books and essays about Miami have tended to stress the importance of politics for Cuban Americans. Yet I am struck by how apolitical, by how rootless, the sound of Miami often seems. After the first years, Cuban politics almost disappears entirely from Miami's music. Only recently, with the anticipation of an end to the Castro dictatorship, have songs begun reflecting specific historical circumstances with some frequency.[12] In fact the sound of Miami tends to be neither "ethnic" nor "nationalistic." That is to say, it tends not to know its place, whether that place be Cuba or Little Havana. Unlike New York salsa, which is firmly grounded in the Hispanic barrio, Miami music favors subjects that are not overtly marked by locale. I do not mean to say that this music does not express the values of the community from which it arises, but rather that one of these values seems to be a studied avoidance of acts of nomination like that in "Salsa Medley."

An example of this avoidance is another song composed by Chirino, "Los diseñadores" (The Designers, 1982), which both celebrates and satirizes the rampant consumerism of the eighties. The speaker is a material man who brags about the many designer items in his possession. One doesn't need to understand much Spanish to get the drift of the lyric:

> Tengo un traje de Yves St. Laurent
> un perfume de Paco Rabanne,
> tres corbatas diseño Cardin
> como toda la gente.
> Dos camisas que son Cacharel,
> tres pañuelos de Coco Chanel,
> cuatro jeans, un reloj y un mantel
> son de Sergio Valente,
> como toda la gente.

> (I have a suit by Yves St. Laurent, / a perfume by
> Paco Rabanne, / three ties designed by Cardin / just
> like everybody else. / Two shirts by Cacharel, /
> three handkerchiefs by Coco Chanel, / four jeans,
> a watch and a tablecloth / are by Sergio Valente /
> just like everybody else.)

Even if the catalogue is carried to parodic extremes (a Cartier bicycle, an Hermenegildo Zegna toothbrush) the tone is affirmative, celebratory. The first word—"Tengo" (I have)—is key, for the catalogue affirms individual acts of material possession. What is more, this seems to be a communal habit, since everybody, "toda la gente," owns the same designer items. If New York salsa unfolds in the barrio, Miami salsa happens in the mall. One will not find many Miami songs that, like Rubén Blades's "Plástico," put down materialism.[13] Money and the things it can buy are recurring themes in the sound of Miami. Chirino has another song called simply "Tengo" (1991), which says:

> Tengo lo que tengo.
> Nadie me lo regaló.[14]

> (I have what I have. / Nobody gave it to me.)

But what I find curious about the list of commodities in "Los diseñadores" is how little it actually tells us about the owner. We know that
he is married (he bought his wife a Valentino handbag) and that he has a
house (he bought a Gucci ashtray for the living room), but that's about
all. Who is this man? How old is he? Where does he come from? Where
does he live? The song catalogues possessions, but it says next to nothing about the social, physical, or temporal setting in which they exist.
Defined by singular, present-tense acts of ownership, this man seems to
have no past, no future, and no place. He lives in a timeless present
filled to the hilt with consumer goods. It may be that for such a person
tengo, I have, substitutes for *soy*, I am. It may be that material possessions compensate for spiritual dispossession. If you don't know who
you are or where you come from, you fabricate your sense of self from
what you own. I buy, therefore I am. In the end, the ostentation of
designer salsa may not be so far from the plaintive cries of early exile
compositions.

The Miami sound is mood-swing music. Expressions of placeless-
ness coincide with acts of nomination. It has always seemed to me
that the "mellowness" of the Miami sound, its preference for ballads
or soft salsa, may be a symptom of the moods it gives vent to.[15] Mellowness may be nothing other than long-standing low-grade depres-
sion. My hunch, based in part on my own reaction to these songs, is
that these ballads give one the opportunity to channel and express
emotions that have other origins. The language of love serves to convey—but also control—political frustrations. Gloria Estefan once
remarked that, for someone of her generation, being attached to Cuba
is "like loving somebody you've never met."[16] My suspicion is that
in Cuban-American love songs the lost lover is a stand-in for the lost
island. When Chirino sings,

> ¿Por qué triunfó la incomprensión
> y se interpuso entre los dos
> una aparente estupidez?
>
> (Why did misunderstanding win out / and an obvious
> stupidity / get between us?)

it is easy to hear "revolución" instead of "incomprensión," and thereby
turn "No debería ser así" (It Shouldn't Be This Way, 1985) into a statement about the rift between residential and nonresidential Cuba. The

political subtext becomes all but explicit with the last line of the lyric, "yo sé que vamos a volver" (I know we will return), which in the song has to do with the lovers' reunion but actually repeats a phrase that for three decades has formed the core theme of Cuban exile culture. Upbeat tunes that celebrate material possessions and plaintive ballads that lament unhappiness in love are but two states of the same underlying condition. Beneath the gloss and the glitz of the Miami sound, a geographical wound festers. At bottom the Miami sound is political through and through; but it is a politics that denies politics, that seeks nonpolitical redress for political grievances.

In the albums after *Evolución* Chirino's elastic music continues to register the differing moods and sounds of Little Havana. His albums contain *sones, guaguancós, merengues, plenas,* boleros, rock-and-roll, and even some flamenco. Like Miami itself, Chirino's music is a crossroads, a mambo jambo, a sonorous stew blended and reblended, combined and recombined, sometimes to the point of zaniness or bewilderment. Both as composer and singer, he is often at his best in novelty numbers like "Los diseñadores" or "Castígala" (Punish Her, 1985), a parody of machismo. One novelty that Chirino has cultivated with some regularity is what one could call *santería*-pop, the kind of music that results when the Miami sound meets Afro-Cuban religion. It goes without saying that the African presence in Cuban music is pervasive, extending to both the rhythmic structure and its subject matter. But it is one thing to hear Celia Cruz intone a *bembé* and quite another to hear it coming from the lips of a white thirty-something like Gloria Estefan, whose "Rhythm Is Going to Get You" is based on Afro-Cuban chants.

Translated to Miami, *santería* is as much a symbol of cultural filiation as a form of religious worship. Like the *azabaches* or good-luck charms that one sees hanging from the necks of many Cuban Americans, *santería*-pop affirms a general attachment to things Cuban in addition to a specific religious conviction. It is perhaps less an article of faith than a consumer article. Since genuine *santería* still exists in Miami, the attenuation of belief is not as marked as it was in Desi Arnaz's "Babalú," which had no ties to a community of believers; but it is noticeable nonetheless. A typical example is Chirino's "Mister Don't Touch the Banana" (1991), about an American man who strays into a religious service for Changó, the Afro-Cuban god of thunder. Noticing a lot of food on a table, the *americano* assumes it's a buffet and eats a banana. Pandemonium ensues. The food is a religious offering, of course, and the banana in particular is one of Changó's favorite fruits.

The votaries faint, cast spells, perform exorcisms, and scold the American for having committed a sacrilege. The refrain of the song, uttered in broken English, cautions: "Mister don't touch the banana, banana belong to Changó." The American, who has no idea what is going on, apologizes in his own macaronic Spanish, "Sorry, excúseme, me no saber que la banana ser de Mr. Chango." [17]

But Chirino's most pointed oxymoronic exercise is "Un tipo típico," another novelty song that raises the Miami sound to a fever pitch of looniness. Released in the fall of 1989 as the lead cut of *Acuarela del Caribe*, "Un tipo típico" has become something like the unofficial anthem of the one-and-a-half generation. The song is an inspired pastiche of Cuban and American music that, like "Soy," draws another vexed self-portrait. But if "Soy" was dispersed and dubitative, "Un tipo típico" is ambivalent and affirmative. The speaker in the earlier song was conflicted because he was placeless; here the speaker is torn between two places, two cultural homes, signified by Cuban and American music. Although he identifies with traditional Cuban music—what is called in fact *música típica*—he also has a "rock-and-roll streak" that makes him a fan of Jimi Hendrix, the Beach Boys, and the Beatles, among others. Depending on his mood, it's salsa or rock. As he puts it at one point, his heart is cleft "between Tito Puente and the Rolling Stones."

Tipo is Cuban slang for "man" or "guy." When the speaker proclaims, "Yo soy un tipo típico," he is setting himself up a Cuban-American everyman, not just a *tipo* but an *arquetipo* defined by his contradictory musical tastes. Cuban tunes like "El son de la loma" and "Seis lindas cubanas" are spliced together with rock-and-roll standards like "Tutti Frutti" or "Sergeant Pepper's Lonely Hearts Club Band." The selection is not incidental, for Chirino makes a point of sampling Cuban songs that describe the nation's identity. "Seis lindas cubanas," for example, is a song about the six provinces of the island (when there were only six; now there are many more). When the speaker blends the melody of "I Get Around" with the words of "El son de la loma" the resulting stew is quite unsettling, since the *son*'s affirmation of rootedness clashes with a rock-and-roll song that, to boot, celebrates a happy-go-lucky nomadism.

What does it mean for the "Son de la loma" to "get around?" Is this harmony or dissonance? Mambo or mumbo? Does a cleft heart make the speaker stronger or weaker; does it enrich or disable him? On this point the song is typically ambiguous, for it seems to say that the same condition can be creatively fruitful and psychologically untenable. Biculturalism makes you smart, but it also makes you crazy. The *tipo típico* is also a *loco ameno*. When the rock-and-roll mood hits him, he "does not know what to do," and when John Lennon's spirit possesses him, he "feels like going mad." Up and down he goes, back and forth he goes. His moods swing with the music. At the end of the song the oscillation speeds up, producing a dizzying succession of sound bites from various artists. The music at this point starts to overcook. Overdone and overseasoned, the sweet-sounding stew degenerates into a nearly indigestible brew. The lyric mixes citations from the Beatles, Little Richard, Celia Cruz, Cheo Feliciano, Rolando Laserie, and others. Even Pérez Prado's grunts put in an appearance! The alternation of samples keeps speeding up until no single item is intelligible and all one hears is a deafening roar.

But the noise is the signal: unlike the Cuban *ajiaco*, the Cuban-American stew can only simmer for so long. At some point the mix turns unsavory and the music becomes unsound. Bicultural harmony can be sustained only for limited periods; after a while the typical *tipo* can no longer negotiate competing demands, and he suffers a cognitive breakdown. The repetition of the phrase "toma chocolate y paga lo que debes" (drink your chocolate and pay what you owe), which is the refrain of a fifties *chachachá*, suggests that biculturalism has a price, that carried to an extreme it breeds monsters. It is perhaps not a coincidence that the song that follows "Un tipo típico" is called "Demasiado" (Too Much). The mixing that in Pérez Prado had been only wildness here becomes insanity. It may be that, ultimately, one needs to choose between Tito Puente and the Rolling Stones.[18] Or perhaps the song's lesson is that diverse cultures cannot be assumed at the same time. A sane biculturalism may consist in alternating cultures, rather than in trying to fuse them.

In the voices of Willie Chirino or Hansel y Raúl, the sound of Miami does not travel well. As Enrique Fernández has pointed out, the Miami version of World Beat stays too close to home to strike an international chord.[19] Chirino's *tipo* is typical only of the Cuban-American baby boomers, those of us born between V-Day and the Bay of Pigs. For one thing, his bilingualism distances him from both non-Hispanic Americans and Latin Americans; for another, non-Cuban U.S. Hispanics can perhaps relate to the general predicament, but most of the Cuban music will be foreign to them. The same limitations apply to Hansel y Raúl and many of the other Miami groups, which draw a loyal following in Miami but have only modest appeal anywhere else. The paradox is that the Miami sound, whose music and words tend to foster a kind of cosmopolitanism, remains firmly anchored in the taste, temper, and distemper of a particular community. Musically and linguistically, the Cuban accent is very much in evidence. Those Clouds do not float freely; they are Clouds of Miami, the name of the band as of 1984.

The one group that has managed to bolt the gilded ghetto of *la sagüesera* is the Miami Sound Machine, which in the mid-eighties was one of the most popular pop groups in America. Like the other Miami groups, MSM got its start a decade earlier as a local party band. Originally the group had six members, including two girl singers (Fig. 8); little by little the original group was whittled down so that by 1986, when "Conga" became a hit, only Gloria and Emilio Estefan and Kiki García remained.[20] Emilio gave up playing for managing shortly thereafter; and García, who had written some of the group's biggest hits (including "Conga"), left at the end of the "Conga" tour. Since then MSM has become essentially Gloria Estefan's solo act, with the ensemble of musicians changing from album to album.

MSM began by cultivating the mellow, pop-oriented strain of the Miami sound. Nearly all of their early Spanish-language hits were ballads in which the only Latin element, besides the Spanish-language lyric, was the occasional use of conga drums and maracas. As Estefan herself has stated, the principal influences in her early career as composer and singer were middle-of-the-road American groups like the Carpenters.[21] Because MSM's first albums offered English and Spanish versions of ballads and soft rock, with an occasional "disco" tune thrown in, it offered a notable change of pace from the Cuban-based rhythms of Hansel y Raúl and others. Younger in taste if not exactly in age, MSM stayed away from songs about milkmen and illegitimate children. Fronted by two Cuban *pepillas* or teenagers, Estefan and Mercy Murciano, MSM sang instead about happiness and unhappiness in love in compositions with such titles as "Quiéreme," "Te quiero, te quiero," "Without Your Love," and "You're All I Have." Nostalgia for Cuba was not an issue, nor was the clash between Cuban and American cultures. Their music was simple, sentimental, and stress-free.

Curiously, in its first incarnation MSM was hardly a "Latin" band. Its considerable popularity in Latin America in the late seventies and

FIGURE 8   *Miami Sound Machine,* Renacer. *Photograph used by permission of Estefan Enterprises.*

early eighties stemmed from the fact that it played American pop music in Spanish. Only later, as part of the effort to "cross-over" into the American market, did MSM take on a "Latin" identity. At first MSM was a hispanophone soft-rock group; later it became an anglophone soft-salsa group. Under both identities, the band's trademark has always been to offer mellow musical exotica—soft rock for Latin America, watered-down salsa for the U.S.A. But as Estefan sees it, MSM's musical tastes respond to the band's personality: "We could get up there and do a legit salsa song, but that's not what's within us, it's not where we are. In a sense we *are* 'watered-down salsa.'"[22]

The Latinization of MSM took place with "Conga" (1985), the band's first big cross-over hit. To those who had followed the band

Miami Sound Machine, Primitive Love. *Photograph used by permission of Estefan Enterprises.*

since its early days, the makeover was quite noticeable. MSM had never sounded so "Cuban" before! The makeover extended to Estefan's looks. MSM's last album had been called *Eyes of Innocence* (1984); the new one, with "Conga" as the lead cut, was called *Primitive Love.* The cover was a closeup of a bejeweled Gloria, with thick dark eyeliner and bright red lipstick, staring straight at you (Fig. 9). Those eyes had nothing innocent about them. At least for publicity purposes, the *cubanita* had grown up into a Latin bombshell. In its first American incarnation, the conga had been imported by Desi Arnaz, the "Cuban conquistador of conga," and another cross-over specialist. Now it was back with Estefan, a female avatar of Arnaz. Like Desi, Gloria was white, good-looking, and well groomed. She may look sultry, but we know that underneath all that makeup she's a nice, middle-class Cuban girl. Like Desi, Gloria purveys sexuality without threat. If Desi was the Latin-lover-as-good-neighbor, Gloria is the Latin-bombshell-next-door.

With its catchy rhythm and snappy lyric, "Conga" topped the dance, pop, Latin, and black charts simultaneously. Its success was aided by a nifty video that showed MSM breaking up a command performance in honor of a stiff, monocled "ambassador" and his obese and snooty wife. With Emilio Estefan on the *tumbadora* and Kiki García on the *timbales*, little Gloria, perky in a one-piece blue jumpsuit, leads the audience in the simple but infectious one-two-three-hump movement. At first all the dignitaries look on in astonishment, but eventually they become links in the Desi Chain.

Everybody gather 'round now,
let your body feel the heat.
Don't you worry if you can't dance,
let the music move your feet.

It's the rhythm of the islands
with the sugarcane so sweet.
If you want to do the conga
you've got to listen to the beat.

Heat/feet/sweet/beat: the monosyllabic rhymes say it all. Like the latunes of the forties, "Conga" keeps the beat basic and the lyric uncomplicated. Because these songs have to be accessible, they rely on the same old stereotypes, which never seem to change. Cuba is the land of sweet sugar and hot rhythms. Another rhyme in the lyric: dance / islands. (Desi Arnaz had sung: "Dance the night away, / that's the Cuban way.") This is spoon-fed salsa, much easier to swallow, say, than the one cooked up by Hansel or Chirino, not to mention someone like Celia Cruz. Desi Arnaz remarks in *A Book* that one thing he learned from Cugat was to make things easier for Americans by including in his troupe dancers whom the audience could emulate.[23] Estefan's song and video exhibit this same practical sense, this combination of *sabor* and savvy. To be successful, the cross-over artist needs to be something of a pedagogue, a cultural emissary. She makes a living by bringing across a certain knowledge, which she then imparts to neophytes. Step by step, she guides the neophytes in the acquisition of new skills. If Cuban Pete taught the rumba beat, Gloria teaches the conga beat.

The contrast between the hybridism of "Conga" and that of "Un tipo típico" is worth noting. Estefan's stereotypes and Chirino's archetype hardly resemble each other. It's not a question of Chirino's more faithful adherence to tradition, since in fact he tampers far more with Cuban music than does Estefan. Except for the English-language lyric, "Conga" sticks fairly closely to its musical roots. The difference resides in how these songs conceive their audience and intent. From the title on, Chirino's song presupposes a community of kindred souls in conflict. For this reason, he shows but does not teach. "Un tipo típico" is data, not explanation. To someone who lacks Chirino's bicultural background, the song must be nearly unintelligible. But as the video makes clear, "Conga" is addressed to an audience of strangers and therefore takes for granted only the most general commonplaces about Cuba and its rhythms. Whatever questions the music raises, the lyric answers. The song "stages" its biculturalism, not only because it puts on a demonstration, but also because the two cultures do not exist simultaneously on the same level. When Estefan says, "It's the rhythm of the islands," she distances the music from the words. Each has its own terrain: the music may be exotic, but the words are plain American. The lyric is the music's passport, a letter of transit that lets the music cross the border. Cuba is the point of departure, but America is the port of arrival. Unlike Chirino's *tipo típico*, Gloria does not attempt to fuse Tito Puente and the Rolling Stones. Rather than rending her heart in the attempt, she assigns separate sites to the two cultures: Cuba in her hips; America on her lips. As a result, she can travel back and forth between cultures, at one moment dancing like a native and at the next explaining in unaccented English the natives' dancing.

Chirino's *arquetipo* is not so fortunate. His problem is that he wants to be, or that he is, Cuban and American at the same time. Instead of being assigned separate roles, the two cultures rub together, creating friction, giving birth to Cuban-American angst. The speaker of "Conga" lives by translation; Chirino's protagonist is driven crazy by it. I like "Conga" very much, and this book shares with the song the ambition to address an audience of strangers. Still, I find Chirino's composition more "typical" of my own experience and perhaps of that of other one-and-a-halfers. About ten years younger than Chirino, Estefan in her music takes enough distance from Cuban culture so as to assume it without conflict, pragmatically rather than existentially. "Conga" treats Cuban culture in the way "Mister Don't Touch the Banana" treats *san-*

tería. "Conga"'s biculturalism seems to me a little too even-tempered, too complacent, too upbeat. It's Ricky Ricardo without the angst. If Chirino swings with the mood, Gloria never misses a beat.

MSM's other *cubano* hits—"Rhythm Is Going to Get You" (1987) and "Oye Mi Canto" (1989)—follow "Conga"'s line by trading happily on Latin stereotypes. Both make the usual connection between Latin rhythms, on the one hand, and freedom and spontaneity, on the other. More interesting is the *cubano* number in *Into the Light* (1991), for unlike their earlier cross-over tunes, "Mama Yo Can't Go" is not a sunny celebration of heat/beat/sweet and feet. The first difference is that the song's fictive audience, the person to whom the lyric is addressed, is also Cuban. The speaker, presumably a young Cuban-American woman, tells her mother that she does not intend to return to Cuba, a country she never really knew. In its rejection of the thematics of *regreso*, the sensibility that speaks here is that of the second generation, the American-Born Cubans or Cuban-Bred Americans. Although the speaker acknowledges spiritual ties to Cuba, return is not an option: "I can't go, I can't go, mama yo no can't go." It was apropos of this song that Estefan remarked that, for someone like her, who left the island at a very young age (she was two), Cuba was like a lover she had never met.

The title of the song conveys this message on more than one level. At first blush the title seems to contain the only Spanish word in the song, the first person pronoun *yo*. Its use signals that to some extent the speaker's sense of self still emerges from her Cuban background: she's a *yo* not an "I." But even this modest grammatical sign of *cubanía* is ambiguous, since "yo" is also an American slang vocative. "Mama yo can't go" may well be English only. Spanish is broken here—by broken English. If this is so, *yo* does not signal deference but disrespect. When was the last time you called your mother by saying "mama yo?" Indeed, turn the words around and what you get is an insult, "yo mama," which accurately translates into the Cuban *tu madre*. As an interlingual pun, *yo* cuts both ways. Wavering between Spanish and English, pronoun and vocative, it underscores the speaker's ambivalent relation toward Cuba. Another MSM song contains the same sort of pun in the opposite direction: "Ay, Ay, I."

In this context, the speaker's renunciation of things Cuban is an understandable attempt to achieve some sort of psychic wholeness. For the one-and-a-halfer biculturalism is not a choice but a fate; but for younger peers the ties to Cuban culture may be substantially more tenuous. If one can actually choose to live in two cultures at once, perhaps it's wiser not to. Better to remove the "ay" from the "I," better not to bear the yoke of a divided *yo*.

Since in this situation my own *yo* identifies more with the Cuban mother than with Cuban-American daughter, I don't necessarily like this song's message, but I think "Mama yo can't go" rings far truer than MSM's earlier *cubano* numbers, for it recognizes that, no matter what your age, being Cuban in America is problematic. It may be troubling that the speaker's declaration of personal and cultural independence should occur in an album entitled *Into the Light*, as if Cuba were the "darkness" from which one needs to emerge, but this song does articulate the point of view of many young Cuban Americans, for whom Cuba is essentially a fiction, the land of *mami* and *papi*'s dreams.

With "Mama Yo Can't Go" the Miami sound nearly merges with the voice of America. Take another little step, remove the drum and pun, and the music becomes plain-vanilla Anglo-pop, which is what happens with artists like Martika, a Gloria Estefan clone, and Jon Secada, an MSM alumnus.[24] But if assimilation is one possible future for the sound of Miami, repatriation is the other. The same year that *Into the Light* came out, Chirino released *Oxígeno*, whose biggest hit, "Ya viene llegando," recounts his life in exile and forecasts the overthrow of Castro's dictatorship. No longer a *tipo típico*, Chirino here sounds Cuban through and through. Jimi Hendrix and the Beach Boys are nowhere in sight; gone are all the references, musical and verbal, to sixties rock. Although Chirino carefully refrains from saying he intends to return to Cuba, the song gives little indication of why it would not be appropriate for him to do so. The song even ends with the playing of the Cuban national anthem, a throwback to those early exile shows at the Dade County Auditorium.

In their recent recordings both Estefan and Chirino seem to be fleeing the hyphen, but in opposite directions. With *Into the Light* the sound of Miami all but loses its accent; with "Ya viene llegando," it reverts to the Cuban *son*. At least conceptually, these two recordings limn the outer limits of Cuban America. But historically also these albums may mark a moment of closure. Even if Chirino, Estefan, Hansel, and the other groups continue recording and performing into the nineties, the Miami sound is essentially a seventies and eighties phenomenon. By now the city's Hispanic population has diversified enough so that the Cuban-American imprint on Miami's culture is no longer as visible as it once was. (The fact that Hansel entitled a recent album *Latinoamericano* is a symptom of this diversification.) Like Estefan and Chirino, respectively, the music of Miami seems to be dissolving into either American pop or Latin American rhythms. As of the beginning of 1993, there were no longer any bimusical radio stations in Miami. Indeed, in the mid-eighties Super Q changed its slogan and stopped playing American music altogether; and in December 1991 the station went off the air. Like the one-and-a-half generation itself, the Miami sound may well have an expiration date.

Mirror, Mirror

MAMBO NO. 5 *One of the landmarks of Cuban Miami is a restaurant called Versailles, which has been located on Eighth Street and Thirty-fifth Avenue for many years. About the only thing this Versailles shares with its French namesake is that it has lots of mirrors on its walls. One goes to the Versailles not only to be seen, but to be multiplied. This quaint, kitschy, noisy restaurant that serves basic Cuban food is a paradise for the self-absorbed: the Nirvana of Little Havana. Because of the bright lights, even the windows reflect. The Versailles is a Cuban panopticon: you can lunch, but you can't hide. Who goes there wants to be the stuff of visions. Who goes there wants to make a spectacle of himself (or herself). All the ajiaco you can eat and all the jewelry you can wear multiplied by the number of reflecting planes—and to top it off, a waitress who calls you mi vida.*

Across the street at La Carreta, another popular restaurant, the food is the same (both establishments are owned by the same man) but the feel is different. Instead of mirrors La Carreta has booths. There you can ensconce yourself in a booth and not be faced with multiple images of yourself. But at the Versailles there is no choice but to bask in self-reflective glory.

For years I have harbored the fantasy that those mirrors retain the blurred image of everyone who has paraded before them. I think the mirrors have a memory, as when one turns off the TV and the shadowy figures remain on the screen. Every Cuban who has lived or set foot in Miami over the last three decades has, at one time or another, seen himself or herself reflected on those shiny surfaces. It's no coincidence that the Versailles sits only two blocks away from the Woodlawn Cemetery, which contains the remains of many Cuban notables, including Desi Arnaz's father, whose remains occupy a niche right above Gerardo Machado's. Has anybody ever counted the number of Cubans who have died in Miami? Miami is a Cuban city not only because of the number of Cubans who live there but also because of the number who have died there.

The Versailles is a glistening mausoleum. The history of Little Havana—tragic, comic, tragicomic—is written on those spectacular specular walls. This may have been why, when the mirrors came down in 1991, there was such an uproar that some of them had to be put back. The hall of mirrors is also a house of spirits. When the time comes for me to pay for my last ajiaco, I intend to disappear into one of the mirrors (I would prefer the one on the right, just above the espresso machine). My idea of immortality is to become a mirror image at the Versailles.

Five

RUM-RUMP-
AND-RUMBA

Although it may be something of
a simplification to say that Oscar Hijuelos is the Gloria Estefan of
Cuban-American literature, their work moves in the same direction.
Like Estefan, Hijuelos is a cross-over artist. Although his novels are
immeasurably richer than Estefan's simple songs, they also aim to
explain Cuban culture to non-Cubans. Hijuelos writes "from" Cuba
but "toward" the United States. I do not mean that he writes literally
from abroad, of course, but rather that Cuban culture is his narrative
point of departure. The voice that speaks in his novels, which one sus-
pects may be close to Hijuelos himself, is that of someone who retains
ties to Cuban culture but who is no longer Cuban. The moral of his
novels might be phrased this way: Cuba breeds Americans. Hijuelos
pays tribute to things Cuban even as he bids them farewell. Although
he remains emotionally invested, ultimately he says, with Estefan,
"Mama yo can't go." His work is a complex and moving valedictory
to the Spanish language, to his Cuban parents, to the island's mores and
its music.

But it is a forced valedictory, the leavetaking of someone who has no
choice but to say good-bye. In Hijuelos's fiction Cuba is unreachable;
but the factors that make it so are cultural rather than political (Miami is
unreachable too). Born in New York in 1951, Hijuelos speaks as someone whose grip on Ricky's "things Cuban" is tenuous. He doesn't command the language and he doesn't know the territory. His novels are
told from the perspective of characters who are the American-born children of Cuban parents. For them, Cuba is a fiction, a fantasy island
known primarily from the stories of parents and relatives. In his novels,

the "last world" is also a lost world. The Cuban feeling is a mix of secondhand nostalgia and firsthand curiosity.

This is not to say that these books do not appeal to Americans for their "Cuban" or "Latin" flavor. Clearly the success of *The Mambo Kings Play Songs of Love*, both novel and film, has to do at least in part with the novel's exoticism. The mambo kings, César and Néstor Castillo, are foreign in an exciting, alluring way. The novel's charm is, to a great extent, their charm. Yet the paradox is that Hijuelos artfully evokes his "home" culture only to show that it is unlivable. He quarries bits and pieces of Cuba and then puts these fragments in a setting where they are woefully out of place. Although he is coeval with the Miami one-and-a-halfers, his outlook is much closer to that of the second generation. Cuba provides Hijuelos with a subject, but it is not constitutive of his writerly stance, of his choice of language, or of his audience. This is perhaps why *Mambo Kings* has had a cool reception among Cuban Americans and other U.S. Hispanics.[1] A Cuban American who reads this novel senses that it is not to him or her that the book is addressed. Even when Hijuelos draws extensively on Cuban or Spanish-American material, he weaves it into a work whose fabric is resolutely anglocentric.

Hijuelos's first novel, *Our House in the Last World* (1983), is an immigrant memoir that follows the fortunes of the Santinio family over several decades. Beginning with the meeting of Alejo Santinio and Mercedes Sorrea in Cuba in 1939, the novel narrates the couple's marriage, their emigration to the United States, the birth of their children, and the family's difficult life in Spanish Harlem. The central consciousness in the novel is Héctor, the Santinio's second son, who (like Hijuelos) was born in New York in 1951. Héctor's upbringing is grim to say the least. Alejo, who arrives in this country with high hopes but can never go further than the kitchen of a restaurant, is a drunk. Héctor's mother Mercedes is a manic-depressive who sees visions and talks to spirits. Resentful of her husband and unhappy with her lot, she becomes withdrawn and bitchy, finally retreating into a fantasy world of Cuban ghosts. (If Héctor is a Latin from Manhattan, Mercedes is a Hecuba from Cuba.) Although Héctor's older brother, Horacio, manages to escape the family's hellish life, Héctor remains trapped until the end. When Alejo drops dead from a heart attack in 1969, the family all but collapses, going from poverty to near indigence. Significantly, the last two chapters are entitled "Ghosts" and "Voices from the Last World." It's as if the family's very materiality required Alejo's physical presence. Once he's gone, Mercedes's hallucinations take over the narrative.

The great theme of Héctor's childhood and adolescence is Cuban manhood—what it means, what it costs, how to achieve it. Over and over Héctor harps on the fact that he's not as "Cuban" as his father or older brother. He doesn't speak Spanish, he's blond, he's frail, and he's a mama's boy. Unlike Horacio, who follows in his father's footsteps by becoming *muy macho*—hard-drinking, brawling, womanizing—Héctor develops into an overweight and shy "American" teenager. As Horacio gloats at one point, "He's just dumb when it comes to being Cuban."[2] Making things worse is his striking physical likeness to his father: "They were like twins, separated by age, with the same eyes, faces, bodies. Except Alejo was from another world—*cubano, cubano*" (145).

As he grows up, Héctor develops the sense that he is a defective replica of his father, a reproduction exact in many outward details but lacking Alejo's Cuban spirit. Too Cuban to be American but hardly Cuban enough to resemble his father, Héctor sees himself as a "freak, a hunchback, a man with a deformed face" (190). He is a "Cuban Quasimodo" (192), a phrase whose linguistic hybridity conveys Héctor's sense of lacking a suitable cultural home. A French Quasimodo is strange enough; but a "Cuban" version of the French character with the Latin name borders on the monstrous.

Yet Héctor is not the only monster in the family. His feelings of inadequacy are complicated by Alejo's habits of excess. "During the night Héctor had screamed out because the monster was prowling in the hall. The monster was Alejo, hanging onto the walls to get from the kitchen to the bathroom" (108). A hard-drinking lothario as a young man, Alejo never renounces his youthful Cuban ways. His wife's recriminations are not enough to stop him from spending most of his free time away from the house, drinking and chasing after women. If Héctor is a freak because he's not Cuban enough, perhaps Alejo is a freak for being too Cuban. At least, this is what his son seems to think.

When Horacio says that his brother is "dumb," we should not overlook the adjective's linguistic meaning, for Héctor's feelings of inferiority have a great deal to do with his poor Spanish. The "real Cubans" (175) are those who speak fluently, without groping for words or stuttering. By contrast, Héctor finds it impossible to generate a good Spanish sentence. When he tries to speak like his gregarious father, he feels that the words and phrases immobilize him, tie him in knots. "He was sick at heart for being so Americanized, which he equated with being fearful and lonely. His Spanish was unpracticed, practically nonexistent. He had a stutter, and saying a Spanish word made him think of drunkenness. A Spanish sentence wrapped around his face, threatened to peel off his skin and send him falling to the floor like Alejo. He avoided Spanish even though that was all he heard at home. He read it, understood it, but he grew paralyzed by the prospect of the slightest conversation" (173). Spanish is an artificial skin, a mask that literally defaces him. If he has a "deformed face," as he remarks, it must be from peeling away the words. Héctor is a sort of mummy, "part Cuban, part American—all wrapped up tightly inside a skin in which he sometimes could not move" (190).

Because for Héctor Spanish is the father's tongue, it is a language that he both desires and avoids. Curiously, even though Mercedes writes poetry, it is Alejo who comes to incarnate the maternal language. When Héctor speaks Spanish, he becomes Alejo; but when he becomes Alejo, he turns into the "monster" who comes home drunk in the middle of the night. Since Spanish focalizes his ambivalent feelings toward his father, it is a wound, a handicap. Spanish is the hump in the hunchback, the twitch in the face. The problem is not only that Héctor's Spanish is monstrous, but that Spanish is the language of monsters. Héctor is a "teratolingual," someone for whom words breed monsters. From his perspective Spanish is inaccessible, ghostly, and oppressive.

The circumstances in which Héctor learned English decisively shape his pathological view of the Spanish language. Without a doubt the most wrenching scenes in the book are those that describe Héctor's prolonged stay in a pediatric hospital when he was only three or four years old (an incident based on Hijuelos's own life). In 1954, shortly after returning to the United States from a trip to Cuba, Héctor becomes seriously ill from a kidney infection and has to spend nearly a year convalescing in a hospital full of terminally ill children. During this period he sees his mother only intermittently and his father not at all. Separated from his parents, he comes under the care of a nurse who takes it upon herself not only to bring him back to health, but also to teach him English. In order to force him to learn the new language, she tries all kinds of scare tactics, even locking him up in a closet from which he's not released until he says, in English, "Let me out!" (103). At first recalcitrant, Héctor eventually gives in. The result, however, is not only that he begins speaking English, but that he develops a distrust for Spanish.

> *"May I have some agua?"*
> *"No! Water."*
> *"May I have some water?"*
> *"Oh yes," she answered. "That's it."*
> *And she kissed him. In time he believed Spanish was an enemy, and when Mercedes came to visit and told him stories about home, he remained silent, as if the nurse were watching him. Even his dreams were broken up by the static of English, like a number of wasps overcoming the corner of a garden. (104)*

By the time he goes back home, Héctor is a different person. "When we left Cuba," Mercedes says, "Héctor was sick but so happy and fat that we didn't know anything. He came back saying *Cuba, Cuba* and spent a lot of time with Alejo. He was a little Cuban, spouting Spanish" (91). A year later, when he is finally released from the hospital, all of this has changed. Héctor is healthy but thin, he no longer speaks Spanish, and he has become distanced from his father, who hardly recognizes him: "Alejo looked at Héctor, wondering if this was his son. There he was, a little blondie, a sickly, fair-skinned Cuban who was not speaking Spanish. He patted the kid on the head, turned around, and took a swig of beer" (195). At the hospital Héctor undergoes a death and rebirth. He loses one nationality and acquires another. That closet is a womb from which he is delivered by the American nurse, who is both mother and midwife, tender and terrible at the same time.

Immigrant memoirs are conversion narratives. "I was born, I have lived, and I have been made over. Is it not time to write my life's story?" The classic opening of Mary Antin's *The Promised Land* (1912) captures the genre's essential movement from birth to rebirth, a process whose model is the religious conversion.[3] Transculturation, the passage from one culture to another, is a secular conversion whose outward sign is the acquisition of a new language. When Antin continues that she is "absolutely other than the person whose story I have to tell," this exaggerated assertion holds truest as regards her use of language. The differences between her native Russian and her adopted English may not be absolute, but they are considerable.

Our House in the Last World follows the conversion model, though it situates the conversion scene in an unusual place. It is typically the school that ushers the young immigrant into the new language, and it is a teacher who replaces the mother or the father.[4] But in Héctor's case the whole experience takes place in a hospital, under the guidance of a nurse. His is not only a conversion, but a cure. This means that Spanish is not merely a language, but a disease. For the rest of his life Héctor will view Cuba, its language and its culture, with a mixture of awe and apprehension. "Cuba gave the bad disease. Cuba gave the drunk father. Cuba gave the crazy mother. Years later all these would entwine to make Héctor think Cuba had something against him" (102). In what is perhaps the most striking image in the book, Héctor compares the X-rays of his diseased kidneys to the map of Cuba (104). His mysterious illness, which his mother attributes to drinking puddled water, is labeled only a "Cuban infection" (88) carried by the everpresent *microbios*, one of the few words in the novel that is almost always written in Spanish.

Héctor's diverse evaluation of Spanish and English helps us to understand the narration's anglocentric bias. Although *Our House* is ostensibly narrated by an anonymous third-person narrator, the narratorial voice is really Héctor's. In a monologue toward the end Héctor acknowledges his desire to become a writer and describes some notebooks where he writes about his family. "When I write in my notebook," he says, "I feel very close to her [Mercedes] and to the memory of my father. I go back to that certain house, I go back to my beginning" (245). These phrases, which evoke the novel's title, leave little doubt that the narration is essentially Héctor's transposition of his notebooks. Significantly, even though the novel is in the third person, the title is in the first—"our house." *Our House in the Last World* is really oblique autobiography. Like many other first novels, this one offers a portrait of the artist as a young man.

Once we realize that Héctor is really the narrator, we can better understand why the text evinces a ruthless effort of translation. The initial sentence of the novel already makes clear that the "last world" of the title will be recreated according to Héctor's peculiar sensibility. "Héctor's mother met Alejo Santinio, his Pop, in 1939 when she was twenty-seven years old and working as a ticket girl in the Neptuna [*sic*] movie theater in Holguín, Cuba" (11). Although Héctor will not appear as a character for several chapters, we are made to realize right away that whatever we see will be from his point of view. The first word— "Héctor's"—already establishes his claim on the account; the possessive tells us that, even when Héctor is offstage, the account belongs to him. This is *his* story. Thus it is significant that his father is labeled, somewhat incongruously, "Pop." From first word to last, the book's opening sentence is filled with Cuban sounds—Héctor, Alejo Santinio, Neptuna, Holguín, Cuba. In the midst of all these Hispanic proper names, the colloquial American "Pop" sticks out like a hump. But given Alejo's importance in the novel, this initial act of nomination is crucial. What should Héctor call his Cuban father in English? Did he, as a child growing up in a Spanish-speaking household, call his father "Pop?" Or was it rather *papá* or *papi*? No, it was always Pop: "I remember my mother and father—'Pop' always 'Pop'" (245). The conversion of a *papá* into a *Pop* entails a decisive (and perhaps derisive) act of translation. Notice that Mercedes, who is identified in the same sentence by the colorless "mother," does not undergo so radical a transformation. I want to suggest that calling Alejo "Pop" is a way of reducing the father to manageable proportions, Héctor's device for removing or neutralizing some of his terror. Translation becomes an art of exorcism. The American name fends off the Cuban monster. Say "Pop" and the paternal ghost collapses.

If we read further in the first page we come upon the following description of Héctor's mother: "Her name was Mercedes Sorrea, and she was the second of three daughters and not married because her last *prometido*, or 'intended,' who worked in a Cuban sour-milk factory, was a louse" (11). "Louse" functions in this sentence in much the same way as "Pop" does in the other one, for it is another monosyllabic epithet that describes a Cuban man, one who almost became Héctor's father. The impact of the monosyllable emerges from the clash between the epithet and its context. The Spanish in the first part of the sentence evokes a Cuban world where young women with names like Mercedes are courted by *prometidos* who work in sour-milk factories. But the last word of the sentence sharply revises the cultural context by designating her womanizing fiancé with another American colloquialism, "louse." It is hardly a coincidence that "louse" is another small disease-bearing organism, for this man is nothing other than a large Cuban *microbio*.

As the sentence unfolds it rattles off one Hispanic marker after another: the girl's name, the Spanish word for "intended," and the reference to the "Cuban sour-milk factory." But this Cuban world so carefully evoked is demolished by that last, monosyllabic barb, "louse," a word that faintly echoes the name of Héctor's homeland: U.S. It's as if Spanish were the language of posturing, of convention, of unkept promises, and English were the language of truth. Spanish is ornate, elegant, but ultimately hollow. Spanish is illusion, *engaño*; English is truth, *desengaño*. In Spanish Mercedes's boyfriend is a *prometido*, in plain English he's just a louse.

When Héctor was a child in Cuba, his aunt prepared a wonderful mysterious brew that Héctor regarded as a "Cuban magic potion"; years later he discovers that the concoction was only Hershey's syrup and milk (177). This incident is typical of the way things Cuban are presented in the novel. Cuban pretense dissolves in the face of American matter-of-factness.

"Pop" and "louse" are paternal names that bear the son's signature. Through them Héctor renders paternal figures in his own words. What is significant about the names is that they both stick out. Neither one fits the sentence in which it appears. They are anomalies, humps of discourse, ill-matching parts of speech. In this they resemble Héctor, who also does not fit inside the "last world" of his parents. These names capture and convey Héctor's ambivalence toward his father in particular and toward Cuba in general. On the one hand, they embody his need to tame his father by anglicizing him; on the other, they reflect his sense of being a misfit, a Cuban Quasimodo.

In *Our House in the Last World* Cuba drifts toward America. Even though most of the characters speak Spanish, the narrator makes little attempt to render the foreignness of their speech. Instead, they all speak idiomatic, unaccented English. At one point Alejo remarks about his brother-in-law, "He is getting fucked by life" (42). Because of its colloquial informality, this brief spoken line, which is inserted in the middle of a long expository paragraph, has an air of authenticity, of being an utterance that reveals Alejo's personality. Yet how could Alejo have said such a thing? He says this while talking to Margarita, his sister-in-law, and therefore it had to be said in Spanish, which has no idiom roughly equivalent to "getting fucked by life." The slang Cuban terms for fucking—*singar* or *templar* or perhaps *joder*—are never used in this kind of construction. Translating Alejo's sentence "back" into Spanish, one would get something like "La vida lo está singando," which in Spanish is not an idiomatic expression but a poetic figure. More likely, Alejo would have said something like "Está jodido" (He is fucked up), which lacks the idea of agency central to the English idiom. Only in English does one get fucked "by life."

These examples illustrate some of the ways in which Hijuelos writes "from" Spanish but "toward" English. Writing in this direction is perhaps common among American "ethnic" writers (Richard Rodriguez and Sandra Cisneros come to mind) but rather atypical of Cuban American writers. By and large, Cuban Americans have so far written for other Cuban Americans. This is the case even when they write in English. Only in the last couple of years, with the appearance of novels by Hijuelos, Virgil Suárez, and Cristina García, have Cuban–American authors sought to reach a broader audience.[5] The language of these recent novels is strikingly different from that of earlier texts.

As a point of contrast, let me quote a passage from another Cuban-American novel, Roberto Fernández's *Raining Backwards* (1988), which also exhibits a kind of translation sensibility, but one with a very different drift. One of Fernández's characters, a woman appropriately named Barbarita, says, "I brought also a few records: The Big Dances of Anthony M. Romeu, Fajardo and His Stars, Congas and Carnival From the Orient, and Jacinto's favorites, The Moor Woman From Syria by Little Barbaro X, and They Are From the Hills by the Moorkiller Trio."[6] The reader of the earlier chapters will recognize some of the names and titles in this peculiar list: *danzones* by Antonio María Romeu, Fajardo y Sus Estrellas, and "El son de la loma" by the Matamoros Trio, among others. What Fernández has done is to translate these names in the most literal way imaginable. Thus, the Cuban province of Oriente becomes "the Orient" and the name of the singer Barbarito Diez becomes "Little Barbaro X." You need to be Cuban, or at least know a fair amount about Cuban culture, to understand this inspired gibberish. Fernández performs the peculiar feat of *writing* with an accent. He proves that "English only" can also be "Spanish first." According to Fernández, *Raining Backwards* (unlike his earlier novels) was written in English in order to reach an anglophone readership; yet to the non-Cuban reader a passage like this is nearly unintelligible. In Fernández's hilarious recastings, everything and nothing is lost in translation. Even when he adopts a foreign tongue, he does not leave the confines of *la sagüesera*, with the result that *Raining Backwards* opens out to anglophone readers only to close itself back up again. Fernández writes English *en clave*; the key to his code can be found only in the Cuban enclave.

By contrast, in *Our House in the Last World* English is an instrument of release, not enclosure. When Héctor was in the children's hospital, only by speaking English ("Let me out!") could he get out of the closet. When he becomes a writer, English will remain the language of release. Growing up with Mercedes and Alejo, Héctor is a closet American. He comes out in his memoirs, which are foreshadowed in the journals that he secretly keeps. No matter what the specific words, the sentences

Héctor writes in his notebooks all say one thing: "Let me out!" The "house" of the title is no less a prison than the closet in the sanatorium. Hector needs to escape both. Someone like Fernández writes what might be termed anglophobic English, a Spanish-English hybrid or "Spanglish" that endeavors to make itself unintelligible to people who don't speak Spanish to begin with. He doesn't say, "Let me out!"—but rather, "I'm not leaving!" Héctor's English goes in the opposite direction. It bolts the barrio. Spanish is the enemy, and the desire is to keep Cuba at a distance—its inflections no less than its infections.

This desire is not completely satisfied. Here is Héctor's reaction to his father's corpse: "The problem was that his body, stretched out in the coffin, was so imposing" (210). Why is this a "problem?" A problem for whom? Héctor's words indicate that defining Alejo as "Pop" is not nearly enough to mitigate the father's oppressiveness. Even in death Alejo remains imposing, an immovable monolingual monolith. But from his young son's perspective, Alejo is immortal: "He was enormous: a size forty-six pants with big muscles. His biceps were like stone in his arms. He was a big Cuban man who was never going to die, even if he said so" (150). In a way this is what actually happens: Alejo dies but he does not pass away. Héctor is unable to unburden himself of his father, an oppressive and unintelligible weight. Alejo remains larger than life, longer than life.

Our House is haunted by the specter of the father, the father's land, and the father's language. After he recovers from his "Cuban illness," Héctor thinks, "Now he looked American and spoke mostly American. Cuba had become the mysterious and cruel phantasm standing behind the door" (106). That cruel phantasm wears Alejo's size forty-six pants. Cuban culture is like Alejo's corpse, lifeless but imposing. Even though the novel succeeds as a subtle, sensitive study of Héctor's struggles to achieve psychic health, to rid himself of spiritual *microbios*, one has the sense that the struggle is finally unresolved. Indeed, the "problem" may be Héctor's bacterial view of Cuba. The memorable image of the island as an infected kidney may itself be a symptom of illness. Perhaps to achieve health, Héctor needs to reconstrue those microbes as life-giving, spermatic. Since Héctor cannot deny that he is his father's son, so long as he sees Cuba as disease he will remain crippled.

The "problem" of paternal presence will be taken up again in Hijuelos's second novel, *The Mambo Kings Play Songs of Love*, which was awarded the Pulitzer Prize for fiction in 1989. *Mambo Kings* will center on another larger-than-life Cuban man, César Castillo, the mambo king, and his nephew Eugenio, who serves as the vehicle for César's story. Notice how the scenario has changed. Here the Alejo-character is not a monster but a king; and the Héctor-character is a nephew rather than a son. Not only is César cast in a more favorable light than Alejo, but Eugenio enjoys an autonomy or distance that Héctor never achieves. Uncles are fathers you can love without fear. When Eugenio says that his project is "the resurrection of a man," his language evokes the ghosts and voices of the earlier novel.[7] Yet César is not a "mysterious and cruel phantasm." Although his portrait is by no means flattering, it is not as one-sided as that drawn in the earlier novel. As befits his name, César Castillo is imposing, but he is not such a problem.

Mambo Kings follows the lives of two Cuban brothers, César and Néstor Castillo, who emigrate to New York in the late forties and form an orchestra called the Mambo Kings, achieving ephemeral fame one night in 1955 when they appear on an *I Love Lucy* episode as Ricky's Cuban cousins. In talent as well as temperament, the two brothers are worlds apart. Néstor is moody and melancholy. His main claim to fame is having written the brothers' greatest hit, "Bellísima María de mi alma" (Beautiful María of My Soul), a bolero or ballad about the girl who broke his heart in Cuba. For years Néstor works tirelessly on this tune, coming up with twenty-two different versions of the lyric; only his death in a car accident puts an end to this obsessive rewriting.[8]

By contrast, César is impulsive rather than melancholy. He is a consummate ladies' man with slicked-back hair, a mellifluous voice, and an irrepressible libido. He's reminiscent not only of Alejo, who possessed many of these same qualities, but also of César's idol, Desi Arnaz. Like Arnaz, César was born in Santiago de Cuba, has a thick Cuban accent and "pretty-boy looks" (33), and plays the conga drum. Like Arnaz, he spends a considerable part of his life chasing women, and comes to regret it. There are many pages of *Mambo Kings*, especially those detailing César's conquests and then his failing health and loneliness, that could have been part of Desi's autobiography. César is Desi without Lucy. In a sense, *Mambo Kings* contains the "lost" chapters of *A Book*, those that the editor left out because they were too depressing.

By 1980 César has ended up, broke and broken, in a seedy New York tenement. On the brink of death, he takes out a stack of old Mambo King records and opens a bottle of rye whiskey. Then he spends his last hours reminiscing, replaying melodies and memories, records and *recuerdos*. As an account of César's final recollections, the novel takes the form of a death watch in mambo time, an agony with words and music.

But the first character we see is not César but Eugenio, the author of the book's fictional prologue and epilogue. The prologue gives his account of seeing a rerun of the *I Love Lucy* episode where César and Néstor appeared, an "item of eternity" that will be replayed throughout the book (3). The epilogue relates Eugenio's visit to Desi Arnaz's ranch in California after his uncle's death. As they sit among the bougainvillea and sip Dos Equis beer, Eugenio and Desi reminisce about the Mambo Kings. The novel closes by rerunning once more the brothers' guest spot on *I Love Lucy*. Much as *Our House in the Last World* "belonged" to Héctor, this novel belongs to Eugenio. Like Héctor, Eugenio is the novel's sentient center, the source of its point of view in the broad sense, that is, of its attitudes and values. Even though he appears only briefly in César's recollections, his presence frames the whole story; he has the first and the last words.

César and Eugenio's relation is crucial. It may seem strange that Eugenio shows a lot more interest in his uncle than in his father; but the point, I think, is that spiritually and emotionally the childless César is Eugenio's real father. The anonymous third-person narration of César's recollections functions as a kind of filter for their sensibilities. César's voice can be heard in the nostalgic tone and in the narration's limitation to events that he witnessed. (Indeed, there are moments when the narration lapses into the first person [53, 161].) Eugenio's voice is heard not only in the epilogue and prologue, but in the interior story as well, which uncannily repeats some of his sentences word for word—and not just any sentences, but his description of the central *I Love Lucy* episode (404–405 and 142–143, respectively). It's not entirely clear what one should make of this duplication, which is inexplicable unless one posits that the *entire* account is Eugenio's fabulation, a suggestive possibility for which the text offers no other evidence.

Without going this far, however, one can at least venture that the duplication gives evidence of the extent to which Eugenio "underwrites" César's memoirs. I use this verb in both of its meanings: to write beneath something and to guarantee. Even if Eugenio is not always responsible for the specific verbal shape of César's recollections, he is at least generally responsible for the memoirs as a whole. Eugenio's name already indicates that he is the source, the genitor of the account. As his uncle's closest relative and the author of the liminar texts, he occupies a position halfway between the narrating "I" and the narrated "he." Perhaps Eugenio is best seen as César's translator, which means that their two voices are formally separate but often hard to tell apart. If *Our House in the Last World* was a third-person autobiography, *Mambo Kings* is a "hetero-autobiography," a text whose narrator and protagonist are in some ways distinct, in other ways indistinguishable.

Eugenio and César's complex filiation suggests the novel's ambivalent embrace of Cuban (and more generally Spanish-American) culture. Although *Mambo Kings* has been termed "the best Hispanic book" ever published by a commercial press in the United States,[9] its connection to things Hispanic is far from simple. From a literary point of view, even as *Mambo Kings* evokes some central works in the canon of contemporary Hispanic fiction, it takes distance from them. Even though it is tempting to read *Mambo Kings* as a "Hispanic book," the novel makes such a reading virtually impossible. In rhetorical terms *Mambo Kings* may be regarded as a sustained traduction, that is, a treacherous, transfigured repetition of certain elements of the Spanish American musical and literary culture. Although the novel bears a certain Hispanic family likeness, it is far from being a chip off the old block.

The family resemblance is evident in two principal ways. Given the episodic plot and the explicitness with which César's sexual exploits are recounted, *Mambo Kings* links up with the Hispanic picaresque, and particularly with the erotic picaresque, a genre that in Cuba includes such texts as Carlos Loveira's *Juan Criollo* (1927) and Guillermo Cabrera Infante's *La Habana para un infante difunto* (1979); the Cuban-American precedent is Desi Arnaz's *A Book*.[10] Like the protagonist of Loveira's novel, César is a Don Juan *criollo*, a creole translation of the Spanish literary type. In the classical picaresque, the protagonist is driven by hunger and spends a large part of his life in the service of a succession of masters. In the erotic picaresque, the moving force is a different kind of appetite; instead of going from master to master the protagonist goes from mistress to mistress—not *de amo en amo* but rather *de amorío en amorío*. César's attitude is exemplified in the motto "rum, rump and rumba" (105), a *cubano* version of the "wine, women, and song" of popular wisdom.[11]

Summing up his life, César remarks: "So I was led around by my prick, so what?" (53). César may not think anything of it, but his "phallocentrism" is the aspect of the novel that has elicited the strongest response from its readers. According to one reviewer, "Although

Hijuelos' narrative is implicitly critical of Castillo's machismo and the conditions that contribute to its psychological makeup, this 'criticism' is undermined by a narrowly male domination of the text."[12] What needs to be added, though, is that the novel's dominant male point of view is refracted through two rather different temperaments. If the text does not endorse César's phallocentrism, it's because his recollections are filtered through his nephew Eugenio, who puts distance between the reader and César's view of himself, as he does more generally between the novel and Cuban culture. Eugenio's mediating presence makes *Mambo Kings* something more than a celebration of César's not-so-private member. When César says, "So what?" this is not a rhetorical question; it is the question that the novel answers in excruciating detail.

If one token of tradition in the book is sex, the other is music, for *Mambo Kings* places itself in the line of descent of a whole spate of recent Spanish-American novels also inspired by popular music. I am thinking generally of works like Severo Sarduy's *De donde son los cantantes* (1967), Lisandro Otero's *Bolero* (1986), Luis Rafael Sánchez's *La importancia de llamarse Daniel Santos* (1989), and even Manuel Puig's *El beso de la mujer araña* (1976), with which Hijuelos's novel also shares the practice of providing explanatory footnotes. More concretely I am thinking of Guillermo Cabrera Infante's *Tres tristes tigres* (1965) and Luis Rafael Sánchez's *La guaracha del Macho Camacho* (1980), two novels reminiscent of *Mambo Kings* in more specific ways. Like *La guaracha del Macho Camacho*, which centers on a tune by the same name, *Mambo Kings* revolves around one song, "Beautiful María of My Soul," one of the cuts in an album from which the book takes its name. Both novels enact a kind of counterpoint between music and text, *música y letra*, that issues in the transcription of the lyric at the end of each book. Cabrera Infante's novel, which also draws heavily on popular music, includes a section entitled "Ella cantaba boleros," a phrase that Hijuelos transposes, since "songs of love" is his English translation of the Spanish "boleros." If she sang boleros, the mambo kings—who are themselves trapped tigers of a sort—play songs of love.

Mambo Kings is a literary latune—English words and Cuban music. But words and music do go together, as the mambo and bolero serve as correlates for the two dominant but discordant emotions in the book, lust and melancholy. The mambo is fast-paced, aggressive, lascivious; it is César's chant of conquest. By contrast, boleros are sad, even whining ballads whose speaker is typically passive and mournful. Like Néstor's "Beautiful María of My Soul," the bolero is a medium for bemoaning unhappiness in love, for questioning the injustice of fate. If the mambo is about conquest, the bolero is about loss. If the mambo is copulative, the bolero is disjunctive. The mambo grunts, the bolero moans. Its great theme is separation anxiety, a male's often infantile longing for a lost love. "Imágenes," a classic bolero by Frank Domínguez about a man who was inexplicably abandoned by his lover, ends:

> *Y desde entonces te ando buscando*
> *para decirte*
> *que cuando te fuiste*
> *como un niño me quedé llorando.*
>
> *(And since then I have been looking for you / to tell*
> *you / that when you left / I was left crying like a*
> *child.)*

Boleros ooze rejection. They are full of helpless posturings, of unanswered questions. Néstor's lyric asks, "Why did she finally mistreat me so? Tell me, why is it that way? Why is it always so?" (406).

The bolero's wordiness sharply contrasts with the mambo's laconism. In fact, the mambo's lovely inarticulateness makes it an odd choice as a model for literary composition. To the extent that *Mambo Kings* takes inspiration from the mambo, it tends toward a kind of expressiveness whose medium is *not* language. Most literary transpositions of popular songs focus on their lyrics—thus it is, for example, with *La guaracha del Macho Camacho* or with *De donde son los cantantes*. But with the mambo, literary transposition is difficult because of the form's instrumental nature. How does one write in grunts? The mambo may be expressive, but it is not articulate.

It is not surprising, for this reason, that what the mambo kings play are not mambos but "songs of love," for in the novel songs of love fill the verbal void left by the mambo. In a bolero rhythm and melody take a back seat to verbal elaboration, as is suggested by Néstor's twenty-two versions of the lyric of "Beautiful María of My Soul." The narrator describes Néstor's composition as "a song about love so far away it hurts, a song about lost pleasures, a song about youth, a song about love so elusive a man can never know where he stands; a song about wanting a woman so much death does not frighten you, a song about wanting that woman even when she has abandoned you" (405). The repetitive intensity of this description, which echoes Néstor's own obsessive rewriting, gives some idea of the bolero's involvement with language. The nostalgic tone of the book has a lot to do with the sensibility of the bolero, which provides the narrator with structures of feeling and forms of expression.

The theme of the novel can be stated as a musical question: Is life a mambo or a bolero? Is it a chronicle of conquest or is it a dirge? The answer, of course, is that life is both. *Mambo Kings* not only takes its title from one of the brothers' albums; Hijuelos labels its two parts "Side A" and "Side B." By patterning the scriptive record after the musical recording, Hijuelos makes the point that there is more than one side to this story. This is borne out in the lives of the two brothers. César, with his "king-cock strut" (47), is the mambo king; Néstor is the spirit of the *letra* of the bolero. As the narrator puts it succinctly, "César was *un macho grande*; Néstor, *un infeliz*" (114). But the irony is that, in the end, the great macho turns out to be no less of an *infeliz* than his brother, for after Néstor's death, César gradually takes on his brother's temperament. Early in the novel Néstor is described as "the man plagued with memory, the way his brother César Castillo would be twenty-five years later" (44). The gradual merging of the two brothers culminates with César's last act, which is to transcribe the lyric of his brother's composition, "Beautiful María of My Soul." When he copies the lyric as if it were his own, César becomes Néstor. This final gesture shows that César has become another man "plagued by memory."

César's impersonation of his brother summarizes the drift of the book. Like the title itself, the novel moves from mambo to bolero, from lust to loss, from conquest to relinquishment. César lives in frenetic mambo time only to discover that life actually follows the languid measures of a bolero. His celebration of rum, rump, and rumba is tempered by the reader's awareness that these chronicles of conquest are actually a derelict's last words. If Néstor composes his bolero in order to get María back (44), César reminisces in order to recapture his life as a *macho grande*; and the narration explicitly plays on the punning relationship between "member" and "remember"—at one point César "remembered a whore struggling with a thick rubber on his member" (393). For César, remembering is a way of re-membering himself, a way of sleeping with the past. But the vitality thus achieved is illusory. Like the bolero composed by Néstor, the novel is very much "a song about lost pleasures, a song about youth." The melancholy is so pervasive that even penises weep: "By evening they were sitting out on a

pier by the sea necking, the head of his penis weeping semen tears"
(99–100).

Néstor's song of love is also an elegy to Cuba. The novel's relation to
things Cuban in general and to the Spanish language in particular is
affectionate but distant. In one sense, Spanish is everywhere in the text:
in the place and character names, in the characters' hispanicized diction,
and in the constant references to Cuban music. In another sense, however, Spanish is nowhere, for Hijuelos has rendered all of the characters'
thoughts and words in English. Indeed, since César's remembrances
make up most of the novel, and since these remembrances were almost
certainly framed in Spanish, the text we read presupposes an invisible
act of translation, somewhat in the manner of *Don Quijote*, which was
supposedly translated by Cervantes from Arabic. The mambo king's
English needs to be read as Spanish in translation; and the source of this
translation must be Eugenio, who then becomes, like Cervantes, the
"second author" of the book. Eugenio's genius, his *ingenio*, is to render
his uncle's recollections in such a way that the reader tends to overlook
the nephew's presence in the uncle's words.

Significantly, the only sustained Spanish passage in the book is the
lyric of the "Beautiful María of My Soul," which appears at the very
end. One cannot overlook the overdetermination of its appearance:
Néstor's song of love, the book's preeminent statement on loss, is tran-
scribed in a language that itself has been lost. The Spanish lyric is a testament to what is lost in translation. And Néstor's beautiful María may
then be an emblem for the maternal language that was left behind in
Cuba. Moreover, since César's last act was to transcribe this lyric, this
Spanish interpolation is literally a testament. When readers finally come
upon these words, they find themselves at a loss. Like Ricky's Spanish
outbursts, the lyric creates a kind of lacuna, a gap in the novel's discur-
sive flow. The bolero, which is one of the novel's principal links to
Hispanic culture, is also the emblem for the loss of that culture, a loss
whose most fundamental manifestation is linguistic.

In a narrow but significant sense, this linguistic loss has been present
throughout the novel in the surprisingly large number of errors in the
spelling of Spanish words and names. For example, Antonio Arcaño,
who is one of the seminal figures in the development of the mambo,
becomes Antonio Arcana (154); the famous singer Bola de Nieve is
strangely transformed into a Pala de Nieve; the equally famous Beny
Moré loses his accent and becomes Beny More (an example of how
"More" can be less). The accentuation throughout is inconsistent: while

César and Néstor lose the accent on their names, other characters keep theirs. Misspelled words are not infrequent: "nalgita" for *nalguita*, "batida" for *batido*, "quatro" for *cuatro*, and so on. Although these errata may be evidence of sloppy editing, they are also typographical reminders of translation as loss, as displacement, as traduction. (Similar mistakes can be found in *Our House in the Last World*.)

Like Hijuelos's first novel, *Mambo Kings* is written "from" Cuba but "toward" the United States. This translational drift is already evident in the title, which goes from the Cuban "mambo" to the English "songs of love." But the beguiling richness of the novel, and what sets it apart from *Our House in the Last World*, stems from the fact that the novel's anglocentrism is not motivated by fear. From Eugenio's perspective, César is not a threatening paternal ghost but a benign avuncular genie. He may be pitiable, but he's not horrific. *Mambo Kings'* considerable achievement is to stage the negotiation between cultures in such a way that the novel neither forsakes nor is enslaved by its family resemblance to things and texts Hispanic. Cuban culture figures in the novel as a distant relation, much as César and Néstor appear on *I Love Lucy* as Ricky's Cuban cousins. The art of *Mambo Kings* resides in knowing how to cultivate distant relations, which means also knowing how to put them in their place. This is the distance that *Our House* was not able to achieve, for Héctor was able neither to slay nor to celebrate his father. Hijuelos's second novel seems to me much more successful in staking out a territory—linguistic, cultural, emotional—that is not overrun by Cuban ghosts.

At one point in *Mambo Kings*, during an interview on a radio show, César Castillo praises Desi Arnaz. The emcee replies: "But no one has ever considered him very authentic or original." To which César counters: "*Bueno*, I think what he did was difficult. For me, he was very Cuban, and the music he played in those days was good and Cuban enough for me" (339). "Good and Cuban enough"—this statement may apply equally well to Hijuclos's second novel, a dance to the music of time that, like Desi and Ricky, loses and finds itself in translation. Perhaps a Cuban Quasimodo never does lose his hump, but at least he can learn not to treat it as a handicap. The motto of the mambo king's Cuban-American progeny might well be: rump, hump, and rumba.[13]

English Is Broken Here

MAMBO NO. 6   *Some years ago a Cuban radio station in Miami aired an advertisement promoting an airline's reduced fares: "Piedmont Airlines quiere limpiar el aire sobre sus bajas tarifas." "Limpiar el aire?" "Clean the air?" This phrase is ungrammatical in two languages. First mistake: perhaps influenced by the Spanish* poner en limpio *(to clean up), the author of the ad must have thought that the English idiom was "clean the air" rather than "clear the air." Second mistake: he then decided that "clean the air" could be translated word for word into Spanish. Third mistake: he rendered "about" as "sobre," which in context sounds too much like "over" or "above." Hence: "Piedmont Airlines wants to clean the air above its low fares." But this sentence does have a certain flighty logic, especially considering that it went out over the airwaves. Piedmont's clean-air act is an interlingual utterance that remains up in the air, that cannot make up its mind whether to land in the domain of Spanish or English.*

Another comedy of grammatical errors will bring us back to earth: there is a Cuban-owned pizza chain in Miami called Casino's Pizza. When Casino's was launched (or lunched) a few years ago, its publicity campaign included a bilingual brochure. I quote the first sentence of the Spanish text: "Su pri-

*mera mirada, su primer olor, su primer gusto le dirá
que usted descubrió La Pizza Ultima." Since "La
Pizza Ultima" (the last pizza) doesn't make much
sense in Spanish (it should have been "la última
pizza" anyway), upon first reading this anglicized
sentence, I had the impression that the final phrase
was an incompletely digested translation of "the ultimate pizza." In order to check out my hunch, I
went to the English text: "Your first sight, your first
smell, your first taste will tell you that you've discovered La Pizza Ultima."*

*So what happened to my hypothetical Ultimate
Pizza? It seems to have been eaten in translation.
The same phrase that sounds like an anglicism in
Spanish is offered as a hispanicism in English! Food
for thought: the English phrase presupposes a Spanish phrase that presupposes an English phrase that
doesn't exist. This is paradox-lover's pizza, one
that consumes itself in the cracks between languages.
Like the Piedmont ad, "La Pizza Ultima" refuses
to be English but cannot be Spanish. If Beny Moré
is the "bárbaro del ritmo," the authors of these ads
must be bárbaros of barbarism. Sometimes the
American dream is written in Spanglish.*

Six

NO-MAN'S-LANGUAGE

If Oscar Hijuelos composes valedictories to Cuba, José Kozer writes so as not to say good-bye. If Hijuelos writes "from" Cuba but "toward" the United States, Kozer writes "from" the United States but "toward" Cuba. Born in Havana in 1940 of Jewish parents, Kozer is the first major poet to have emerged from the contemporary Cuban diaspora. Although his first book of poetry, *Padres y otras profesiones* (1972), was not published until he was in his thirties, since then he has produced a steady stream of volumes that now number more than a dozen.[1] With the appearance in 1983 of *Bajo este cien*, a generous selection of his work published by the prestigious Mexican publishing house Fondo de Cultura Económica, his work acquired a visibility that has continued to the present day. His poems are widely anthologized and studied.[2] Among living Cuban poets perhaps only Heberto Padilla and Eugenio Florit (who are much older) enjoy a comparable stature.

Upon leaving Cuba in 1960, Kozer settled in New York, where he has lived for over thirty years. He attended New York University, specializing in Brazilian and Latin American literature; since 1965 he has taught Spanish at Queens College. Like Hijuelos, Kozer is a Cuban-American writer from New York. Yet viewing Kozer in this light seems strangely inappropriate, for someone who comes to his poems without any information about their author would be hard-pressed to locate this poet in New York. Although Kozer's poems make fully and painfully evident that he is a Cuban exile, they say very little about the country where he has lived most of his life. Like some of the songs we sampled in Chapter 4, Kozer's poetry is loquacious about Cuba but strangely silent about the United States. Unlike other hispanophone U.S. writers, Kozer does not write about the anglophone world that surrounds him. His poetic universe seems disconnected from the place where he lives and works.

This sparseness of topical reference is all the more striking given the autobiographical slant of many poems. Indeed, he has recently published a book of self-portraits, *Trazas del lirondo* (1993). As Kozer himself has said, his poetry confounds the "biographical I" with the "poetic I."[3] Yet since Kozer's poetic persona speaks from a virtual point in space without a name or an address, he does not seem to live anywhere in particular. When Cuba is the subject, Kozer's poems teem with toponyms. But when it comes to New York City, where the poet has now lived for most of his life, they are far more reticent. To judge from his poetry, Kozer has a past but no present. The only map in his work is that of Havana, and particularly of Santos Suárez, the neighborhood where he grew up. Kozer's nonretrospective poems tend not to leave his house. Rather than society-at-large, they occupy a sanctuary of interior, domestic spaces: doorways, stairwells, dining rooms, and bedrooms instead of streets, subways, highrises, schools, and supermarkets. The poet's vision reaches beyond the walls of his house only when it looks back to Cuba. Kozer looks back and looks in, but he seldom looks out. He may reside in New York, but he does not live there, if by living we mean engaging the time and place and culture of his surroundings.

But my intention here is not to criticize or question Kozer's choice of spiritual habitat. Rather, I am interested in appreciating his isolationism, that is, in understanding its value by examining the dynamics of inwardness in his poetry. In the last chapter Hijuelos's novels took us to one of the borders of Cuban America, the point at which it crosses over into the American mainland. In this chapter I want to explore Cuban America's other border, contiguous with Cuba. If the American border raises the issue of assimilation, the Cuban border raises the issue of regression (again, in the allied senses of *regreso* and *regresión*), or what Kozer terms "contraction."

These borders are also, of course, generational divides. Second-generation Cuban Americans, who keep the hyphen but lose the accent, inhabit the American border. The Cuban border is occupied by first-generation Cuban exiles, who could not sound like Americans even if they tried (but who, for the most part, don't try). In his own very personal way, Kozer embodies the attitudes and values of the first generation. For Kozer, as for Cuban exiles, Cuba is not just a historical point of departure but a constant frame of reference. The great theme in his poetry is the presence and presentness of the past. As we will see, many of Kozer's poems are exercises in recollection, attempts to save in writing a world that no longer exists in history.

But two things set Kozer apart from most other Cuban-exile writers. First, he is Jewish. For this reason, his evocations of *la Cuba de ayer* contain elements missing from other portrayals. A significant portion of Kozer's extensive *oeuvre* is given over to highlighting the Jewish ingredients in the Cuban *ajiaco*. For Kozer, just as there is a Cuban counterpoint, there is a Cuban-Jewish counterpoint. As he put it in a recent essay, "Esto (también) es Cuba, Chaguito" (This Is [Also] Cuba, Chaguito).[4] Moreover, as a Jew, Kozer's grasp of exile is deeper and more faceted than that of most of his compatriots. For him exile is familiar, even routine. His parents were themselves exiles; the Havana of his childhood was his Russian father's *orbis ultima*. Some of his most striking poems deftly contrast the father's disorientation upon reaching Cuba and the son's nostalgia upon leaving it. Joining his Cuban and Jewish heritage, Kozer sees himself as a *cubano errante*, a "Wandering Cuban" who continues a centuries-old Jewish tradition of itinerancy.

Kozer also stands apart from other first-generation Cuban exiles in that he became a writer *after* leaving Cuba. Somewhat older than the Cuban baby boomers but somewhat younger than his generational peers, Kozer might be described as belonging to the "one-and-a-quarter" generation (Hijuelos, by contrast, would belong to the "one-and-three-quarters" generation). This fractional refinement may be meaningless in the case of most people, but it helps to define the blend of tendencies in Kozer's poetry. Older Cuban-exile poets and novelists—Padilla, Florit, Gastón Baquero, Guillermo Cabrera Infante, Hilda Perera, and many others—became writers in Cuba. Their writerly vocation is firmly rooted in a national context. But Kozer is an exiled writer who did not publish his first poems until the mid-sixties and his first book until 1972, a dozen years after he left the island. Whatever his youthful poetic exercises, Kozer's poetic voice was shaped in exile and, more importantly, *by* exile. Would he have been a poet in Cuba? Perhaps. But his poetry seems unimaginable without the experience of exile. I do not

know for sure whether exiles write more than other people, but sometimes it does seem that way. Miami is crawling with poets. At least in
its initial phases, exile breeds writers. The shelves of La Universal, the
biggest bookstore in Little Havana, are filled with books written by
Cuban exiles, bearing titles like *Flores del destierro, Raíces del olvido,
Ardor de palmeras*. Had the Cuban Revolution not sent my family into
exile, right now I would probably be tending a store, not writing a
book.

Because Kozer became a writer in exile, his Spanish has a peculiar
accent. Kozer's language is rich, copious, supple, precise, but it does not
sound quite Cuban. If one thinks again of other Cuban exile writers,
this is somewhat unusual, for an exile's iterative gestures extend to his
use of language. Just as he tries to recreate his home in a foreign land,
he tries to recreate his home's language. Just as he holds fast to the old
places, he holds fast to the old words. This is particularly so when the
writer lives in a society that speaks a language different than his own.
Wrenched from its natural surroundings, language tends to freeze rather
than evolve. Sephardic Jews whose ancestors were thrown out of Spain
in 1492 still sing medieval Spanish ballads. The Spanish spoken by
Cubans in Miami has an "archaic" flavor (circa Havana 1959) lacking in
its contemporary mainland counterpart.

But what happens to a young exiled writer who is trying to develop
a voice and a vocabulary in a "foreign" language, that is, in a language
different from that of the place where he resides? And what if he doesn't
even live in an ethnic enclave like Little Havana, where his native tongue
is still a *lingua franca*, but in a babelic but English-dominant city like
New York? Where does such a writer find his words? Where does he
pick up speech patterns, slang, intonations? How does he ascertain that
he is working with a living language? Even more important, how does
he locate his *nation* within his *voice*?

Kozer gives these questions complicated, sometimes contradictory,
answers. Even when he writes about Cuban subjects, his Spanish has
acquired an odd "international" flavor. Even if the matter is Cuban, the
medium is not entirely so. Or rather, it is Cuban, but it is also Spanish,
Mexican, and Peruvian. Bringing together words and locutions from
widely dispersed regions of the Hispanic world, Kozer writes an Esperanto Spanish, a no man's language that testifies to the author's condition
as an exile. If, as Elias Canetti has said, a language is a place, Kozer's is a
utopia, a no-place. His is a virtual language, words bereft of commu-

nity. His idiolect is not a subset of some group's sociolect, unless one takes the group to be Spanish speakers as a whole. I do not mean that Kozer's Spanish is different from the everyday variety in the way in which "poetic" language is different from "ordinary" speech. Although his language can be quite abstract and metaphorical at times, it is also earthy, colloquial, full of slang. It's not that forms of popular speech are absent from his idiolect, but that they are used without regard for geographical boundaries. His poems mingle idioms and vocabulary from all over the Spanish-speaking world. They presuppose a speaker who contains within himself several Hispanic nationalities. A line in one autobiographical poem says, "Su ambición es una: todo el vocabulario" (He has one ambition: the whole vocabulary; *BEC*, 42). The problem is that when you possess all the words, you end up speaking and writing a language that no one else speaks or writes. The overreaching ambition to know all of the words generates a language that is remarkable because of its richness as well as because of its artificiality. The speaker of Kozer's poems inhabits a linguistic utopia that cannot be traced back to a specific community of speakers.

Kozer's Esperanto Spanish is both a symptom of uprootedness and a shield against it. Since he has lived most of his life surrounded by the sounds of English, his exile is linguistically precarious. Only sustained, deliberate cultivation could have produced his abundant Spanish. Every writer cultivates language, of course, but a hispanophone writer in the United States needs to do it more deliberately than most. It is telling that in his poems Kozer does not show any fear of becoming less Jewish; yet his work is haunted by the possibility of losing its mother tongue. Because Spanish is for Kozer a way of life, the cornerstone of his identity as a writer, he cannot afford to be casual about it. In the prologue to an anthology of hispanophone U.S. poetry, Kozer writes that what unites these poets (of whom he is one) is their decision to maintain their Spanish:

> In all [of these poets] there persists the conscious desire to safeguard the mother tongue, to the point that the Spanish language (more than Spanish culture) becomes a way of protecting one's personal identity, thereby establishing a conscious state of separation from the Anglo-Saxon environment. . . . The desire to live in Spanish, in spite of the persistent threat constituted by the cosmopolitan and supercivil-

*ized Anglo-Saxon environment which these poets
inhabit, is, to our mind, a capital factor in this new
Latin-American poetry.*[5]

Kozer then goes on to relate the anecdote that the Spanish poet Juan
Ramón Jiménez never learned English because he feared that for each
new English word he learned he would forget three words in Spanish.
Since these poets view Spanish and English as vying for the same
domain, their literary vocations require the dissociation of life and
work. The instrument of dissociation is Spanish, which insulates the
writer from American influences. In Hijuelos's *Our House in the Last
World*, Cuban culture is seen as an enemy. In Kozer the allegiances are
reversed, for it is the United States that becomes the enemy. But the
antagonistic view of culture contact remains the same. Kozer employs
vaguely military rather than specifically medical metaphors: the mother
tongue needs to be "safeguarded" from the "threat" of American
culture. If Héctor feared Cuban infections, Kozer fears American
invasions.

His striking phrase for the decision to write in Spanish is *la voluntad
de vivir en español* (literally, the will to live in Spanish). By conceiving of
language in spatial terms, this phrase conflates living with writing: just
as other people live in a house, Kozer lives "in" Spanish. However,
because he distinguishes between language (*el español*) and nationality
(*lo español*), his linguistic residence does not correspond to any national
entity. As the label "Anglo-Saxon" (for "American") also suggests,
the borders of this territory are cultural rather than territorial. Kozer's
language constructs what he calls a "superior geography" whose confines are simply those of the Spanish-speaking world.[6] Paradoxically,
although Spanish effectively separates Kozer from anglophone America, it also distances him from Cuba. For someone in his situation, linguistic and national identity do not easily merge. He can assert his non-
Americanness only by hedging on his Cubanness.

Kozer once described his poetry as expressing a "continuous state
of alarm."[7] The foregoing suggests that the sense of alarm perhaps
emerges from the encroachment of America—its ways and its words—
on his work (and perhaps also on his life). Let's remember that an alarm,
from the Italian *all'arme*, is literally a call to arms. Kozer's weapon
against the Mac-attacks of American culture is language. If you can't
beat them, translate them. His work offers an example of what Michael
Fisher has called "ethnic anxiety," the ethnic American's fear of decul-

turation, of losing old–country roots.[8] It is this anxiety that makes Kozer a Cuban-American writer, a label he probably would not accept, preferring instead "Cuban" or simply "Latin-American." But in my view, Kozer is too anxious to be simply Cuban, with or without the Jewish component. Even if Juan Ramón Jiménez was scared to death of losing Spanish, his fear was exaggerated. Keeping his language vital may have required some effort, but Jiménez could not have been anything other than what he was before he left Spain, a Spanish poet from Andalusia. But because Kozer became a writer after leaving Cuba, his vocational foundations are far more shaky. His self-image as an exiled *writer* is an identity that Kozer will have to construct in his poems, which are then both the result of his vocation and its condition of possibility. Yet in order to make himself into a Cuban writer in exile, Kozer has had to turn his back on the society in which he has spent all of his adult life. His refusal of English in particular and of things American in general will be a recurring, if not always explicit, theme in his work. The difference between his "biographical I" and his "poetic I" is that the former has spent two-thirds of his life in a world that the latter is bent on ignoring.

Kozer's poetry abhors a vacuum. Not partaking in the least of the Mallarmean cult of blankness, he looks upon the scriptless page as a cavity that needs to be filled with words. As a "judío agrio y coleccionista" (sour and collecting Jew; *BEC*, 76), Kozer errs on the side of excess rather than aridity. His poems develop by accretion or accumulation; one word generates another, one line generates another, one poem generates another, one book generates another in a seemingly unstoppable proliferation. Since he knows all the words, he uses all the words. Not satisfied with the *mot juste*, Kozer will look for the imprecise but suggestive term that unleashes a series of associations: "Y la veleta en la bóveda del templete, ristra incorpórea (orla) la saeta en el aire" (And the vane on the vault of the temple, incorporeal string [fringe] the arrow in the air; *BEC*, 100). The weather vane is named in four different ways: *veleta, ristra, orla,* and *saeta.* Not content with the bare name, *veleta,* the speaker follows with two metaphors, *ristra* and *orla,* before returning to the concreteness of the *saeta.*

A different kind of amplification appears in "Santos Suárez, 1956," an evocation of the neighborhood where the poet spent his childhood and adolescence:

Esta romanza
a las marmitas, destapa: y en las tarteras, serrucho
en escabeche
y mil glorias y mil orines el vecindario, el lebrel y la
    verja, tío
Sidney
que perseveró con los dijes, las alcancías, de un hijo
    mayor y el canario que perseveraba
(salmodia).

(This song
to casseroles, uncover it: and in the pans, swordfish
in brine
and the neighborhood a thousand glories and a
    thousand urines, the greyhound and the grate,
    uncle
Sidney
who persevered with the trinkets, the piggy banks, of
    an eldest son and the canary that persevered
[psalmody].) (BEC, 19)

The whole poem consists of an enumeration of domestic utensils and events, a "song to casseroles," as the speaker says. What Kozer "uncovers" to the reader is a string of small things: his mother's pots and pans, the noises and smells of the neighborhood, relatives who come and go. The jumbled enumeration conveys the hustle and bustle of the household. Unlike what often happens in exile poetry, there are no large themes here, no vapid generalities about expatriation or nostalgia, for the poet is shrewd enough to let the details do the talking. At his best, Kozer is a poet of trifles and trinkets, of *shashkes* or *cachivaches*. His titles reveal his preferences: "Album de familia" (Family Album), "Gramática de papá" (Papa's Grammar), "Todas las puertas dan al comedor de la casa" (All the Doors Open to the Dining Room), "Retrato (en sus quehaceres) de mamá" (Portrait of Mother [Doing Her Chores]), "Limpieza general" (House Cleaning), "Pascua en La Habana" (Passover in Havana), and so on.

Poems like these are exercises in recollection, a term I intend in both its temporal and physical meanings. They not only memorialize; they gather, assemble, string together: *and* this *and* that *and* the other: "y mil glorias y mil orines el vecindario, el lebrel y la verja, tío Sidney." Kozer loves to enumerate, to count. He is the *cantor* as *contador*, the bard as accountant: a teller, in both senses. Not surprisingly, he describes himself as a "quantitative poet," a label that applies both to his prolificity and to the enumerative strain within his poems, which are full of numbers: "a thousand glories, a thousand urines." One of his first books was called, *Este judío de números y letras* (*This Jew of Numbers and Letters*); a volume in English is entitled *The Ark upon the Number*; and the title of his best-known volume is *Bajo este cien* (*Under This Hundred*), where *cien* sums up the number of poems in the book. The expected phrase in Spanish would have been *Bajo este cielo* (Under This Sky). But in Kozer's world we are enveloped not by skies but by poems. His is truly a uni-verse.

The numerical afflatus that inspires individual poems has infused Kozer's whole career. In 1988 he calculated that over the previous fifteen years he had written 2,300 poems and that in spite of the dozen volumes of poetry he had published up to that time his published output represented only a small fraction of all the poems he had written.[9] What I find remarkable is not only the size of the *oeuvre* but the very fact of keeping count. How long did it take him to count 2,300 poems? But for Kozer numbers count, quantity changes quality. Each new poem is an additional hedge against the void, another roof over our heads, a little verbal parapet that protects us. Kozer accumulates poems the way he accumulates objects within his poems. When he remarks that Kafka was "vast in excess" (*BEC*, 129), this nearly redundant phrase describes Kozer's own capaciousness. "In poetry," Kozer says, "everything fits [*cabe todo*]."[10] Significantly, the world of his childhood is described in exactly the same terms: "Todo cabía, entonces" (Then everything fit; *BEC*, 41). Like the world of his childhood, a poem is a universe of capacious diversity, a kind of receptacle that accommodates the most heterogeneous materials. This is why Kozer's poems are full of containers—pots, pans, vessels, vases, jars, jugs, bottles, bags, boxes, etc.[11] "Santos Suárez, 1956" begins as a "song to casseroles," and then goes on to mention baking pans and piggy banks. If Kozer's poems abhor a void, they love receptacles, which enclose the void. Once enclosed, the void can be filled to the hilt with objects.

The most explicit justification of Kozer's aesthetics of capacious diversity is contained in "Gaudeamus," a striking apologia for his life and art. The title, a fragment of the Latin hymn "Gaudeamus Igitur" (Let Us Then Rejoice), sets the exultant hybrid tone of the poem, which celebrates the poet's mixed cultural heritage. "Gaudeamus" is poetry as mixed bag, as multicultural collectanea. The speaker's monologue takes the form of an imaginary reply to his critics:

En mi confusión
no supe ripostar a mis detractores, aquellos
que me tildan
de postalita porque pronuncio la ce a la manera
　　castellana o digo tío por tipo (me privan) los
　　mestizajes
(peruanismos) (mexicanismos)
de la dicción y los vocablos: ni soy uno (ni otro) ni
　　soy recto ni ambiguo, bárbaramente
romo
y narigudo (barbas) asirias (ojos) oblicuos y vengo del
　　otro lado
del río: cubano
y postalita (judío) y tabernáculo (shofar y taled)
　　violín de la Aragón o primer corneta
de la Sonora Matancera: qué
más quisiera uno que no haber sido ibis migratorio
　　(ludibrio) o corazón
esporádico.

(In my confusion
I didn't know how to answer my detractors, those
who brand me
a poseur because I pronounce the c in the Castilian
　　manner or I say fellow instead of guy [I love]
　　miscegenations
[peruvianisms] [mexicanisms]
of diction and vocabulary: I am neither the one [nor
　　the other] neither straight nor ambiguous,
　　barbarously
flat-nosed
and big-nosed Assyrian [beards] oblique [eyes] and I
　　come from the other side
of the river: Cuban
and vain [a Jew] and tabernacle [shofar and taled]
　　violin of the Aragon or first trumpet
of the Sonora Matancera: what
more could one have wished than not to be a
　　migratory ibis [scorn] or a sporadic
heart.) (BEC, 44)

Derided for his Castilian pronunciation and his use of regionalisms from different countries, Kozer is stigmatized as a "postalita," a Cuban slang term for a *poseur*. Kozer's accusers, who by their choice of insult reveal themselves to be Cuban, make fun of the fact that he does not sound or speak like a typical Cuban. Although Kozer says that he does not know how to reply, simply repeating the criticism is his best reply. His "riposte"—a word that cunningly echoes the derisive epithet "postalita"—is not to renounce hybridism but to revel in it. Feigning remorse, he responds to the accusation of affectation by accumulating "affectations," of which the most salient is the liturgical Latin title, which seems singularly inapt for the self-portrait of a Jew. But the whole poem makes obvious that the speaker has hardly gotten over his "confusion." Cuban and Jew, Castilian and Cuban, Mexican and Peruvian, he contains multiple identities.

In its mix of languages (Latin with Spanish with Hebrew), "Gaudeamus" illustrates Kozer's ambition to know all the words. The result is a shifting idiolect that is both translational and transnational. When Kozer says that he comes "from the other side of the river," he is translating the literal meaning of "Hebrew." When he says that his nose is "barbarously" flat, he is punning on the Greek root of the adverb, since as an outsider who speaks and writes an unacceptable language Kozer is indeed a barbarian in the old cultural and linguistic senses. Not only that; he is a barbarian with a beard, a *barba*, another word that derives from the same etymon. The whole poem is filled with multilingual barbs.

In "Gaudeamus" even the parentheses are barbed. Although a parenthetical utterance usually stands in apposition to the main clause, here parentheses lose their appositional function. This creates a kind of grammatical insubordination, a joust between syntax and punctuation:

> *(me privan) los mestizajes . . .*
> *ni soy uno (ni otro) . . .*
> *(barbas) asirias (ojos) oblicuos . . .*
>
> *([I love] miscegenations . . .*
> *I am neither the one [nor the other] . . .*
> *Assyrian [beards] oblique [eyes] . . .)*

In each of theses phrases the punctuation segregates words that are syntactically linked—verb and predicate, matching parts, noun and adjective. In order to grasp the sense one has to read through the parentheses, thus joining syntactically phrases that are typographically distinct. Of course, Kozer's confused punctuation is yet another way to underscore the theme of the poem, which is the mixing of things that are usually held apart. The clever phrase "(me privan) los mestizajes" not only does what it says, but contains another sly pun, this one on *privar*, which literally means to deprive or set apart. The whole poem mounts an attack on the notion of the privative, the exclusionary. Kozer's non-privative use of parentheses is one way in which this attack is carried forth.

The reasons for Kozer's frequent, and frequently unconventional, use of parentheses are not difficult to discern. For one thing, parentheses enclose supplementary or alternative utterances: para-theses. Parentheses are the logical abode of minority discourses. As a Cuban Jewish writer, Kozer is himself parenthetical. In the title "This Is (Also) Cuba, Chaguito," the cultural specificity of Cuban Jews is signified in the parenthetical "(Also)." Kozer locates himself inside that parenthetical indication of supplementarity. The other reason for their use is formal: parentheses are containers, typographical casseroles, open-lidded receptacles that allow him to stuff the poem with words. Like pots and pans, parentheses are *útiles*, utensils that can be used to accumulate and keep verbal stores. When he writes, in another typical image,

> las coles en las marmitas
> (todas las puertas abiertas de par en par)
>
> (the cabbages inside the casseroles
> [all of the doors wide open]) (BEC, 30)

he is explaining, within parentheses, the function of this device. Parentheses are indeed "open doors" through which additional text can enter the poem. The roundness of the containing casseroles is recovered visually in the curves of the typographical marks.

If anything, the rest of "Gaudeamus" is even more "confused" than the first part. After Kozer splits into two people, an "I" and a "he," the poem's catalogue of contradictory attributes becomes increasingly difficult to construe.

> . . . qué
> más quisiera uno que no haber sido ibis migratorio
> (ludibrio) o corazón

esporádico

hecho al escándalo de quien a la hora nupcial, a la
  hora

del festín

cruza el umbral y aspira un olor a jarabes (olor) a
  frutas tropicales y eneldo: pues

soy así, él

y yo, cisterna y limbo (miríadas) las manos que
  trepan por la escala contaminan

el pensamiento

de tiña y verdín (aguas) imperturbables: sin nación,
  quieto

futuro

y jolgorio de marmitas redondas (mis manos) son mi
  raza que hurgan en la crepitación

de la materia.

(. . . what

more could one have wished than not to be a
  migratory ibis [scorn] or a sporadic

heart

made for the scandal of whom at the nuptial hour, at
  the hour

of the feast

crosses the threshold and inhales a scent of potions
  [scent] of tropical fruits and dill: well

that's how it is, he

and I, cistern and limbo [myriads] the hands that
  climb the scales contaminate

thought

with ring-worm and scum [waters] imperturbable:
  nationless, quiet

future

and mirth of round casseroles [my hands] are my race
  that

dig into the crepitation

of matter.)

The poem that began with confusion ends with connubium. Like the lines that precede it, the description of the wedding feast suggests union, a conjugal coming together of the speaker's multiple identities, his "I" and his "he." Those *marmitas* are melting pots. What is being stirred up in Kozer's ever-present containers is a Cuban-Jewish *ajiaco*. Itinerancy nurtures, hybridity nourishes. In yet another etymological pun, when Kozer calls himself a "sporadic heart," he reminds us of the link between "sporadic" and "diaspora," since both words have to do with dissemination, the scattering of seeds. Kozer's sporadic heart is an organ that thrives in dispersion. The final image of the hands in the pot of crackling matter attests to the vitality of such scatterings.

                          Although "Gaudeamus" bears rich witness to the fruitfulness of Kozer's "will to live in Spanish," his poems are not always so approving of "confusion." The dynamic of his work encompasses a double movement, expansive and contractile. In its expansive phrase, his poetry is capacious, receptive, joyously hybrid, lustfully in love with otherness. "Gaudeamus" is a Cuban-Jewish *I Love Lucy*, with Kozer's sporadic heart a reminder of Lucy and Ricky's heart-shaped logo. In its contractile phase, however, Kozer's poetry retreats from otherness and desists from opening doors and crossing thresholds. Unlike "Gaudeamus," these poems give voice to Kozer's anxiety at the "threat" of the "Anglo-Saxon environment." Instead of being expansive and celebratory, they contract. The containing spaces in these poems are hermetic rather than open: cloisters rather than casseroles.

I take the notion of contraction from a recent poem entitled "Uno de los modos de resarcir las formas" (One of the ways of mending the forms), where "contraction" designates the poet's reaction to inclement cold weather. In the middle of a snowstorm, the speaker "opts for contraction," that is, he bundles up against the cold and imaginatively leaves the unnamed street in the unnamed city where he is walking.

> *Amago, la nevisca me contrae.*
> *Estas calles opto por contraerme en el cuadrante*
>   *tercera*
>   *fase, volver.*[12]
>
> *(I feint, the snow contracts me.*
> *These streets I opt for contraction in the quadrant*
>   *third*
>   *phase, return.)*

Next thing we know he's in Calzada, a street in the neighborhood of El Cerro, in Havana.

> *Opto o me descuajeringo: mi contracción bajo un*
> *paraguas en*
> *medio del aguanieve tengo un gorro*
> *de lana con borla el frío*
> *opíparo me devolvió a la anochecida*
> *del portal o me redujo a las dos*
> *macetas de la entrada (ahí) discuten*
> *viandero y casera.*
> *Discutan discutan que yo vivo: Calzada, estoy vivo.*

> *(I opt or fall apart: my contraction under the umbrella*
> *in the midst of the sleet I have a cap*
> *of wool with a tassel the cold*
> *opiparous returned me to the evening*
> *in the porch or reduced me to the two*
> *flower pots at the entrance (there)*
> *the vendor and the housewife argue.*
> *Let them argue argue I am alive: Calzada, I am*
> *alive.)*

Physical retreat opens the way for imaginary recovery. As the body contracts against the cold, the imagination expands and the speaker is transported back to the Havana of his childhood. It is striking, and typical, that in this poem only Cuban places have a name; the wintry cityscape (probably New York) remains anonymous. The whole poem exemplifies the process of exilic substitution: Cuban *calzadas* replace New York avenues; indeed, by the end of the poem, the northern snowstorm has turned into a tropical hurricane, "el ciclón del '44." The operative words are *devolver*, to return, and *reducir*, which literally means to lead back. The poem's title underscores the function of substitution: imaginative transport is "one of the ways to mend the forms," that is, a mechanism for repairing the speaker's dislocation. The imagination makes amends to the poet for the storms of history.

"Opto o me descuajeringo," he says: either I opt for contraction or I fall apart. The colloquial "descuajeringo," which refers strictly to a relaxation of joints and muscles, is the exact opposite of contraction. The problem, though, is that full contraction may not be possible, with the result that the imagined or interior landscape does not completely blot out the real world. Even though the setting of "Uno de los modos . . ." never does return overtly to the United States, the last phrase of the poem, "solavaya el viento" (dammit the wind), applies both to the remembered hurricane and to the actual snowstorm. The speaker's mind may be in Cuba, but his feet are still walking down the snowy streets of New York.

The impossibility of sustained or complete contraction is the perhaps unintended lesson of "Home Sweet Home," a poem from *El carillón de los muertos* (1987) that I want to discuss in some detail. Like "Un modo de resarcir las formas," this poem unfolds in the midst of bad weather, but this time the speaker is holed up in his house. Instead of voyaging mentally to another place, he will withdraw into the sweet security of his home. The "reduction" here will be introspective rather than retrospective. Rather than looking back, he will be looking in.

With the rain falling outside, the house in the poem becomes a kind of Ark that shelters him and his family (one of Kozer's books is entitled *The Ark upon the Number*). From the first lines, the poem establishes a tense opposition between outside and inside, between the threatening exterior world and the domestic sanctuary.

> *Ya pasaron: aquellos días de verdadera agitación.*
> *Hay una gotera en el cuarto de la niña, dejó de*
>   *rezumar (pese a que llueve)*
>   *(llueve) está ahí la gotera,*
>   *no rezuma, el Bendito.*
> *En casa, hay cinco relojes: detenidos.*
>
> *(They passed already: those days of real agitation.*
> *There is a leak in our daughter's room, it stopped*
>   *leaking [even though it rains]*
>   *[it rains] the leak is still there*
>   *it doesn't drip, thank God.*
> *In the house, there are five clocks: stopped.)* [13]

This house seems to exist outside time and space: because the leak has been sealed, the rain can't come in; and because the clocks don't work, time has stood still. (A few lines later the speaker will disclose that he doesn't even know what month it is.) Since the opposite of "agitation" is inactivity, everything inside the house appears reduced to stillness. The verbs in this stanza communicate either the cessation of activity—*pasaron, dejó*—or passive states of being: *hay, está.* The rain stays outside, a separation indicated by the ever-present parentheses.

Nonetheless, the status quo does not last long. As the poem continues, little things begin to disturb the stillness of the household. Cicadas buzz, a neighbor gets a phone call, the phone rings. And the one clock that actually works throws the speaker into a fright:

> *No obstante el que funciona, espeluzna: son así*
> *estas cosas estas noches (lapsos)*
> *o la luna a franjas por la persiana*
> *o el respaldo en sombras a travesaños*
> *de la silla, en la pared (una reja).*

> *(Nonetheless, the one that works terrifies: that's how,*
> *these things are these nights [lapses]*
> *or the moon in stripes through the blinds*
> *or the shadows across the back*
> *of the chair, on a wall [a grate].)*

Perhaps the best description for the speaker's mindset in these lines is the phrase "a continuous state of alarm." The strong word *espeluzna*, which literally means to make your hair stand on end, not only expresses his apprehension but also reveals anagrammatically the causes of his alarm: *luz* and *luna*. Just as time cannot be made to stand still, the light of the moon cannot be kept out. As the speaker mentions, there are "lapses" in the house's hermeticism, for the shutters in the window have cracks that allow the light to filter in. Were it not for the moon's illumination, the house would be totally dark.

But since the light does come in, what does he do? Does he accept or does he resist what he calls the "visits" and "signals" from the outside?

> *¿Aceptemos?*
> *Personalmente, yo me niego (claro, es un lujo que me*
> *puedo dar yo tengo mi casa) soy*
> *propietario de un chalet de*
> *ladrillos tejado a dos aguas*
> *azotea que si no fuera por los*
> *chapapotes los cuartos de casa*
> *se nos mojaban.*

¿Y?
Seríamos peces sábanas recién blanqueadas seres
  hospitalarios lavados por el
  agua viva que rezuman las
  mamposterías (y qué otra
  cosa tiene uno sino cuatro
  paredes): bien que reflejan
  su sombra en la pared las
  macetas del alféizar la
  begonia florida sobre la
  antigua cómoda Shaker
  del dormitorio.

(Shall we accept?
Personally, I refuse [of course, it's a luxury I
  can afford I have my house] I am
  the owner of a brick chalet
  tiles on two levels
  a roof that if it weren't for all
  the tar the rooms in the house
                would get wet.

And?
We would be fish just-whitened sheets hospitable
  beings washed by the
  running water that drips from
  the masonry [and what else
  does one have but four
  walls]: well does the shadow
  of the flowerpots on the sill
  reflect on the wall the
  flowering begonia on top
  of the old Shaker chest
  in the bedroom.)

These lines are central to Kozer's existential and writerly stance. Although the speaker recognizes that the house is not impermeable, he still opts for enclosure. His reply is unambiguous: "¿Aceptemos? Personalmente, yo me niego" (Shall we accept? Personally, I refuse). The reason for the refusal is that the price of acceptance seems too high. Let the rain come in, he says, and we will all be carried away by the current.

We would become fish, we would lose ourselves. But this imagery cuts two ways, for if on the one hand it suggests homelessness and denaturing, on the other it connotes cleansing and renewal. The same water that drenches also irrigates. Perhaps this is why the speaker quickly stanches the flow of water and returns to a contemplation of the static objects inside the house. With the references to the flowerpot and the chest of drawers, we are back to familiar Kozer territory: an interior space crowded with containers. The speaker's philosophy is summed up in the aside "(y qué otra cosa tiene uno sino cuatro paredes)" ([and what else does one have but four walls]), where the affirmation of immurement is appropriately walled-in between parentheses.

Once the threat from the outside has been averted (or rather, denied) the poem turns sharply inward, ignoring any further external signals. The speaker will now enumerate in loving detail the furnishings and routines that make up life inside those four walls. In its cult of domesticity, "Home Sweet Home" is reminiscent of the Santos Suárez poems; the difference, however, is that the Cuban house was not hermetically sealed. In fact, it welcomed intrusions from the outside: "las coles en las marmitas (todas las puertas abiertas de par en par)" (the cabbages inside the casserole [all the doors wide open]). This line from "Julio" (*BEC*, 30) establishes a counterpoint between enclosure and openness: the cabbages are enclosed inside the pots, but the doors are open to the outside. It is always thus in Estrada Palma 515, Kozer's childhood home. Even when Kozer stresses the disjunction between the Gentile world of the street and the Jewish world of the household, he also highlights the exchanges and negotiations between the two realms. The outside is a source of nourishment, the source of cabbages and kettles. Unlike the family in "Home Sweet Home," the members of the Cuban household move back and forth between the two worlds. A lovely poem about his father concludes:

> *Recuerdas, Sylvia, cuando papá llegaba de los*
> *almacenes de la calle Muralla y todas las mujeres*
> *de la casa Uds. se alborotaban.*
> *Juro que entraba por la puerta de la sala, zapatos de*
> *dos tonos, el traje azul a rayas, la corbata de*
> *óvalos finita*
> *y parecía que papá no hacía nada.*

(Remember, Sylvia, when father used to come from
the big stores on Muralla Street and all the women
of the house, all of you ran to riot.
I swear that when he used to come through the door,
two-tone shoes, blue pin-striped suit, thin oval
stamped tie
it seemed father never did anything.) [14]

By contrast, in "Home Sweet Home" no one enters and no one leaves. This household has none of the lively agitation of the Cuban home. Surrounded by four walls and numberless *cachivaches* (bric-a-brac), the speaker, his wife, and their daughters inhabit a *hortus conclusus*, a paradise for shut-ins. Their lives seem to transpire in silence and in darkness. There is intimacy, but there doesn't seem to be much life. There is peace, but it borders on inertness. The poem ends by describing the parents and the children going to bed.

> . . . *bonito peldaño*
> *que acaba de crujir (supongamos*
> *que duermen) (supongamos que la*
> *maternidad las arrulló) (entra)*
> *(entra) la habitación (nos ajusta).*

> *(. . . pretty stairstep*
> *that just crackled [let's suppose*
> *they sleep] [let's suppose that*
> *maternity lulled them to sleep] [come in]*
> *[come in] the bedroom [surrounds us].)*

As the living room gives way to the bedrooms, the family retreats further into seclusion. Now even parents and children are separated from each other. But in some ways this is a comforting scene, and it is artfully depicted, with parentheses enclosing the verbs of enclosure and the spouses' dormitory caught or cradled in the middle.

I am moved by this poem and I sympathize deeply with the desire to seek relief from bad weather and agitation, to circle the family's wagons and make the world go away. Nonetheless, I am troubled by how easily and repeatedly the outside punctures the domestic bubble. As the last lines suggest, the whole poem is built on "suppositions," which perhaps is another way of saying that it is built on wishful thinking. Just as the speaker "supposes" that his daughters are asleep, he supposes that his four walls insulate and protect the household. But the poem itself tells us that the outside cannot be kept out for very long; that perhaps it cannot be kept out at all. Amplifying on the American commonplace that "a man's home is his castle," the speaker aims to construct an impregnable fortress for himself and his family. But in Spanish a man's home is not a castle but a *casa*; and a *casa* is impregnable in the other sense: capable of being impregnated. There is not enough tar, there are not enough words, to seal all of the cracks.

The paradoxical English-language title already makes this point. The phrase "Home Sweet Home" blurs the distinction between outside and inside, for it renders the commonplace of the home as haven in a "foreign" language, in the language of the society that the poet endeavors to exclude. Even as it names the cloister, the title points to the world that lies beyond it. Characteristically, the speaker does not indicate the location of his home; but he doesn't have to, for "Home Sweet Home" is address enough. Of all of the intrusions from the outside, the English-language title is perhaps the most alarming, since it shows that Kozer's will to live in Spanish cannot be sustained indefinitely. English may not reach into the house itself, but it appears on the lintel or the doormat. After a while, the mother tongue begins to yield before the other tongue. After a while, those alarming intrusions from the outside become the norm. As he goes to bed with his wife, the speaker assumes that his daughters are sleeping peacefully; but perhaps what they are really doing is whispering on the phone to their American boyfriends.

As Kozer's work evolved during the 1970s and 1980s, it began to resemble that closed but not quite hermetic house. The straightforward conversational manner and style of his best early poems—"Te acuerdas, Sylvia," "Julio," or "Santos Suárez, 1956"—have gradually receded before dense, obscure meditations. Because the windows and doors have been closed, these poems transpire among shadows. If Kozer's early poetry was notable for its joyous transparency, his most recent work is notable for its somber hermeticism. His language is as copious as ever, but it has become opaque, foreboding, full of enigmatic images and undecipherable references: not clutter, but murk. Kozer's always long verse-lines swell into verse paragraphs that span a page or more. At its most indulgent, this type of writing turns the poem into a nearly impenetrable wall of words:

La sombra del repartidor de leche nos blanqueaba: los
geranios
   de harina los enjambres de esporas blancas
a su paso: y la espuma creciente de la
palabra leche (un aviso) su llegada: llegó,
consecutivo el cisma de la reproducción
(cuajada, los pechos repletos de semillas
el embrión de los sementales rojos junto
a las madres) se nos llamaba órganos
reproductores: éramos niños a veces
(indistintos) de delantal (amábamos los
tules) alguna mosca muerta hace poco sobre
el ácido encaje de los objetos moribundos,
del aparador: nos llaman. El marbete de la
hoz azul en el resalte de los cuatro platos
con los cuatro tazones a dos asas, falta
alguien: con su bata de felpa roja vierte
la leche hervida tres veces los tazones
dieron las tres oímos el aviso (la oíamos,
llamarnos): y quedaba el vacío en aquel
espacio un nimbo obligatorio encima del
tazón del ausente . . .

(The milk dealer's shadow whitens us: geraniums of
flour
   the swarm of spores white at his step: and
the rising froth of the word milk [warning]
his arrival: he came, following the schism of
reproduction [curdled, breasts full of seed
the breeders' red embryo next to the mothers]
we were called reproductive organs: children
sometimes [indistinct] of apron [we loved the
bulrushes] a fly already dead awhile on
the acrid lace of dead objects, of the
cupboard: they call us. The label a blue
scythe in relief off the four plates with
four cups and two handles, someone's
missing: with her red plush gown she

> boils the milk three times the cups
> signal three we hear the warning [we heard
> her, calling us]: and the empty was left
> in that space obligatory nimbus over
> the cup of the missing . . .)[15]

The uninterrupted column that makes up this poem continues for twenty more lines. Even typographically the poem looks like a wall of words. Although the reader realizes that Kozer is once again talking about his childhood, the setting and the characters are shadowy, indistinct, with the mass of words occluding rather than clarifying. In its puzzling associational drift, the poem itself becomes an "acrid lace of dead objects."

Kozer's early poetry was topical in the sense that it was firmly grounded in a place, even if that place existed only in recollection; but during the eighties his poetry became atopic or utopic, for it seemed to lose its mooring in Santos Suárez. It is not surprising that after so many years the Cuban recollections, whether remembered or invented, should become fuzzy, for as the period of exile lengthens, the old nourishing images lose their sharpness, and the exiled poet begins to lose his place.

What is surprising, perhaps, is that a writer as capacious as Kozer has not made room in his poems for any habitation other than Cuba. Except for an occasional reference, the United States just does not appear in his work. It is striking, for example, that the encompassing gestures of "Gaudeamus" do not allude to Kozer's prolonged residence in this country. After two decades in the United States (the poem was published in 1983), Kozer must be not only Cuban and Jewish and Castilian and Venezuelan and Peruvian, but also a little bit American. Yet it is as if living in this country has no impact on his sense of self. A similar example is his essay "Esto (también) es Cuba, Chaguito," which was published in 1992 and written in the late eighties. This is a fine and revealing essay, but it is also oddly anachronistic, for its point of departure is a promotional slogan that was popular in Cuba during the fifties. The "esto es" is a deictic that should denote proximity, but the world to which it points is distant in time and space. "This is" should really be "that was," for Kozer's Cuba has not existed for decades.

Kozer's hermeticism is part and parcel of his persistent "will to live in Spanish" in a world where such a life is next to impossible. But it's less a question of writing in English than of living in American. Juan Ramón Jiménez never learned English because he thought he was just a man passing through. But the Cuban-American writer who came to this country as a child or young adult and who has done most or all of his writing here is not just passing through. More likely than not, he is here to stay. For him to achieve psychic balance, for him to find his place, *bio* and *grafía* need to make a better fit. They have to understand each other, they have to speak the same language. There are times when residence should precede essence.

After all, this is precisely what one learns from "Gaudeamus" and similar poems. The irony is that Kozer embraces certain kinds of hybridity, certain types of *jolgorio*, only to eschew other kinds. The Cuban-Jewish *ajiaco* is in, but the Cuban-American stew is out. The house in Havana opens out, but the house in New York shuts in. Kozer's poetry is both capacious and cramped. The amount of material that Kozer puts into his poems is matched only by the amount of material that he leaves out. In poem after poem and book after book he has erected an admirable hispanophonic fortress to protect himself from the threat of what he perceives as a hostile "Anglo-Saxon" takeover. In a poem entitled "Legacy," he says, "Quise regir con unos pobres sustantivos los hechos" (I wanted to rule over the facts with a few poor nouns).[16] This statement, which also applies to poems like "Uno de los modos de resarcir las formas" and "Home Sweet Home," captures the exile's need to substitute remembrance for reality, words for things. But as Kozer here recognizes, language is not up to this task. No amount of verbal invention can successfully cover up the fact of displacement. It was Cuba *ayer*, and it may be Havana *mañana*, but it's U.S.A. today. Real feet cannot walk in imaginary gardens. Remembered hurricanes cannot insulate you against oncoming blizzards. Indeed, the more one insists on erecting a house of words, the more visible the cracks in the foundations. He who lives by the word dies by the cliché: "Home Sweet Home."

Perhaps the key is to achieve a balance between the past and the present, between yesterday's Cuba and today's U.S.A., by replacing alarm with alertness. Alertness is alarm without apprehension. To be alert is to be wary rather than worried. The alert individual does not strut blindly into the future, but neither does he hole himself up in the past. This word also has an Italian root, *all'erta*, on the rise or the ascent. Alertness is not a call to arms but a wake-up call. In "Home Sweet Home" everything tends toward sleep; the poem begins with a cessation of activity and ends with the whole family in bed. Alarm and somnolescence are not mutually exclusive. In fact, closing one's eyes may be the definitive way of shutting the world out. But does it work? One can imagine the protagonist of this poem, stirring in his bed, jumping up at every little noise in the house. What if the roof leaks? What if the phone rings? What if someone knocks on the door?

I would replace restless alarm with calm alertness. If one can write well from a state of alarm, one can write even better from a state of alertness. Open your eyes, open your windows, and cautiously welcome the flood. Better acceptance than resistance. Better alert than inert. Better drenched than dry. It may be that getting swept away by the current, going with the flow, is not such a bad thing. In the poem's own terms, the water does not simply blanch, it cleanses. Besides, the danger of blanching, of losing your identity, is exaggerated. There is no discoloration without recoloration. There is no deculturation without reculturation. We are all people of color. You lose one color, one culture, but you gain another. The process is not dying but dyeing, not death but change. Since the water is going to seep in anyway, it may be far healthier to let it soak your pores. Ricky Ricardo once said: You can lead a horse to water, but you can't make him a drink. At their best, Cuban Americans not only lead the horse to water; they make him a *mixed* drink.

Cuban-American culture is a feat and a feast of alertness. Alarm breeds premature closures; it cements exile or abets assimilation. It makes your hair stand on end. But alertness keeps you on your toes, lets you dance the conga without missing a step. Desi is alert, not alarmist. Chirino is alert, not alarmist. The mambo is alert, not alarmist. (Pérez Prado's grunts are wake-up calls.) Life on the hyphen has a price, of course, but for someone who has been in this country as long as many of us have, no amount of Cuban color is going to erase our Carolina blues. And my American horse sense tells me that it's always a good idea to choose what you cannot avoid. *Amor fati*: first a fate, then a feat, then a feast. So embrace otherness, love Lucy, mix it up. Elect what you cannot elude. Opt for attraction, not contraction. Make your home an aviary, not a nest. Make your words a byway, not a wall. Look in, look back, but most of all: Look out!

Conclusion   # LAST-MAMBO-IN-MIAMI

Soy un ajiaco de contradicciones.
I have mixed feelings about everything.
Name your tema, I'll hedge;
name your cerca, I'll straddle it
like a cubano.

I have mixed feelings about everything.
Soy un ajiaco de contradicciones.
Vexed, hexed, complexed,
hyphenated, oxygenated, illegally alienated,
psycho soy, cantando voy:
You say tomato,
I say tu madre;
You say potato,
I say Pototo.
Let's call the hole
un hueco, the thing
a cosa, and if the cosa
goes into the hueco,
consider yourself en casa,
consider yourself part of the family.

(Cuban-American mí:
I singo therefore I am, sí.)

Soy un ajiaco de contradicciones,
un puré de impurezas,
a little square from Rubik's Cuba,
que nadie nunca acoplará.
(Cha-cha-chá.)

Notes

INTRODUCTION

1. Steve Dougherty, "One Step at a Time," *People*, June 25, 1990.

2. Enrique Fernández, "Spitfires, Latin Lovers, Mambo Kings," *New York Times*, April 19, 1992.

3. Desi Arnaz, *A Book* (New York: William Morrow, 1976), 61–62. This claim is not uncontested. In *Rhumba Is My Life* (New York: Didier, 1948), Xavier Cugat also takes credit for having introduced the conga to America (198). So does Arthur Murray, who claims to have brought it over from France (Sylvia G. L. Dannett and Frank R. Rachel, *Down Memory Lane. Arthur Murray's Picture Story of Social Dancing* [New York: Greenberg, 1954], 140)! These assertions need to be taken cautiously, especially given that Arthur Murray also liked to claim that he "created most of the steps used in the rumba" (163). In *The Latin Tinge* (New York: Oxford University Press, 1979), John Storm Roberts points out that by the week of New Year's 1937–1938, which is when Arnaz claimed to have introduced the conga, Eliseo Grenet's "La Conga" had been published in English under the title "Havana Is Calling Me" (82). The publication of a song is something different from the introduction and popularization of a dance, however. The dance instructor Rudolfo D'Avalos has also been credited with introducing the conga (Angela M. Rosanova, *Ballroom Dancing Made Easy* [New York: Vantage, 1954], 84).

4. For a historical overview of the Cuban presence in the United States, see Carlos Ripoll, *Cubans in the United States* (New York: Eliseo Torres, 1987).

5. Rubén G. Rumbaut, "The Agony of Exile: A Study of the Migration and Adaptation of Indochinese Refugee Adults and Children," in *Refugee Children: Theory, Research, and Services*, ed. Frederick L. Ahearn, Jr., and Jean L. Athey (Baltimore: Johns Hopkins University Press, 1991), 61. On the importance of adolescence as a dividing line among immigrants, see also Michael

Piore, *Birds of Passage* (Cambridge: Cambridge University Press, 1979), 65–69.

6. See Ralph Beals, "Acculturation," in *Anthropology Today*, ed. A. L. Kroeber (Chicago: University of Chicago Press, 1953), 621–641; Gonzalo Aguirre Beltrán, *El proceso de aculturación* (Mexico City: Universidad Nacional Autónoma de México, 1957); and Fernando Ortiz, "Del fenómeno social de la transculturación y de su importancia en Cuba," *Revista Bimestre Cubana* 46 (1940): 272–278.

7. Lisandro Pérez, "Cuban Miami," in *Miami Now! Immigration, Ethnicity, and Social Change*, ed. Guillermo J. Grenier and Alex Stepick III (Gainesville: University Press of Florida, 1992), 83–108.

8. Ricardo Pau-Llosa, "Identity and Variations: Cuban Visual Thinking in Exile since 1959," in *Outside Cuba / Fuera de Cuba*, ed. Ileana Fuentes-Pérez, Graciella Cruz Taura, Ricardo Pau-Llosa (New Brunswick: Office of Hispanic Arts, Mason Gross School of the Arts, Rutgers University, 1988), 41.

9. I should perhaps emphasize that I will make no attempt to survey or study Cuban-American literature as a whole. To my mind, Kozer and Hijuelos are the two most significant contemporary Cuban-American writers, but they are not necessarily representative of the dominant tendencies. There are several useful anthologies of Cuban-American literature, including the Spanish-language *Veinte años de literatura cubanoamericana*, ed. Silvia Burunat and Ofelia García (Tempe, Ariz.: Bilingual Review Press, 1988); and the English-language *Cuban American Writers: Los Atrevidos*, ed. Carolina Hospital (Princeton, N.J.: Ediciones Ellas, 1988). We do not yet have a good overall survey of Cuban-American literature. For useful, though partial, studies, see José Sánchez Boudy, *Historia de la literatura cubana en el exilio* (Miami: Ediciones Universal, 1975); Elías Miguel Muñoz, *Desde esta orilla: Poesía cubana en el exilio* (Madrid: Betania, 1988); and Pablo Le Riverend, *Diccionario biográfico de poetas cubanos en el exilio* (Newark, N.J.: Ediciones Q-21, 1988).

10. Jorge Mañach, *Historia y estilo* (Havana: Minerva, 1944), 64.

11. Fernando Ortiz, "Los factores humanos de la cubanidad," *Revista Bimestre Cubana* 21 (1940): 161–186. I have discussed this issue in *The Cuban Condition: Translation and Identity in Modern Cuban Literature* (Cambridge: Cambridge University Press, 1989).

12. Among them I should mention the following, in order of publication: A.J. Jaffe, Ruth M. Cullen, and Thomas D. Boswell, *The Changing Demography of Spanish Americans* (New York: Academic Press, 1980); José Llanes, *Cuban Americans: Masters of Survival* (Cambridge, Mass.: Abt Books, 1982); Thomas D. Boswell and James R. Curtis, *The Cuban-American Experience* (Totowa, N.J.: Rowman and Allanheld, 1984); Alejandro Portes and Robert L. Bach, *Latin Journey: Cuban and Mexican Immigrants in the United States* (Berkeley: University of California Press, 1985); Thomas Weyr, *Hispanic U.S.A.* (New York: Harper and Row, 1988); Alejandro Portes and Rubén G. Rumbaut, *Immi-*

grant America: A Portrait (Berkeley: University of California Press, 1990); and Grenier and Stepick, *Miami Now! Immigration, Ethnicity, and Social Change*. Earl Shorris's *Latinos* (New York: Norton, 1992), which aims at a general audience, is a compendium of errors and misrepresentations (see my review in the *Washington Post Book World*, November 1, 1992).

13. Joan Didion, *Miami* (New York: Simon and Schuster, 1987); David Rieff, *Going to Miami: Exiles, Tourists and Refugees in the New America* (Boston: Little, Brown and Company, 1987). See also T. D. Allman, *Miami, City of the Future* (New York: Atlantic Monthly Press, 1987). A category apart is what one might term documentary fiction about Miami, which includes John Sayles, *Los Gusanos* (New York: HarperCollins, 1991); and Christine Bell, *The Pérez Family* (New York: W. W. Norton, 1990). And then there are also novels about Miami (in Spanish or English) by Cuban exiles. Two notable examples are Celedonio González, *Los cuatro embajadores* (Miami: Ediciones Universal, 1973), which takes its title from a hotel and apartment complex in Miami; and Roberto G. Fernández, *Raining Backwards* (Houston: Arte Público Press, 1988), a satirical look at the mores of Little Havana.

1. I LOVE RICKY

1. There are several accounts of the show's genesis. See Desi Arnaz, *A Book* (New York: William Morrow and Company, 1976), 199–224; Bart Andrews, *The "I Love Lucy" Book* (New York: Doubleday, 1989), 1–33; Jim Brochu, *Lucy in the Afternoon* (New York: Simon and Schuster, 1990), 92–102; Charles Higham, *Lucy: The Real Life of Lucille Ball* (New York: St. Martin's Press, 1986), 101–115; Joe Morella and Edward Z. Epstein, *Forever Lucy: The Life of Lucille Ball* (New York: Berkeley Books, 1986), 81–91; and Max Wilk, *The Golden Years of Television* (New York: Delacorte Press, 1976), 246–256. Two recent biographies are Warren G. Harris, *Lucy & Desi* (New York: Simon and Schuster, 1991); and Coyne Steven Sanders and Tom Gilbert, *Desilu: The Story of Lucille Ball and Desi Arnaz* (New York: William Morrow, 1993).

2. "Why Millions Love Lucy," *New York Times Magazine*, March 1, 1953.

3. Other sitcoms emulated the title of *I Love Lucy: I Married Joan* (1952–1955), starring Joan Davis and Jim Backus; *I Dream of Jeannie* (1965–1970), with Barbara Eden and Larry Hagman; and *I Married Dora* (1987–1988), with Daniel Hugh-Kelly and Cuban-born Elizabeth Peña. In all of these cases the "I" refers to the male member of the couple, but the show's protagonist, its real subject, is the female.

4. The following essays and books all deal, at least in part, with the series: Alexander Doty, "The Cabinet of Lucy Ricardo: Lucille Ball's Star Image," *Cinema Journal* 29, no. 4 (Summer 1990): 3–22; Joann Gardner, "Self-Referentiality in Art: A Look at Three Television Situation-Comedies of the

1950s," *Studies in Popular Culture* 11, no. 1 (1988): 35–50; Gerard Jones, *Honey, I'm Home. Sitcoms: Selling the American Dream* (New York: Grove Weidenfeld, 1992); David Marc, *Comic Visions: Television Comedy and American Culture* (Boston: Unwin Hyman, 1989); Diana M. Meehan, *Ladies of the Evening: Women Characters in Prime-Time Television* (Metuchen, N.J.: Scarecrow Press, 1983), 21–26; Patricia Mellencamp, "Situation and Simulation: An Introduction to *I Love Lucy*," *Screen* 26 (1985): 30–40; Patricia Mellencamp, "Situation Comedy, Feminism, and Freud: Discourses of Gracie and Lucy," in *Studies in Entertainment: Critical Approaches to Mass Culture*, ed. Tania Modlevski (Bloomington: Indiana University Press, 1986), 80–95; Patricia Mellencamp, *High Anxiety* (Bloomington: Indiana University Press, 1992); John Carlos Rowe, "Metavideo: Fictionality and Mass Culture in a Postmodern Economy," in *Intertextuality and Contemporary American Fiction*, ed. Patrick O'Donnell and Robert Con Davis (Baltimore: Johns Hopkins University Press, 1989), 214–235; Lauren Rabinovitz, "Television Criticism and American Studies," *American Quarterly* 43 (1991): 358–370; and Lynn Spigel, *Make Room for TV* (Chicago: University of Chicago Press, 1992). Although many of these studies are useful, some are hampered by an insufficient acquaintance with the show. Thus, for example, John Carlos Rowe finds it significant that Lucy and Ricky move to a suburb in California and states that little Ricky was played by Desi, Jr. (222). In fact the Ricardos moved to a suburb in Connecticut (how could Ricky have commuted from California to his nitery in New York?) and Desi Arnaz, Jr., never played little Ricky, who was played mostly by Richard Keith. About Ricky and Lucy's move to California, Rowe concludes: "The suburban homeliness of the family in California thinly disguises the aristocratic pretensions of the upwardly mobile Ricardos. . . . Ricky and Lucy assume their status as the new, postmodern aristocrats, prefiguring such economically powerful celebrities in our own decade as Bill Cosby and Michael Landon" (222). As Ricky might say: "¡Ay, ay, ay, ay, ay!"

5. In Allen L. Woll and Randall M. Miller's survey of Hispanic characters in American film and television, Ricky Ricardo is not mentioned at all. See "Hispanic Americans" in Woll and Miller, *Ethnic and Racial Images in American Film and Television* (New York: Garland Publishing, 1987), 243–251.

6. This and the following statistics come from various publications by Bart Andrews, who has practically made a career of chronicling the series. His *The "I Love Lucy" Book*, which contains an episode-by-episode synopsis of the series, is an indispensable guide to the program. Andrews's books include *Lucy & Ricky & Fred & Ethel: The Story of "I Love Lucy"* (New York: E. P. Dutton, 1976); (with Thomas J. Watson) *Loving Lucy* (New York: St. Martin's Press, 1980); and *The "I Love Lucy" Book*.

7. Bart Andrews, "Lucy Ricardo," *Special Report: The 50 Most Influential TV Characters* (May–July, 1991), 13.

8. Andrews, *Lucy & Ricky & Fred & Ethel*, 5.

9. Jack Sher and Madeline Sher, "The Cuban and the Redhead," *American Magazine* 154 (September 1952): 100.

10. Cecilia Ager, "Desilu, or from Gags to Riches," *New York Times*, April 20, 1958.

11. In 1952, when one of Adlai Stevenson's political speeches preempted an *I Love Lucy* episode, Stevenson received a letter saying: "I love Lucy, I like Ike, drop dead." This anecdote comes from Erik Barnouw, *Tube of Plenty* (New York: Oxford University Press, 1975), 210.

12. Ricky's difficulties with English echo those of Desi Arnaz, who had a sign on his dressing room door that said, "English is broken here." I will refer to the episodes by title and date of original broadcast.

13. This number was included in one of the first episodes of the series, "The Diet" (October 29, 1951).

14. The first recorded usage of the term "ethnicity" apparently occurs in 1953; see Werner Sollors, *Beyond Ethnicity* (New York: Oxford University Press, 1986), 22.

15. These were the writers' code words for Lucy's patented expressions. When the script called for Lucy to react in a certain way, the writers just wrote in the code word for the desired facial expression. See Andrews, *The "I Love Lucy" Book*, 158.

16. This piece is included in the compilation *Lucy's Lost Episodes* (Good Times Home Video Corp., 1989). There may well have been some real personal animosity underlying this comic exchange, since Desi Arnaz, in the rough draft of his autobiography, includes Bob Hope in a list of men with whom he thinks Lucille Ball had an affair during their marriage. The list was deleted from the published version of *A Book*.

17. Mellencamp, "Situation and Simulation," 34.

18. Mikhail Bakhtin, *Rabelais and His World*, trans. Hélène Iswolsky (Cambridge, Mass.: M.I.T. Press, 1968), 7. Bakhtin states: "In fact, carnival does not know footlights, in the sense that it does not acknowledge any distinction between actors and spectators. Footlights would destroy a carnival, as the absence of footlights would destroy a theatrical performance. Carnival is not a spectacle seen by the people; they live in it, and everyone participates because its very idea embraces all the people. While carnival lasts, there is no other life outside it. During carnival time life is subject only to its laws, that is, the laws of its own freedom."

19. David Marc, *Comic Visions: Television Comedy and American Culture* (Boston: Unwin Hyman, 1989), 59.

20. It is important to stress that Ricky's role is no less fixed than Lucy's. If Lucy is incompetent in the nightclub, Ricky is incompetent in the home. Thus, it is only partially true, as Marc suggests, that the episodes highlight Lucy's incompetence (*Comic Visions*, 93). Not infrequently Lucy is the one who "wins." In "The Audition" (November 19, 1951), for example, it is she who gets the TV contract; in "Home Movies" (March 1, 1954), it is her movie that is

called a work of genius; in "Lucy Tells the Truth" (November 9, 1953), she wins the bet and Ricky pays up; in "Equal Rights" (October 26, 1953), Ricky agrees to equal rights. The point seems to be that both Lucy and Ricky should stick to what they know best. Thus, when Ricky and Fred try to bake a cake, the results are no less funny than when Lucy tries to sing opera. Lastly, even if the episodes stress Lucy's shortcomings more than Ricky's, this emphasis is all but negated by the viewer's awareness that, time after time, Lucy steals the show. It is difficult to overlook Lucille Ball's enormous skill at acting incompetent. As Patricia Mellencamp points out, "if Lucy's plots for ambition and fame narratively failed, with the result that she was held, often gratefully, to domesticity, performatively they succeeded" ("Situation Comedy, Feminism, and Freud," 88).

21. The new furniture was occasionally written into the episodes, as in "Redecorating" (November 24, 1952) or "Lucy Wants New Furniture" (June 1, 1953). After little Ricky's birth, the Ricardos moved to a "larger" apartment, but the only change in the living room was the addition of a curtained window ("The Ricardos Change Apartments," May 18, 1953).

22. Although some of the material in the pilot was incorporated into one of the first season's shows ("The Audition"), the pilot itself was not shown on television until recently. Supposedly Desi kept a print of the pilot under his bed until the day he died. In the pilot Lucy and Desi played themselves, since the characters of Lucy and Ricky Ricardo did not exist yet. Although the Ricardos "moved" to a bigger apartment after little Ricky was born, little Ricky's room was seldom shown.

23. Victor Turner, *Dramas, Fields, and Metaphors* (Ithaca: Cornell University Press, 1974), 13.

24. In the movie *The Mambo Kings* Club Babalú is the name of the club where the Castillo brothers perform.

25. Ricky's full name was Ricardo Alberto Fernando Ricardo y Acha ("Hollywood Anniversary," April 4, 1955). De Acha was actually Desi's matronymic; Alberto was his middle name. Of the characters in the show, only Fred allows Ricky a more grown-up variant of his name by calling him Rick. It is not surprising that Fred would address Ricky differently, for in some ways Fred is a paternal figure. Ricky and Fred have several things in common. Like Ricky, Fred had a show business career (as part of the "Kurtz and Mertz" duo in vaudeville); unlike Ricky, he has retired from show business and settled into a life of domesticity. In this sense Fred is a harbinger of Ricky's future; when Ricky buys the Tropicana, he becomes a property owner like Fred. At the same time, however, Fred collaborates with Ricky to resist domesticity (and even domestication). His calling him "Rick" may be part of this effort, as is their joint opposition to Lucy and Ethel's many schemes.

26. Michael Fisher, "Ethnicity and the Post-Modern Arts of Memory," in *Writing Culture: The Poetics and Politics of Ethnography*, ed. James Clifford and George E. Marcus (Berkeley: University of California Press, 1986), 194–233.

27. The Brazilian standard "Mamãe Eu Quero," of which there is also a popular Spanish version, was a mainstay of Miranda's act; it was one of the first songs she recorded upon her arrival in the United States in the late thirties and she sang it in her first Hollywood movie, *Down Argentine Way* (1940). In Carmen Miranda's last film, *Scared Stiff* (1953), Jerry Lewis, wearing a *baiana* and five-inch platform shoes, lip-syncs "Mamãe Eu Quero," but whereas Lucy's mimicry is funny, Lewis's is only grotesque. Although Carmen Miranda never appeared on *I Love Lucy*, she and the Arnazes had a friendship that went back to their Hollywood days in the forties, when Miranda was a frequent visitor at their apartment. By 1951 Miranda's career was nearly over; she died only a few years after this episode was filmed, in August 1955. There is an informative biography of Carmen Miranda in English by Martha Gil-Montero, *Brazilian Bombshell: The Biography of Carmen Miranda* (New York: Donald I. Fine, 1989). For a lucid discussion of Miranda's films, see Ana M. López, "Are All Latins From Manhattan?: Hollywood, Ethnography, and Cultural Colonialism," in *Unspeakable Images: Ethnicity and the American Cinema*, ed. Lester D. Friedman (Urbana: University of Illinois Press, 1991), 404–424.

28. See Jack Burton, *The Blue Book of Hollywood Musicals* (New York: Century House), 140. Under the title "I Want My Mama," Al Stillman provided English lyrics for the song.

29. This is not the first time, however, that Carmen Miranda is taken for Cuban. In *Weekend in Havana* (1941), she plays the part of Rosita Rivas, a Cuban entertainer. When Lucy impersonates Ricky's mother, she is playing the part of Carmen Miranda playing the part of Rosita Rivas.

30. The program's emblem was inspired by a heart-shaped diamond lapel watch that Desi gave Lucy for her twenty-ninth birthday a few weeks after they met.

31. Arnaz, *A Book,* 270.

32. An important difference between Ricky and Danny, however, is that, since Danny did not have an accent, another way to highlight his "ethnicity" had to be found. This may be why *Make Room for Daddy* included Danny's very Lebanese Uncle Tonoose as a recurring character: Uncle Tonoose is Danny's accent. *I Love Lucy* needed no such character because Ricky's accent spoke for itself.

33. The lyric, written by Harold Adamson, runs in its entirety:

> *I Love Lucy and she loves me.*
> *We're as happy as two can be.*
> *Sometimes we quarrel but then,*
> *oh, how we love making up again.*
>
> *Lucy kisses like no one can.*
> *She's my missus and I'm her man.*
> *And life is heaven you see,*
> *'cause I love Lucy, I love Lucy, and Lucy loves me.*

This and other songs by Arnaz are available in *Babalú Music!* (Columbia 48507, 1991); also in *The Best of Desi Arnaz* (BMG 66031–2, 1992).

2. THE MAN WHO LOVED LUCY

1. Bob Hope speaks this line to Ricky/Desi during a skit on Hope's television show, included in *Lucy's Lost Episodes* (Good Times Home Video Corp., 1989).

2. In 1974 Arnaz attempted a comeback to television with a pilot entitled "Dr. Domingo," about a small-town doctor who moonlighted as the local coroner. The pilot was an episode in the *Ironsides* series, but it didn't sell.

3. The most famous example of this was the birth of little Ricky on Monday, January 19, 1953, which was timed to coincide with that of little Desi (Lucy delivered via cesarean, so the date for the delivery was set on a Monday, the day the show came on). But there are many, many others. For example, both the Arnazes and the Ricardos were married in Connecticut in November 1940. Lucy was Desi's pet name for Lucille. In "The Moustache" (March 3, 1952), Ricky shows a talent scout Desi's scrapbook, explaining that he, Ricky, got his start on Broadway in a show called *Too Many Girls*, which of course was Desi's Broadway show and later his first movie. As noted in the last chapter, even the show's logo was based on a heart-shaped lapel watch that Desi gave Lucy back in 1940, shortly after they started going together.

4. Desi Arnaz, *A Book* (New York: William Morrow and Company, 1976), 9. Other page references are given in the text.

5. John Carlos Rowe, "Metavideo: Fictionality and Mass Culture in a Postmodern Economy," in *Intertextuality and Contemporary American Fiction*, ed. Patrick O'Donnell and Robert Con Davis (Baltimore: Johns Hopkins University Press, 1989), 222.

6. In the liner notes to *The Best of Desi Arnaz* (BMG 66031–2, 1992).

7. For more on the *vivo*, see my *The Cuban Condition* (London: Cambridge University Press, 1989), chap. 2.

8. Quoted in Penny Stallings, *Forbidden Channels* (New York: Harper Perennials, 1991), 101. Lucy once remarked: "If I'd stayed mad at every woman Desi had an affair with, I'd have been angry with half of the nicest girls in Hollywood." Quoted in Jim Brochu, *Lucy in the Afternoon* (New York: Pocket Books, 1990), 144.

9. Cugat, who later took credit for "the making of Desi Arnaz," describes Arnaz as "a young, mild-mannered, handsome Cuban from Santiago" who "had a talent that matched his exuberance" (*Rhumba Is My Life* [New York: Didier, 1948], 118). Arnaz gives an account of his early years in the United States in "America Has Been Good To Me," *American Magazine* 159 (February 1955): 22–23, 82–87.

10. Arnaz, *A Book*, 132–133. In 1940 *Variety* described Arnaz as RKO's "prospect for buildup to star billing" ("Films' Latin-American Cycle Finds Congarhumba Displacing Swing Music," *Variety*, November 6, 1940).

11. "*Too Many Girls*," *Time*, November 11, 1940.

12. Bosley Crowther, "*Too Many Girls*," *New York Times*, November 21, 1940.

13. Philip T. Hartung, "*The Navy Comes Through*," *Commonweal*, November 17, 1942.

14. Arnaz, *A Book*, 145.

15. Arnaz, *A Book*, 164.

16. "*Cuban Pete*," *Variety*, July 22, 1946.

17. In the forties Arnaz also made several film shorts—with titles like *Jitter-rhumba*—which were essentially excerpts from his nightclub act.

18. "*Holiday in Havana*," *Variety*, October 5, 1949.

19. Touzet is a Cuban composer of boleros (and other music) who in the late forties was briefly a member of Arnaz's orchestra. He appears in the movie as one of the band's two piano players (the other is, of course, Marco Rizo).

20. Valdés recorded "Babalú" with Xavier Cugat's orchestra in 1941, several years before Arnaz, who did not include this song in his repertoire until after the war (see John Storm Roberts, *The Latin Tinge* [New York: Oxford University Press, 1979], 108; Arnaz, *A Book*, 164). "Babalú" (most often written "Ba-Ba-Lu") was also featured in movies like *Pan-Americana* (1945) and *Variety Time* (1948).

21. On the Latin American musical, see Allen Woll, *The Hollywood Musical Goes to War* (Chicago: Nelson-Hall, 1983), 105–120. Some of this same material is also included in Woll's earlier *The Latin Image in American Film* (Los Angeles: UCLA Latin American Center Publications, 1977).

22. It is a curious coincidence that in *Moonlight in Havana* William Frawley, who later became Fred Mertz, played the part of the owner of a Havana nightclub.

23. According to film historians Jay Robert Nash and Stanley Ralph Ross, a young Fidel Castro appears in several crowd scenes during this movie. See *The Motion Picture Guide, 1923–1983* (Chicago: Cinebooks, 1986), 1252.

24. Allen Woll, in his indispensable *The Latin Image in American Film*, exaggerates somewhat when he states that "the performers from South America rarely managed to marry the hero or the heroine" (63). There's no question that maraca musicals are ethnocentric, but they are actually fairly democratic when it comes to intercultural romance. César Romero, Desi Arnaz, Fernando Lamas, and Ricardo Montalbán did often wind up with the girl.

25. Lucy Ricardo's mother would have agreed. When she hears that Ricky is being hailed in Hollywood as a new Valentino, she remarks that Ricky "couldn't hold the edge of his [Valentino's] burnoose" ("California Here We Come," January 10, 1955). But Mrs. Trumbull, the Ricardos' neighbor, has a differ-

ent view: "I used to be a Rudolph Valentino fan," she says, "now I'm a Ricky Ricardo fan" ("Homecoming," November 7, 1955).

26. Richard Griffith and Arthur Mayer, *The Movies* (New York: Simon and Schuster, 1957), 141.

27. On the type of the caballero, see Arthur G. Petitt, *Images of the Mexican American in Fiction and Film* (College Station: Texas A&M University Press, 1980), 138–140. The best-known example of the caballero occurs, oddly enough, in Walt Disney's feature-length cartoon *The Three Caballeros* (1945).

28. Basil Woon, *When It's Cocktail Time in Cuba* (New York: Horace Liveright, 1928). As Woon's title indicates, Cuba's appeal was enhanced by the passage of the Halstead Act in 1919. Another of Woon's chapters is called "Where Everyone Is Drinking and Not a Soul Is Drunk!" Cuban time was cocktail time, and it's always cocktail time in Cuba.

29. Helen Lawrenson, "Latins Are Lousy Lovers," *Esquire*, 6, no. 4 (October 1936): 36–37, 198; reprinted in Lawrenson, *Latins Are Still Lousy Lovers* (New York: Hawthorn Books, 1968), 23–32. Page references are given in the text.

30. In Valentino's first hit movie, *The Four Horsemen of the Apocalypse* (based on a popular novel by the Spaniard Vicente Blasco Ibáñez), Valentino plays a gaucho and does a hot tango with Helena Domingues. Before becoming an actor, Valentino worked as a *danseur mondain* at a tango bar in New York. On the "Mediterranean" Latin lover, see Woll, *The Latin Image in American Film*, 23. This is not to say, of course, that the screen's Latin lovers were genuinely "Latin." Ricardo Cortes's real name was Jake Stein. The other "Cuban" lover was César Romero, who claims to be José Martí's New York–born grandson, and who also played a comic and harmless blade. Romero achieved greatest fame in such movies as *Viva Cisco Kid* (1940) and *The Gay Caballero* (1940), where he did not play Cubans. For a perceptive discussion of Valentino and his epigones, see Joan Mellen, *Big Bad Wolves: Masculinity in the American Film* (New York: Pantheon, 1977), 51–55.

31. I am referring here to the American rumba, which is actually the American name for the Cuban *son*. The Cuban *rumba* is an entirely different story.

32. The title of one of the songs in Cole Porter's *Let's Face It* (1943).

33. Jack Gould, "Why Millions Love Lucy," *New York Times Magazine*, March 1, 1953.

34. This is not the first time that a Desi Arnaz character has vehicular problems. In *Holiday in Havana* Carlos also makes a cross-country trip (but in a different country) when he has to drive the beat-up band bus from one end of the island to the other. The bus's mechanical problems combined with Carlos's lack of experience as a driver make for an eventful trip.

35. "*The Long, Long Trailer,*" *Commonweal*, March 5, 1954. Bosley Crowther, who never liked any of Arnaz's movies, was less witty but no less caus-

tic: "[*The Long, Long Trailer*] is an hour and a half of the sort of nonsense you might get in one good, fast Lucy show . . . And there isn't much peril that the sequence of adventures will be mistaken as drama on any but the lowest slapstick plane" ("*The Long, Long Trailer*," *New York Times*, February 19, 1954). Other reviews, however, were more positive. *Time* called it a "a wonderfully slap-happy farce" ("*The Long, Long Trailer*," *Time*, February 22, 1954); *Saturday Review* thought it was a "very funny" movie that should dissuade anyone from purchasing a trailer (Hollis Alpert, "SR Goes to the Movies," *Saturday Review*, February 20, 1954); and *Newsweek* concluded that the comedy was so well done that it made "Mack Sennett look, in retrospect, like a reticent disciple of Ibsen" ("*The Long, Long Trailer*," *Newsweek*, February 8, 1954). Vincente Minnelli, who was the director, has some interesting remarks on the making of the movie in his memoir *I Remember It Well* (Garden City: Doubleday and Company, 1974), 275–278. Historically *The Long, Long Trailer* is significant because it marked the first time that actors who had become famous on television crossed over to the "big screen." Until then the cross-over was always in the opposite direction: fading movie actors or actresses (like Lucille Ball) attempted to turn their fame as motion picture stars into success on television. MGM was originally lukewarm about the Arnaz-Ball "vehicle" for fear that audiences would not be willing to pay for what they could get at home for free.

36. The movie's incoherence was pointed out by several reviewers. See John McCarten, "Woe and Insecticide," *New Yorker*, February 18, 1956; also "*Forever, Darling*," *Time*, March 12, 1956; and "Any Way You Spell It," *Newsweek*, February 13, 1956.

37. This scene also resonates with Lucy and Desi's own troubled marriage. When Larry laments that he and Susie have drifted apart, one feels that his words apply equally well to Lucy and Desi, whose marriage by 1956 was also on the rocks. In this light, *Forever, Darling* is a cruelly ironic title.

38. Tracy Johnston, "A Book," *New York Times Book Review*, January 25, 1976.

39. Respectively, "A Book," *Publishers Weekly*, December 8, 1975; and Johnston, "A Book," 29.

40. Eva Hoffman, *Lost in Translation* (New York: Penguin Books, 1989), 186.

41. In this sense, *A Book* weaves together two different first-person genres, the immigrant autobiography and the erotic memoir. As an erotic memoir, it is related to such Cuban classics as Carlos Loveira's *Juan Criollo* (1927) and Guillermo Cabrera Infante's *La Habana para un infante difunto* (1979).

42. Jean Starobinski, "The Style of Autobiography," in *Autobiography: Essays Theoretical and Critical*, ed. James Olney (Princeton: Princeton University Press, 1980), 82.

43. As quoted in Warren G. Harris, *Lucy & Desi* (New York: Simon and Schuster, 1991), 302–303.

3. A BRIEF HISTORY OF MAMBO TIME

1. "Hey Mambo," a duet by Manilow and Kid Creole, in Manilow's *Swing Street* (Arista AL-8527, 1987).

2. See Ed Regis, *Great Mambo Chicken and the Transhuman Condition: Science On the Edge* (Reading, Mass.: Addison-Wesley, 1990).

3. "La música popular cubana," *Signos* 2, no. 3 (May–August 1971): 12.

4. Fernando Ortiz, *Los bailes y el teatro de los negros en el folklore de Cuba* (Havana: Publicaciones del Ministerio de Educación, 1951), 80.

5. Fernando Ortiz, *La Africanía de la música folklórica de Cuba* (Havana: Publicaciones del Ministerio de Educación, 1950), 232–233, 241. See also Lydia Cabrera, *El monte* (Havana: Ediciones C.R., 1954), 127; and Robert Farris Thompson, *Flash of the Spirit* (New York: Random House, 1982), 110–111. Although a fair amount has been written on the mambo, there is no full-fledged discussion of the subject. For many years Robert Farris Thompson has been promising a book on the mambo that will surely be the most thorough and perceptive discussion of the topic that we have. The best general introduction in English is John Storm Roberts, *The Latin Tinge* (New York: Oxford University Press, 1979). Also very informative is Isabelle Leymarie's "Salsa and Latin Jazz," in *Hot Sauces: Latin and Caribbean Pop*, ed. Billy Bergman (New York: Quill, 1985), 95–115. In Spanish there are three useful histories of popular Cuban music: Cristóbal Díaz Ayala, *Música cubana del Areyto a la Nueva Trova* (San Juan, Puerto Rico: Editorial Cubanacán, 1981); Natalio Galán, *Cuba y sus sones* (Valencia: Pre-Textos, 1983); and Elena Pérez Sanjurjo, *Historia de la música cubana* (Miami: La Moderna Poesía, 1986). Of these three, Galán—an accomplished musician and composer in his own right—is the most insightful and lively.

6. Although Natalio Galán attributes this composition to Orestes López's brother, "Cachao," this seems to be an error. In an interview with Cachao I conducted in August 1990, he confirmed that it was his brother who composed "Mambo." Odilio Urfé gives 1935 as the date of composition, although he adds that the piece was not played with any regularity until 1939 ("Danzón, mambo y chachachá," *Revolución y Cultura* 77 [January 1979]: 57). See also Rosa Ileana Boudet, "Arcaño y Sus Maravillas," *Revolución y Cultura* 25 (September 1974): 33–35. Because Orestes stayed in Cuba after the Revolution but Cachao left, accounts of their contributions are sometimes distorted by politics. Although Cachao is himself an important composer and arranger (particularly known for the *descargas* or jam sessions he recorded in the fifties), he is hardly ever mentioned in post-1959 writings emanating from Cuba. Orestes López, in a 1976 interview with Leonardo Acosta, says nothing about his brother's existence, let alone his musical contributions to Arcaño's band (Leonardo Acosta, *Del tambor al sintetizador* [Havana: Editorial Letras Cubanas, 1983], 43–50).

7. "La primera persona que yo le oí decir la palabra mambo fue a Arsenio Rodríguez. Arsenio se ponía a tocar y en cierto momento durante la pieza miraba para atrás y le decía a los dos trompetas '¡mambo! ¡mambo!' Y entonces los trompetas se ponían de acuerdo y salía la primera frase, que es lo que llaman diablo y después mambo. El mambo o diablo es una inspiración natural sin arreglo ninguno" (The first person from whom I heard the word "mambo" was Arsenio Rodríguez. Arsenio started to play and at some point during the piece he looked back and he said to his two trumpet players, "Mambo! Mambo!" And then the trumpet players would get together and make the first phrase, which came to be called *diablo* and then mambo. The mambo or *diablo* is a natural inspiration without any arrangement; Rolando Laserie, interview with the author, Miami, Florida, August 14, 1990). René Touzet's recollections agree with Laserie's: "El mambo la primera vez que se oyó fue en la orquesta de Arsenio Rodríguez. Lo de Arcaño no era mambo, era danzón" (The first time the mambo was heard was in the orchestra of Arsenio Rodríguez. Arcaño's was not a mambo, it was a *danzón*; René Touzet, interview with the author, Miami, Florida, August 13, 1990).

8. Manuel Cuéllar Vizcaíno, "La revolución del mambo," *Bohemia* 40, no. 2 (May 30, 1948): 20–21, 97–99.

9. "Todos los músicos, con excepción del bajista y del tumbador, están autorizados para hacer lo que les dé su real gana, inspirándose o improvisando aires a la diabla, de modo que se establece lo que llamaríamos una caprichosa e informal conversación entre el piano, la flauta, el violín, el güiro, el timbal y el cencerro, mientras el bajo y la tumbadora regañan rítmicamente como para poner la casa en orden."

10. Odilio Urfé, "La verdad sobre el mambo," *Inventario* 1, no. 2 (May 1948): 12.

11. "Para que se produzca el mambo se requiere fundamentalmente que todos, absolutamente todos los que participan en su formación, toquen de manera distinta a lo que tienen escrito. Más claro, todos deben de ejecutar lo que no está escrito dentro de lo que está escrito. Para obtener un genuino mambo los instrumentistas deben emplear solamente en el 'clímax' o 'nudo' efectos rítmicos. Ritmo contra ritmo. Nada de tonadas ni melodías definidas. No debe haber ritmo fijo en ningún instrumento" (Urfé, "La verdad sobre el mambo," 12).

12. Ortiz, *La Africanía de la música folklórica de Cuba*, 246.

13. Quoted in Cuéllar Vizcaíno, "La revolución del mambo," 97.

14. Earl Leaf's *Isles of Rhythm*, also published in 1948, gives a long list of Cuban rhythms—*rumba, conga, son, danzón, danzonete, guaracha, guajira, zapateo, bolero, pregón*—but makes no mention of the mambo. Leaf does mention that in voodoo rituals the priestess is called "mambo," but makes no connection to Afro-Cuban music or ritual. See Leaf, *Isles of Rhythm* (New York: A. S. Barnes and Company, 1948), 41–56. The composer Bobby Collazo traces the mambo's

popularity in Havana back to the end of 1946; see his *La última noche que pasé contigo* (Puerto Rico: Editorial Cubanacán, 1987), 264. Writing in 1950, however, Juan J. Remos remarks that the mambo is a "new form" that has just "irrupted" on the scene in Cuba ("La virtud del mambo," *Diario de la Marina*, December 27, 1950). To this day "mambo" also remains the term for a part of an arrangement, which explains why many songs that are not mambos in the strict sense (most of them are *guarachas* or *sones*) nevertheless carry this label. The continuing appeal of the word has turned the mambo into something like an all-purpose salsa.

15. Galán, *Cuba y sus sones*, 342. With the current popularity of the mambo, several other claimants for the title of "mambo king" have appeared, notably Machito, Mario Bauzá, and Tito Puente. Even Desi Arnaz, who never played a mambo in his life, has now been dubbed, for marketing purposes, the "mambo king."

16. Different sources give varying years of birth for Pérez Prado, ranging from 1916 to 1921. I am following here Helio Oronio's *Diccionario de la música cubana* (Havana: Editorial Letras Cubanas, 1981), 32.

17. "Estoy preparando un estilo musical nuevo que creo que va a gustar mucho: el 'son mambo.' El primer número lo titularé 'Pavolla.' Ya sólo falta un 'pase' al piano y, tal vez, alguna corrección. La firma Vda. de Humara y Lastra está esperándolo como cosa buena para grabarlo y lanzarlo al mercado. Vamos a ver qué sale de ahí." This interview is reproduced in Betancourt's *Apuntes para la historia* (San Juan, Puerto Rico: Ramallo Bros. Printing, 1986), 110–113. I have not been able to find "Pavolla" within Pérez Prado's extensive discography. In the interview Pérez Prado reports that Desi Arnaz "is a great guy who loves Cuba a lot."

18. Rolando Laserie tells the amusing anecdote that Cuban musicians, especially trumpet players, were afraid of Pérez Prado because of the difficulty of his trumpet parts: "Pérez Prado era un artista muy moderno y había que ser muy buen músico para trabajar con él. Sobre todo los trompetas, porque les ponía muchas notas altas que eran difíciles de tocar. Los músicos en Cuba veían llegar a Pérez Prado y decían: 'Dios mío, ahí viene Beethoven,' porque él fue el Beethoven del mambo" (Pérez Prado was a very modern artist and you had to be a very good musician to work with him. Especially the trumpet players, because he gave them many high notes that were difficult to play. In Cuba when musicians saw Pérez Prado coming they used to say, "My God, here comes Beethoven," because he was the Beethoven of mambo; Laserie, interview with the author, Miami, Florida, August 14, 1990).

19. See Nat Hentoff, "Mambo Rage Latest in Latin Dance Line," *Down Beat*, December 1, 1954.

20. Ralph J. Gleason, "Prado's New Mambo Is Sweeping the Americas," *Dancing Star*, 2, no. 3 (January 1952): 4, 16.

21. Robert Farris Thompson, "Mambo with Pantomime," *Dance* 32, no. 6 (June 1958): 68.

22. For an enlightening discussion of Pérez Prado's orchestra, see Acosta, *Del tambor al sintetizador*, 49. See also Díaz Ayala, *Música cubana*, 194–195.

23. Pérez Prado drew attention to the importance of the trumpet and sax parts: "The interpretation of the mambo is based on the saxophones. They carry the basic rhythm pattern. The rhythm section accentuates that pattern and the brass has a number of variable functions it can perform. The brass can sing out the pure melody over the saxes and rhythm; the brass can play contrapuntal lines against the sax lines; the brass can just accentuate rhythmically the figures the saxes are playing; or you can switch and have the brass carry the rhythm pattern while the saxes play the melody" (as quoted in Nat Hentoff, "Prado Tells How Mambo Made It But Not How He Makes It Tick," *Down Beat*, December 1, 1954).

24. Roberts, *The Latin Tinge*, 128.

25. Respectively, from "El Mambo," *Newsweek*, September 4, 1950; "Mambo King," *Ebony* 6 (September 1951): 46; Marshall Stearns, *The Story of Jazz* (New York: Oxford University Press, 1956), 182; and Bill Smith, "Pérez Prado Ork," *Billboard*, August 7, 1954. His grunting is the subject of the mambo number in the movie *Damn Yankees* (1958), "Who's got the pain when they do the mambo?"

26. *Dilo (Ugh!)* became the title of one of his records (RCA Victor LPM 1883, 1958); for Pérez Prado's explanation, see Oscar Berliner, "Latin Americana," *Down Beat*, January 22, 1955. In the liner notes to *Dilo*, Watson Wilie remarks tongue in cheek (I think), "Not the least intriguing aspect of Prado's musical war cry is how he manages to make 'Dilo!' sound like 'Ugh!' The exact technique is his own secret, but it would appear to the analytic ear that he accomplishes this transition by removing the vowels and the consonants from the word before exhaling."

27. The songs labeled "rumbas" or "rhumbas" in the United States are, for the most part, *sones*. The Cuban *rumba* is only distantly related to its American namesake. I will distinguish the Cuban *rumba* from the American rumba by putting the former in italics.

28. Referring to "Cherry Pink," the rock historian Arnold Shaw says, "replete with low, throbbing, pedal tones in the trombones, high flying trumpets, cowbells, and grunts, it was a mambo—a Latin dance that was to the rumba what the jitterbug was to the fox trot" (*The Rocking '50s* [New York: Hawthorn Books, 1974], 123). Nonetheless, grunts and cowbells do not a mambo make.

29. Alejo Carpentier, *Ese músico que llevo dentro*, 3 vols. (Havana: Editorial Letras Cubanas, 1980), 2:344. In his three-volume compilation of musical journalism, Carpentier mentions Pérez Prado or the mambo only one other time

when he remarks, perhaps condescendingly, "Me encanta cierta música popular urbana, tan llena, a veces, de auténtica gracia. Me gusta la melodía de 'Silbando el mambo' de Pérez Prado, y también la canción—tan insinuante, indolente—de 'La balandra Isabel'" (I love a certain Cuban popular music, so filled, at times, with authentic grace. I like the melody of "Silbando el mambo" by Pérez Prado, and also the song—so suggestive, so indolent—"La balandra Isabel"; 3 : 177).

30. Díaz Ayala, *Música cubana*, 227. Yet, according to Juan J. Remos, the mambo "has not been born on our soil, although its author is from Matanzas: it has come from abroad and it has been brought to us by its inventor and exponents from other countries" ("La virtud del mambo," 5).

31. Roberts, *The Latin Tinge*, 128.

32. Galán, *Cuba y sus sones*, 342.

33. I take this information from Roberts, *The Latin Tinge*, 124. According to Albert and Josephine Butler, in 1944 Anselmo Sacasas made a record called "The Mambo" ("Mambo As It Is Danced at Broadway's Palladium," *Dance*, 24, no. 3. [March 1950]: 32). I have not been able to confirm this, but it is possible that Sacasas's recording was a cover of Orestes López's old *danzón*. In his list of "milestones of mambo," Ernest Borneman cites the 1946 mambo concerts at Sweet's Ballroom in Oakland, California ("Big Mambo Business," *Melody Maker*, September 11, 1954). Another New York musician, Joe Loco, once claimed that he had been playing mambo in Harlem as early as 1936 (see *Metronome* 71 [May 1955]: 12), but this is surely not true (he was not called "Loco" for nothing). In 1948 *Dance News* reported, "The mambo is the most popular of all the steps danced in the New York night spots at the present time" (Don LeBlanc, "The Mambo," *Dance News*, 13, no. 4 [October 1948]: 8).

34. *Time*, April 9, 1951; *Variety*, August 29, 1951; Ralph Gleason, "Prado's West Coast Tour a Huge Success," *Down Beat*, October 5, 1951. Gleason adds: "It's a shame that all the bandleaders who have been bellyaching about the disappearance of the dancing American weren't on hand. Prado's audience dances, my friends—young and old they all kick out. Frequently the band shaded down so low you could hear the shuffling rhythm of the dancers above the conga drum beat. How long is it since you've heard that in a joint the size of Sweet's?"

35. Hentoff, "Prado Tells How Mambo Made It But Not How He Makes It Tick," 3.

36. Respectively, from Walter Waltham, "Mambo: The Afro-Cuban Dance Craze," *American Mercury* 74 (January 1952): 17; and Barbara Squier Adler, "The Mambo and the Mood," *New York Times Magazine*, September 16, 1951.

37. "Mambo King," *Ebony* 6 (September 1951): 45; Adler, "The Mambo and the Mood," 22.

38. Respectively, from "Mambo King," 46; and "Pérez Prado Shines on Coast," *Down Beat*, January 13, 1954. Undoubtedly there was an element of racial typing in all of this. Already in Cuba the mambo had been labeled "an

africanization" of the *danzón* (Cuéllar Viscaíno, "La revolución del mambo,"
98). *Time* reported that the mambo combined "the subtle trickery of the Latin
with the simplicity of a society-band beat" ("Darwin and the Mambo," September 6, 1954). *Life's* cover story for December 1954 bore the title "Uncle
Sambo, Mad for Mambo."

39. Albert Butler and Josephine Butler, "Mambo Today," *Dance* 27, no. 12
(December 1952): 52.

40. Mrs. Arthur Murray, "What the Heck Is the Mambo," *Down Beat*,
December 1, 1954.

41. Sylvia G. L. Dannett and Frank R. Rachel, *Down Memory Lane. Arthur
Murray's Picture Story of Social Dancing* (New York: Greenberg, 1954), 174.

42. See Robert Luis, "Rumba's Anniversary," and Dorothea Duryea Ohl,
"Mambo Not a Dance?" in *Dance Magazine* 32, no. 6 (June 1958): 66–68. Pérez
Prado believed that the mambo should be danced *ad libitum*: "You should dance
the mambo the way you feel" (Hentoff, "Prado Tells How Mambo Made It But
Not How He Made It Tick," 3). In 1959 the mambo was still going strong at
the Palladium; see Robert Farris Thompson, "Palladium Mambo," *Dance Magazine* 23, no. 9 (September 1959): 73–75.

43. Walter Waldman, "Mambo: Afro-Cuban Dance Craze," *American Mercury* 74 (January 1952): 20.

44. "Embullo parabólico" is Fernando Ortiz's phrase for the slow buildup of
enthusiasm in Afro-Cuban music (*Los bailes y el teatro de los negros en el folklore
de Cuba*, 150).

45. "Uncle Sambo, Mad for Mambo," *Life*, December 20, 1954.

46. See José Arteaga, *La salsa* (Bogotá: Intermedio Editores, 1990), 88.

47. Ernest Borneman, "Mambo '54," *Melody Maker*, January 1, 1955. Someone tuning in to Perry Como's television show in 1954 could have seen him not
only sing this song but attempt to dance it with Peggy Lee (when it comes to
Cuban motion, Perry is no match for Peggy). This clip is now available in *TV
Variety XXV* (Shokus Video #466, 1990).

48. "Mambo Fever Hits Peak in Music Biz, with More to Come," *Variety*,
October 20, 1954.

49. Respectively, from Smith, "Perez Prado Ork," 46–47; and "Night Club
Reviews," *Variety*, August 4, 1954. See also Bill Coss, "Prado Means Mucho
Mambo," *Metronome* 70 (October 1954): 19.

50. See Nat Hentoff, "The Mambo!! They Shake A-Plenty with Tito
Puente," *Down Beat*, October 6, 1954. See also Michael McSorley, "'Killer Joe'
Piro: Past and Present," *Dance* 29, no. 10 (October 1955): 40–41, 84; and José
Torres, "The Palladium," *New York*, December 21–28, 1987. Piro, who was
regarded as one of the very best mambo dancers, claimed to have taught 90,000
mamboniks.

51. The original recording has been reissued in *15 grandes éxitos de Pérez
Prado y su orquesta* (RCA International 6411-4-RL, 1983); the 1960 version is

available in *Mambo Night Fever* (BMG Music 495–593, 1989); it was originally released in *Big Hits by Prado* (RCA Victor 2104, 1960).

52. Oronio, *Diccionario de la música cubana*, 33.

53. Ortiz, *Los bailes y el teatro de los negros en el folklore de Cuba*, 81.

54. In Cuba the mambo had been an embattled genre from the first. Because of its lack of "nativeness," Cuban composers such as Eliseo Grenet and Bebo Valdés came up with "Cuban answers to the mambo" like the *sucu-sucu* and the *batanga*, respectively. In addition there was the practical impediment that the Pérez Prado "sound" required an unfeasibly large orchestra. As played by Pérez Prado, the mambo was a big-band commodity that most Cuban *conjuntos* simply could not afford. Then too, the mambo was tough to dance—even for Cubans. As a result, in Cuba this music was predominantly a jukebox and show phenomenon. One could listen to mambos on the Victrola or one could go to nightclubs like Tropicana to see professional mambo dancers like "Las mulatas de fuego" or "Las mamboletas."

55. "New Terps Bet Hot-Cha Cha," *Variety*, March 9, 1954.

56. "Cha–Cha–Cha Old Hat Says Pérez Prado," *Billboard*, September 10, 1955.

57. Sammy Kaye, "To Heck with the Mambo," *Down Beat*, April 20, 1955; Barry Ulanov, "After the Mambo, What?" *Metronome* 71 (February 1955): 21, 35.

58. Pérez Prado continued to record into the sixties, seventies, and eighties, producing such lamentable albums as *Pérez Prado A-Go-Go* (Orfeon LP-12-448) and the pseudo-psychedelic *Pérez Prado está IN-creíble* (Arcano DKLI-3514). Beginning in the mid-fifties Pérez Prado also tried his hand at longer compositions, *Voodoo Suite* (1955), *Concierto para bongó* (1960), and *Exotic Suite of the Americas* (1962). He died in Mexico City on September 14, 1989.

59. After its heyday in the early fifties, the mambo did not disappear altogether, since it lived on in what came to be called salsa music. The *chachachá* fared somewhat better, since it was incorporated into rock music. My favorite *chachachá* band after the Orquesta Aragón is the Beach Boys; my favorite *chachachá* after "La engañadora" is "Don't Worry Baby." The honor roll of "cha-cha-rock" is a long one.

4. SALSA FOR ALL SEASONS

1. The lyric of "Flagler Street" began: "Flagler, Flagler Street,/me recuerda a San Rafael a mí./Las cubanitas lucen bonitas/cuando pasean por Flagler Street, cosita buena." The complementary song was Rosendo Rosell's "Callecitas de mi Cuba," which lovingly enumerated streets in Havana and elsewhere.

2. Los Jóvenes del Hierro, *Si tienes vergüenza no me hables más* (Sound Triangle Records STS-7788, 1974).

3. I will be using the term "salsa" in the broad sense as the now-current generic label for Caribbean-derived music in this country. Historically the term is closely identified with the music of the Hispanic urban ghetto of New York. The term began to gain currency in the late sixties. After the heyday of the mambo, Latin music in New York went back to the ghetto, there to be enriched by new genres like the *pachanga*, the Latin-rock fusion called boogaloo, and old Caribbean rhythms like the Puerto Rican *plena* and the Dominican *merengue*. What emerged in the mid-sixties was called "salsa." But from the beginning the term was more of a marketing tool than a musical label, as salsa encompasses a variety of different rhythms. The best-selling salsa album of all time, Rubén Blades and Willie Colón's *Siembra* (1978), includes *sones, plenas*, and *merengues*, as well as a couple of cuts that are most directly indebted to North American rock.

Even semantically the term "salsa" is equivocal, for almost invariably it is translated "sauce." More than one salsa album has had on its cover a life-size Warhol-like bottle of ketchup, *salsa de tomate*. Nowadays the word "salsa" conjures up the notion of a sauce like the one in the ubiquitous salsa and chips combination. Yet the musical use of the word apparently goes back to Ignacio Piñeiro's 1928 *son* "Echale salsita," where the word means gravy rather than sauce. And in the fifties when the redoubtable Beny Moré sometimes yelled out "¡Salsa!" in the middle of a number, the sense was not sauce but gravy. Nonetheless, once the term gained currency in the United States, it became identified with the spicy red sauce familiar to Americans. By now, salsa is sauce forever. No wonder that Tito Puente once remarked, "The only salsa I know comes in a bottle. I play Cuban music."

The most complete survey of salsa music is César Miguel Rondón, *El libro de la salsa* (Caracas: Editorial Arte, 1980). Also useful are Robert Farris Thompson, "New York's Salsa Music," *Saturday Review*, June 28, 1975; Jorge Duany, "Popular Music in Puerto Rico: Toward an Anthropology of *Salsa*," *Latin American Music Review* 5, no. 2 (Fall–Winter 1984): 186–216; Guillermo Cabrera Infante, "Salsa para una ensalada," in *Literatures in Transition: The Many Voices of the Caribbean*, ed. Rose S. Minc (Baltimore, Md.: Ediciones Hispamérica, 1982); Charley Gerard with Marty Sheller, *Salsa: The Rhythm of Latin Music* (Crown Point, Ind.: White Cliffs Media Company, 1989); José Arteaga, *La salsa* (Bogotá: Intermedio Editores, 1990); Olavo Alén Rodríguez, *De lo afrocubano a la salsa* (San Juan, Puerto Rico: Editorial Cubanacán, 1992); and Vernon W. Boggs, ed., *Salsiology: Afro-Cuban Music and the Evolution of Salsa in New York City* (New York: Greenwood, 1992).

4. In my mind the jingle connects with the fight song of Ricky Ricardo's alma mater, which featured a similar interlingual rhyme: "Arriba, arriba, Havana U./No hay nadie en el mundo/que sea como tú" ("Lucy Hires an English Tutor").

5. The song is included in *Miguel, Oscar y La Fantasía* (Suntan Records

STLP-001, 1985). This idea was subsequently used in the musical *Salsa* (1988), a Hispanic *Saturday Night Fever*, where "Good Loving" is performed by choreographer Kenny Ortega; but Miguel y Oscar's "original" version is far more spicy.

6. The term "Miami sound" has also been used to label hip-hop groups like Exposé, some of whose members are Cuban American, but musically they bear slight resemblance to the bands I will discuss here.

7. Their discography includes *Charanga 76: Encore* (TR Records 128, 1977), *Con la lengua afuera* (Suave K712, n.d.), *Charanga 76 en el 79* (TR Records 145, 1979), *Hansel & Raúl y La Charanga* (Top Hits TH-AM 2133, 1981), *Hansel & Raúl* (Top Hits TH-AMF 2169, 1981), *Hansel & Raúl* (Top Hits TH-AMF 2211, 1982), *Hansel & Raúl* (Top Hits TH-AMF 2271, 1983), *Hansel & Raúl* (Top Hits TH-AMF 2317, 1984), *La magia de Hansel y Raúl* (RCA International 5701-4-RL, 1986), *Tropical* (RCA International 5701-4-RL, 1986), *Hansel y Raúl y la Orquesta Calle Ocho* (RCA International 6670-1-RL, 1988), and *Blanco y negro* (CBS International 80016, 1988). Hansel's solo albums include *Solo* (CBS International 80148, 1989), *El Gato* (CBS International 80469, 1990), and *Latinoamericano* (SONY 80806, 1992). By himself Raúl has recorded *El gallo de la salsa* (Gayo Productions C-11, 1989).

8. Daisann McClane, *New York Times*, June 10, 1990.

9. His discography: *One Man Alone* (GEMA 5014, 1974), *Chirino* (GEMA 5026, 1975), *Chirino 3* (Borinquen AAD-1323, 1976), *Evolución* (Borinquen AAD, 1339, 1978), *Come into My Music* (Oliva-Cantú OOC-211, 1979), *Diferente* (Oliva-Cantú OCC-214, 1980), *La salsa y yo* (LAD 365, 1981), *Chirinísimo* (LAD 377, 1982), *Subiendo* (Top Hits TH-AMF-2268, 1983), *Zarabanda* (CBS International 10394, 1985), *Amándote* (CBS International 10542, 1988), *Acuarela del Caribe* (CBS International 80228, 1989), and *Oxígeno* (CBS International 80600, 1991). Chirino has also recorded with other artists like Lissette, Marisela Verena, and Angela Carrasco and has put together several compilations of "Greatest Hits."

10. For a perceptive discussion of "Son de la loma," see Roberto González Echevarría, *La ruta de Severo Sarduy* (Hanover: Ediciones del Norte, 1987), 102–107.

11. Roberto Fernández was one of the first to begin writing about Miami from a perspective different than that of the exile. His first book, *Cuentos sin rumbo*, dates from 1975. He has also written *La vida es un special* (1982), *La montaña rusa* (1985), and *Raining Backwards* (1988).

12. Some examples are Hansel's "Los balseros,' Titti Sotto's "La Habana espera," Carlos Oliva's "Canción de amor (no de protesta)," and Chirino's "Ya viene llegando" and "Habana D.C." (where "D.C." stands for "después de Castro" or "después del Caballo"). In the aftermath of the *Mariel* boatlift in 1980 there was also a brief burst of patriotic musical feeling, most notably Gustavo Rojas's "Yo soy el cubano" and "Soy de allá," both from his *Gustavo Rojas* (CBS International DML 10305, 1980).

13. "Plástico," the lead cut in Rubén Blades and Willie Colón's *Siembra* (1978), mounts a savage attack on a "plastic" couple, who think only about creature comforts. Unlike the Miami sound, which speaks for a politically conservative and upwardly mobile class, New York salsa embodies the values and vexations of the working-class barrio. According to Duany, "The backbone of salsa music is the Puerto Rican proletariat . . . the best salsa songs voice the problems of this disadvantaged class" ("Toward an Anthropology of *Salsa*," 207). Only Hansel y Raúl sometimes come close to representing the point of view of the "proletariat."

14. Ironically, *Tengo* (1964) is also the title of a book of poems by Nicolás Guillén.

15. Carlos Oliva, the founder and leader of Los Sobrinos del Juez, defines the Miami sound as a "soft salsa" that blends "jazz, Cuban music, Caribbean music, and rock" ("Carlos Oliva y su formidable grupo musical," *Alerta*, March 23, 1987); see also "Carlos Oliva: Precursor del Crossover," *Cartel* 4, no. 3 (1992): 2–5. According to Thomas D. Boswell and James R. Curtis, the Miami sound "is perhaps best described as a mellow form of salsa, in which commercial American rock and jazz elements are emphasized, more so than in New York-based salsa" (*The Cuban-American Experience* [Totowa, N.J.: Rowman and Allanheld, 1983], 141).

16. Quoted in Hank Bordowitz, "Gloria Estefan," *VisàVis* 1 (June 1992): 59.

17. "Mister Don't Touch the Banana" was composed by Chirino and Marisela Verena. Other examples of *santería*-pop are Chirino's "El collar de Clodomiro" (1980), "Muéveme el coco" (1982), "Wilfredo el mago" (1982), and "San Zarabanda" (1985); and Carlos Oliva and Los Sobrinos del Juez, "Ekelecuá" (1991). These songs were all written by Titti Sotto, a prolific Cuban-born composer whose work has been recorded by many Miami artists.

18. Within weeks of its original release, "Un tipo típico" was withdrawn because Chirino had neglected to pay royalties for his extensive sampling of copyrighted material. The album *Acuarela del Caribe*, where "Un tipo típico" was the lead cut, was then rereleased with another song, "Pobre diabla," in its place. Ironically, "Un tipo típico" did not obey its own injunction to discharge one's debts (the cost would have been prohibitive). But apparently Chirino has now paid up, since the song appears in a collection of his greatest hits, *Willie Chirino: Un tipo típico y sus éxitos* (Sony-Globo Records 80824, 1992).

19. Enrique Fernández, "Worlds Collide," *Village Voice*, November 10, 1992. For many years now Fernández (in his *Village Voice* column and elsewhere) has been an alert and knowledgeable chronicler of the vicissitudes of Cuban music inside and outside the island. On the Miami sound, see also his "The Miami Sound," *Village Voice*, January 28, 1986.

20. The original members of the band were Gloria and Emilio Estefan, Raúl and Mercy Murciano, Juan Marcos Avila, and Kiki García. A list of MSM's most important recordings includes *Renacer* (Audiofon AUS 5426, 1977), *Miami*

Sound Machine (Top Hits TH-AM 2187, 1978), *Miami Sound Machine* (CBS International 10311, 1980), *Rio* (CBS International 10330, 1982), *A toda máquina* (CBS International 10538, 1983), *Eyes of Innocence* (CBS-Epic ET-39622, 1984), *Primitive Love* (CBS-Epic BFE-40131, 1985), *Let It Loose* (CBS-Epic ET-40769, 1987), *Cuts Both Ways* (CBS-Epic ET-45217, 1989), *Exitos de Gloria Estefan* (CBS International 80432, 1990), *Into the Light* (Epic EK-46988, 1991), and *Gloria Estefan: Greatest Hits* (Epic EK-53046, 1992).

21. Grace Catalano, *Gloria Estefan* (New York: Saint Martin's Press, 1991), 36.

22. Quoted in Catalano, *Gloria Estefan*, 76.

23. Desi Arnaz, *A Book* (New York: William Morrow and Company, 1976), 50.

24. More interesting to me than Martika or Jon Secada are Nuclear Valdéz, a Cuban-American rock band, and the Mavericks, a country music group led by Raúl Malo. Although the sounds of these bands have almost nothing to do with Cuban music, every once in a while their songs discuss Cuban-exile subjects (as in "Summer" by Nuclear Valdéz and "From Hell to Paradise" by the Mavericks). I should also mention the Cuban-American rapper Mellow Man Ace, who calls himself "the Ricky Ricardo of rap" and is best known for "Mentirosa," which is spoken in "Spanglish."

5. RUM, RUMP, AND RUMBA

1. See Enrique Fernández's review, "Exilados on Main Street," *Village Voice*, May 1, 1990.

2. *Our House in the Last World* (New York: Washington Square Press, 1983), 178. Other page references are given in the text.

3. Mary Antin, *The Promised Land* (Boston: Houghton Mifflin, 1912), xii.

4. In this respect and others one might usefully contrast Hijuelos's novel with Richard Rodriguez's *Hunger of Memory*. Here is the corresponding scene in Rodriguez: "The nun said, in a friendly but oddly impersonal voice, 'Boys and girls, this is Richard Rodriguez.' (I heard her sound out: *Rich-heard Road-ree-guess*.) It was the first time I had heard anyone name me in English. 'Richard,' the nun repeated more slowly, writing my name down in her black leather book. Quickly I turned to see my mother's face dissolve in a watery blur behind the pebbled glass door" (*Hunger of Memory* [New York: Bantam, 1982], 11).

5. Suárez is the author of *Latin Jazz* (New York: William Morrow, 1989) and *The Cutter* (New York: Ballantine Books, 1991). García has published *Dreaming in Cuban* (New York: Alfred A. Knopf, 1992).

6. Roberto Fernández, *Raining Backwards* (Houston: Arte Público Press, 1988), 48–49.

7. Oscar Hijuelos, *The Mambo Kings Play Songs of Love* (New York: Farrar, Straus, Giroux, 1989), 8. Other page references are given in the text.

8. Alejo Santinio also had a brother, Héctor (after whom his son was named), who died in an accident (*Our House*, 63).

9. Nicolás Kanellos, "*The Mambo Kings Play Songs of Love*," *Americas Review* 18, no. 1 (1990): 113.

10. According to Guillermo Cabrera Infante, *La Habana para un infante difunto* is "una suerte de memoria erótica" (quoted in Rosa María Pereda, *Guillermo Cabrera Infante* [Madrid: EDAF, 1979], 141).

11. César's success with women is so phenomenal that it has even spilled out from the pages of the novel. A few months after *Mambo Kings* was published Hijuelos was sued for libel by a singer named Gloria Parker, who appears briefly in the book as the leader of "Glorious Gloria Parker and Her All-Girl Rumba Orchestra," a real band that Gloria Parker actually led during the fifties. Parker's suit alleged that Hijuelos portrayed her and her colleagues as sluts. The suit quoted from the novel, which states that César "made it with three of the musicians who played with Glorious Gloria Parker and Her All-Girl Rumba Orchestra, among them a Lithuanian trombone player named Gertie whom he made love to against a wall of flour sacks" (198). But this passage, which gives the notion of "deflouring" an entirely new meaning, apparently was not enough to prove Gloria's case and the suit was dismissed.

12. Laura Frost, "*The Mambo Kings Play Songs of Love*," *Review* 42 (January–June 1990): 65. Referring to the novel's sexual content, Hijuelos has said: "I intended a little bit of parody of the super-sexual virility that men are obsessed with in macho cultures. I was having fun with it. Also, for me, it's a play on mortality, and on the body and how one can be hyperphallic—built like the Empire State Building—and it won't make any difference to the ultimate issues of love or family or death" (quoted in Michael Coffey, "Oscar Hijuelos," *Publishers Weekly*, July 21, 1989).

13. This chapter was completed before the publication of Hijuelos's third novel, *The Fourteen Sisters of Emilio Montez O'Brien* (New York: Farrar, Straus and Giroux, 1993), which continues the drift away from Cuba. Born in the United States of an Irish father and a Cuban mother, Emilio and his fourteen sisters are American through and through (the exception is Isabel, who marries a Cuban man, but who hardly figures in the novel). The firstborn, Margarita, thinks of Cuba as "that troublesome country of her mother's birth" (416), and the youngest, Emilio, is regarded by his mother as "an absolute American" (296).

6. NO MAN'S LANGUAGE

1. Kozer's books include *Padres y otras profesiones* (1972); *De Chepén a La Habana* (with Isaac Goldemberg; 1973), *Poemas de Guadalupe* (1973), *Este judío de*

números y letras (1975), *Y así tomaron posesión en las ciudades* (1978), *La rueca de los semblantes* (1980), *Jarrón de las abreviaturas* (1980), *Antología breve* (1981), *Bajo este cien* (1983), *Nueve láminas (glorieta)* (1984), *La garza sin sombras* (1985), *Díptico de la restitución* (1986), *El carillón de los muertos* (1987), *Carece de causa* (1988), *Prójimos* (1990), *De donde oscilan los seres en sus proporciones* (1990), and *Trazas del lirondo* (1993). Selections from his poetry have appeared in *Ultima poesía cubana,* ed. Orlando Rodríguez Sardiñas (Madrid: Hispanova, 1973); *Los paraguas amarillos: Los poetas latinos en Nueva York,* ed. Iván Silén (Hanover, N.H.: Ediciones del Norte, 1983); *Antología de la poesía hispanoamericana (1915–1980),* ed. Jorge Rodríguez Padrón (Madrid: Espasa-Calpe, 1984); *Poetas cubanos en Nueva York,* ed. Felipe Lázaro (Madrid: Betania, 1988); and *Veinte años de literatura cubanoamericana,* ed. Silvia Burunat and Ofelia García (Tempe, Ariz.: Bilingual Review Press, 1988). For a sampling of his poems in English translation, see José Kozer, *The Ark upon the Number* (1982) and *Anthology of Contemporary Latin American Literature,* ed. Barry Luby (Rutherford, N.J.: Farleigh-Dickinson University Press, 1985). Page references to *Bajo este cien* (Mexico City: Fondo de Cultura Económica, 1983) are included in the text (as *BEC*). Except where I indicate otherwise, the translations from the Spanish are my own.

    2. On Kozer's poetry, see Rose S. Minc, "Convergencias judeo-cubanas en la poesía de José Kozer," *Cuadernos Americanos* 142, no. 5 (September–October 1980): 111–116; Rose S. Minc, "Revelación y consagración de lo hebraico en la poesía de José Kozer," *Chasqui* 10, no. 1 (November 1980): 26–35; Jorge Rodríguez Padrón, "José Kozer: El texto como teoría y como experiencia," *Cuadernos Hispanoamericanos* 399 (September 1983): 162–166; Sabas Martín, "José Kozer: Pasión y transfiguración de la palabra," *Chasqui* 13, nos. 2–3 (1984): 60–64; Pedro López-Adorno, "Teoría y práctica de la arquitectura poética kozeriana: Apuntes para *Bajo este cien* y *La garza sin sombras,*" *Revista Iberoamericana* 52 (1986): 605–611; and Jorge Rodríguez Padrón, "Cauce de comunión: *Carece de causa* de José Kozer," *Inti* 29–30 (1989): 89–99. See also my "Noción de José Kozer," *Revista Iberoamericana* 152–153 (July–December 1990): 1247–1256. Kozer has dicussed his work and life most extensively in an interview with Miguel Angel Zapata, "José Kozer y la poesía como testimonio de la cotidianeidad," *Inti* 26–27 (Fall–Spring 1987–1988): 177.

    3. Roberto Reis, "Entrevista: José Kozer," *Chasqui* 6, no. 1 (November 1976): 97.

    4. "Esto (también) es Cuba, Chaguito," *Papeles de Enlace* (Summer 1992): 3–4.

    5. "En todos [estos poetas] persiste la voluntad consciente de salvaguardar la lengua madre, en tal grado que el español (más que lo español) llega a constituírse en un modo de proteger la identidad personal, estableciéndose un estado consciente de separación con el medio ambiente anglosajón. . . . La voluntad de vivir en español, a pesar de la persistente amenaza que constituye el medio ambiente anglosajón, cosmopolita y supracivilizado en que se desenvuelven

estos poetas, es según nuestra opinión, factor capital para agrupar esta nueva poesía latinoamericana" (José Kozer, "Breve antología de poetas latinoamericanos en Estados Unidos," *Norte* 11 [1970]: 141–142).

6. Kozer, "Breve antología de poetas latinoamericanos en Estados Unidos," 143.

7. Interview with Elizabeth Pérez-Luna, quoted by Rosa Minc, "Convergencias judeo-cubanas en la poesía de José Kozer," 111. Although this phrase has been widely quoted, Kozer has recently claimed that he never said it, attributing it instead to Isaac Goldemberg, with whom he co-authored *De Chepén a La Habana* (see Zapata, "José Kozer y la poesía como testimonio de la cotidianeidad," 177–178). See also Alberto Luis Ponzo, "Un continuo estado de alarma," which is the prologue to Kozer's *Poemas de Guadalupe* (Buenos Aires: Ediciones Por la Poesía, 1973). As we will see, this striking phrase (whether Kozer's or somebody else's) describes precisely a crucial element in his poetry.

8. Michael M. J. Fisher, "Ethnicity and the Post-Modern Arts of Memory," in *Writing Culture*, ed. James Clifford and George E. Marcus (Berkeley: University of California Press, 1986), 194–233.

9. José Kozer, "The Poetic Experience: The Logic of Chance," in *Philosophy and Literature in Latin America*, ed. Jorge J. E. Gracia and Mireya Camurati (Albany: State University of New York Press, 1989), 100; and Zapata, "José Kozer y la poesía como testimonio de la cotidianeidad," 185.

10. Reis, "Entrevista: José Kozer," 97.

11. Kozer's ample lexicon of receptacles would include *alcancías, almacenes, arcones, botijas, búcaros, canastas, cántaros, cestas, cestos, cuencos, cuévanos, escudillas, espuertas, graneros, lebrillos, macetas, marmitas* (many *marmitas*), *ollas, silos, tarteras, tibores, tiestos,* and *trojes.*

12. *Carente de causa* (Buenos Aires: Ediciones Ultimo Reino, 1988), 147–148.

13. *El carillón de los muertos* (Buenos Aires: Ediciones Ultimo Reino, 1987), 13.

14. I quote both original and translation of "Recuerdas, Sylvia" (Remember, Sylvia) from José Kozer, *The Ark upon the Number*, trans. Ammiel Alcalay (Merrick, N.Y.: Cross-Cultural Communications, 1982), 18–19. This poem also appears in *Bajo este cien*, 32.

15. Both the original and the English translation of "La blanca ambigüedad de las horas" (White Ambiguity of Hours) come from *Prójimos/Intimates*, trans. Ammiel Alcalay (Barcelona: Les plaquettes del Carrer Ausiàs, 1991), no pagination.

16. *El carillón de los muertos,* 11.

Index

INDEX

Permissions
Acknowledgments

*Grateful acknowledgment is made to the following for permission
to reprint previously published material:*

Lucie Arnaz: Lyrics of "I Love Lucy" by Harold Adamson and Eliot Daniels, published by Desilu Music; text excerpts from the manuscript of *A Book* by Desi Arnaz.

Willy Chirino: Excerpts from "Soy," "Tengo," "No debería ser así," and "Los diseñadores" by Willy Chirino. Used by permission of the author.

Dutton/New American Library/Penguin Books USA Inc.: Excerpts from *Latins Are Still Lousy Lovers* by Helen Lawrenson. Copyright © 1968 by Helen Lawrenson. Used by permission of the publisher, Dutton, an imprint of New American Library, a division of Penguin Books USA Inc.

Estefan Enterprises/Foreign Imported Productions: Lyrics of "Conga" by Enrique García, published by Foreign Imported Productions. Used by permission of Music Publishing, Estefan Enterprises.

The Johns Hopkins University Press: Excerpt from "The Agony of Exile: A Study of the Migration and Adaptation of Indochinese Refugee Adults and Children" by Rubén G. Rumbaut; in *Refugee Children: Theory, Research, and Services*, edited by Frederick L. Ahearn, Jr., and Jean L. Athey. Copyright © 1991 by The Johns Hopkins University Press. Reprinted by permission.

José Kozer: Excerpts from the poetry of José Kozer. Used by permission of the author.

Music Sales Corporation: Lyrics of "Papa Loves Mambo" by Al Hoffman, Dick Manning, and Bix Reichner. Copyright © 1954 (Renewed) Al Hoffman Songs, Inc., Shapiro Bernstein & Co., Inc., and Dick Manning Music (ASCAP). International Copyright Secured. All Rights Reserved. Used by permission.

Peer International Corporation: Excerpt from the lyrics of "El Bilingüe" by Germán Bas. Copyright © 1975 by Peer International Corporation. International Copyright Secured. All Rights Reserved. Used by permission.

William Morrow & Company, Inc.: Excerpts from *A Book* by Desi Arnaz. Copyright © 1976 by Desi Arnaz. By permission of William Morrow & Company, Inc.